Crane Island Journal Part Four

Sumar (Summer)

A Memoir of a Remarkable Daily Life
on a Small Island in the Salish Sea

By John Ashenhurst

Walt's Fourth Blessing

Flood-tide below me!

I see you face to face!

Clouds of the west—sun there half an hour high—I see you also face to face.

Crowds of men and women attired in the usual costumes, how curious you are to me!

On the ferry-boats the hundreds and hundreds that cross, returning home, are more curious to me than you suppose,

And you that shall cross from shore to shore years hence are more to me, and more in my meditations, than you might suppose.

From "Crossing Brooklyn Ferry" by Walt Whitman

Sumar (Sumer)	1
Dedication	3
Introduction	4
Two-hundred-sixty-nine: Welcome	16
Two-hundred-seventy: Whales of July	20
Two-hundred-seventy-one: Head in the Clouds	24
Two-hundred-seventy-two: Fond Farewell	28
Two-hundred-seventy-three: Crabby	32
Two-hundred-seventy-four: Birthday Launch	36
Two-hundred-seventy-five: Sail Ready	40
Two-hundred-seventy-six: Curb Your Enthusiasm	44
Two-hundred-seventy-seven: Jones Island	49
Two-hundred-seventy-eight: Victoria	53
Two-hundred-seventy-nine: Magic Garden	58
Two-hundred-eighty: Crossing the Straight	61
Two-hundred-eighty-one: Off and On	66
Two-hundred-eighty-two: Crossing the Line	70
Two-hundred-eighty-three: Chipper	74
Two-hundred-eighty-four: Pictures	77
Two-hundred-eighty-five: Flexibility	81
Two-hundred-eighty-six: Back Home	84
Two-hundred-eighty-seven: Picnic	88
Two-hundred-eighty-eight: Departures	92
Two-hundred-eighty-nine: The Fort	96
Two-hundred-ninety: Hornets	101
Two-hundred-ninety-one: Sailing	108

Two-hundred-ninety-two: Swarms	113
Two-hundred-ninety-three: Day of Rest	117
Two-hundred-ninety-four: Comparisons	121
Two-hundred-ninety-five: People	125
Two-hundred-ninety-six: Girdled Branches Mystery	129
Two-hundred-ninety-seven: Home Improvement	133
Two-hundred-ninety-eight: Leaks	138
Two-hundred-ninety-nine: Book Sale	143
Three-hundred: A Dangerous Situation	148
Three-hundred-one: Rules and Goals	153
Three-hundred-two: New Car	156
Three-hundred-three: Keeping an Eye Out	160
Three-hundred-four: Disappearing View	164
Three-hundred-five: Success	168
Three-hundred-six: Memories	172
Three-hundred-seven: See It Through	176
Three-hundred-eight: The Good Rain	180
Three-hundred-nine: They're Back	183
Three-hundred-ten: Fact Finding	187
Three-hundred-eleven: Duck Soup	191
Three-hundred-twelve: Earth Light	196
Three-hundred-thirteen: Tess	199
Three-hundred-fourteen: Wine Tasting	203
Three-hundred-fifteen: Rethinking	207
Three-hundred-sixteen: The Cable Guy	211
Three-hundred-seventeen: Collaboration	215

Three-hundred-eighteen: Turning	221
Three-hundred-nineteen: Veterans	225
Three-hundred-twenty: Arrival	230
Three-hundred-twenty-one: Kayaking	235
Three-hundred-twenty-two: Departure	242
Three-hundred-twenty-three: Cutting Up	247
Three-hundred-twenty-four: More Wood, More Wood	251
Three-hundred-twenty-five: Cleaning Up	255
Three-hundred-twenty-six: Earthquake	258
Three-hundred-twenty-seven: Exploring	261
Three-hundred-twenty-eight: East Shore UUs	265
Three-hundred-twenty-nine: Frustration	269
Three-hundred-thirty: Bzzzz, Bzzzz	273
Three-hundred-thirty-one: Chores	278
Three-hundred-thirty-two: Bang!	282
Three-hundred-thirty-three: Wings	287
Three-hundred-thirty-four: Island Farmers	292
Three-hundred-thirty-five: Preparing for Winter	296
Three-hundred-thirty-six: Discovery	300
Three-hundred-thirty-seven: Break In	306
Three-hundred-thirty-eight: Another Break In	310
Three-hundred-thirty-nine: Heightened Security	316
Three-hundred-forty: Harstine Island Rumpus	320
Three-hundred-forty-one: Ocean Shores	325
Three-hundred-forty-two: Running on Empty?	330
Three-hundred-forty-three: Windy Return	335

Three-hundred-forty-four: More Wood	340
Three-hundred-forty-five: To Town	344
Three-hundred-forty-six: Dirty Job	349
Three-hundred-forty-seven: Beachcombing Treasure	353
Three-hundred-forty-eight: First Fire	357
Three-hundred-forty-nine: Evacuation	361
Three-hundred-fifty: Sitting, Thinking, Learning, and Writing	366
Three-hundred-fifty-one: Recital	370
Three-hundred-fifty-two: Loss	375
Three-hundred-fifty-three: Disturbance	379
Three-hundred-fifty-four: Slogging	383
Three-hundred-fifty-five: Looking and Not Seeing	388
Three-hundred-fifty-six: Report	393
Three-hundred-fifty-seven: Change in the Weather	398
Three-hundred-fifty-eight: Birthday and Farewell	402
Three-hundred-fifty-nine: Smaller Portions	406
Three-hundred-sixty: Can You Hear It Now?	410
Three-hundred-sixty-one: Who Are We?	414
Three-hundred-sixty-two: Here and There	418
Three-hundred-sixty-three: Chetzemoka Visits	424
Three-hundred-sixty-four: A Day in Town	428
Three-hundred-sixty-five: Ready, Set, Go	434
Afterword	438
What's next?	442

Sumar (Summer)

Sumar (Summer)

A Memoir of a Remarkable Daily Life on a Small Island in the Salish Sea

By John Ashenhurst

Crane Island Journal is a four-part memoir beginning with *Haust* and continuing with *Vetur*, *Vor*, and ending with *Sumar* (autumn, winter, spring and summer in Old Norse)

Publisher: Classics Unbound

V1.00 02/20/2025

Copyright © 2025 by John Ashenhurst

ISBN 978-0-9904563-6-0

All rights reserved. Created in the United States of America. No part of this book may be reproduced in any manner whatsoever without written permission except in the case of brief quotations embodied in critical articles and reviews. For information, address Classics Unbound, 5615 24th Ave NW, #43, Seattle, WA 98107

All photographs are the property of the author unless otherwise indicated.

For more information see www.craneislandjournal.com.

Dedication

For Corrina Celeste Mehiel — loving, loved, missed

Introduction

> *"There is nothing — absolutely nothing — half so much worth doing as simply messing about in boats." — "The Wind in the Willows" by Kenneth Grahame*

I grew up in Chicago and its western suburbs and from an early age was acutely aware of the yacht harbors along Lake Michigan, the white sailboats promising something special and mysterious and I had heard about the annual Chicago Yacht Club race to Mackinac (pronounced Mack-i-naw) Island, located between lower and upper Michigan in Lake Huron, a sometimes dangerous 333 mile competitive sail, but other than occasionally fishing with my grandfather, Carl, on the Chain O' Lakes near Waupaca, Wisconsin and happily handling the oars, I had no access to a boat of any kind until friend, Vince, then at the University of Chicago Circle Campus Medical School and me at the University of Chicago in Philosophy Graduate School, decided to jointly buy a small styrofoam-core sailboat. It did float, was easy to transport on the top of any car but in much of any wind could not resist it, even with tacking, and would go backward, and on one occasion, when I was trying to impress a young woman on Lake Geneva, Wisconsin, forcing me to ingloriously land far from my car so we could beach the boat, walk to the car, drive back, pick up the sailboat, and drive back to Chicago.

In 1978 when Yvonne, daughter Jeni and son Eric blended with me and son Noah in Boulder, Colorado and then added our son James, born in 1986, other boat opportunities arose. In 1980, Yvonne and I parked the kids with their other parents and took the Princess Marguerite to Victoria. I was transfixed.

Introduction

1968: Underway, sort of

SS Princess Marguerite on the way to Victoria, B.C. in 1980. Notice Ouspensky's The Fourth Way on the table in front of Yvonne

Introduction

We all visited Yvonne's mother Opal every summer in Seattle and made a point of taking the Washington State Ferry to Bremerton or Bainbridge Island, the latter where we would wander through the Winslow marina, me imaging us with a sailboat or small trawler.

Winslow Harbor on Bainbridge Island with cousin Gina

In 1987, at a small resort in Maine with the whole family, we took turns with sailboards and a Sunfish, the three older kids deliberately capsizing and then pulling it upright to continue on with the fun.

In 1997, living in Boulder, we unexpectedly and without much of a reason bought a "summer house" in Deer Harbor on Orcas Island, and surprising Yvonne, I switched into "buy a boat" mode and talked to business colleagues on the East and West Coasts for suggestions. I wanted to sail but also wanted to go fast enough to get from place to place and to do some boat camping. And I knew I did not want a project boat. We'd need space only for James, still at home, and Samantha the Dog.

Eric and Noah experiment with a sailboard in Maine

Simrishamn I

I settled on a MacGregor, a water ballast, trailerable, 20 knot motoring-sailboat with a 50 hp outboard, a versatile boat that could do everything sort of but nothing very well and I began enjoying — as well as coping with — the realities of being on the water. Living in Boulder, I had a trailer hitch welded to our Ford Windstar van, and we picked up our new MacGregor at Blue Water Yachts in Seattle and then loaded it up with various boating and other supplies on the way north to the San Juan Islands ferry landing in Anacortes.

Introduction

1999 with our MacGregor on the way to the Orcas ferry.

1999 - James, right, and Boulder friend, enjoying dock boating.

Gumption

In 2000, after retiring, selling our house in Boulder and buying a condo there, we began spending much of our time in Deer Harbor, meeting more people, becoming active with the Deer Harbor Community Club, the Unitarian Universalist Fellowship, and the Orcas Island Yacht Club, and our MacGregor began to feel inadequate: we wanted to cruise long distances, maybe to Alaska. We liked the looks of pocket (modest sized) trawlers and tugs. Nordic tugs were an option but we wanted a flybridge helm and deck for nice weather as well as a warm and dry inside helm. We also wanted a semi-planing hull for decent milage and speed, a good use of space and amenities in the house, and great visibility outward. We found a Canadian-made, 31' Camano Troll, in Friday Harbor on San Juan Island and after an inspection, bought it, and brought it to Orcas and neighborhood Cayou Quay Marina where we had moored our MacGregor summers — the MacGregor wintering in our boathouse (with woodshed and my office). The *Gumption* was a good boat, with a useful bow thruster making docking much easier, could cruise at 10 knots, got about three miles per gallon diesel, and never disappointed. We were all over the San Juan Islands and up into the Gulf Islands, to Vancouver Island and Victoria, as far north as Desolation Sound and as far south as Olympia where we could approach Noah and Natasha's beach on Harstine Island. The Volvo four-cylinder diesel engine smoked and an expert mechanic who claimed he could fix it couldn't. And it wasn't much of a sailboat. Time for another change.

Introduction

Christening the Gumption at Blakely Island with the Orcas Island Yacht Club's spring boat cleaning cruise

2006 in Reid Harbor, Stuart Island

Introduction

Simrishamn II

So in 2006 we bought a project-boat, a Finnish, Baltic-bred 33' two-masted Nauticat pilothouse with a second, outdoor helm. Lots of room inside for six people to sleep, a big, reliable Ford diesel, and a good-looking rounded stern. I spent the next year sanding, varnishing, cleaning, and repairing the Nauticat and eventually we sold the *Gumption* and motored and sailed up and down, round and round the San Juans and Gulf islands in *Simrishamn II*.

2007 May - Intermittently at work in a tent at Boatworks in Deer Harbor

2007 August — Oyster Bay on North Pender Island

Huginn

And then we moved to Crane Island and we needed a commuter boat — something versatile, fast and small — with an enclosed helm. Our Deer Harbor home buyer had just what we needed for sale — a 19′ Sea-Sport, a popular brand in the San Juan Islands and especially on Crane Island. Though we had some mechanical problems over time, we used our SeaSport to make daily trips to Orcas, sometimes more, to the ferry landing, to Friday Harbor, and to Sucia and Stuart Islands. The *Huginn* (Thought, one of Odin's two Raven's) was our floating F150.

2009 — Huginn at the Crane dock - (by Corrina Mehiel)

Discovery

On Deer Harbor Road in 2008 coming round the bend at Massacre Bay we saw an attractive orange Ranger sailboat for sale, made in Kent Washington, south of Seattle. The price was right, we could store it winters in our yard, and it seemed a good idea to have a daysailer for neighborhood use, so we towed the Ranger to the Deer Harbor Cayou Quay boat ramp, backed the trailer into the water, released the *Discovery*, and towed it to the Crane Island dock, bringing the trailer by barge later. It turned out to be a great boat for casual, no fuss sailing and everyone liked going for a round-Crane spin.

Introduction

2009 - The Ranger has an elegant slipper shape. It's a classic.

Introduction

2009 - The Ranger is surprisingly capacious and a pleasure to sail.

Two-hundred-sixty-nine: Welcome

"Rain is grace; rain is the sky descending to the earth; without rain, there would be no life." – John Updike

About 8:30 Yvonne came into the living room and told me she had heard water burbling and dripping in the bathroom. Oh no! And then I realized she was hearing water from the downspout outside flowing into the 450 gallon catchment tank outside the bathroom. It was raining. I offered that she was hearing the sound of a double benefit — the direct rain on her garden and water being saved to use later on the garden. She said there was a third benefit — she wouldn't have to draw from the Crane Island water system.

Outside the living room windows water dripped from the eves onto the deck. The madrona and salal leaves glistened below a grey sky and cloud fragments drifted through the forest of fir and cedar two miles away at the ferry landing. Outdoors the air was fragrant as it always is after a dry spell, the flowering ocean spray decidedly so. The Pacific Northwest is especially beautiful when it's sunny and when it's wet.

Son, James, and his partner, Keith were flying into SeaTac from LAX and would arrive before mid-morning and be picked up by Keith's father, John, mother, Susan, and brother, Andrew, Keith's family, coming from a week's vacation in central Oregon. James called to tell us he and Keith were on the ground and expected to be picked up by the Hall's in about an hour. They'd easily make the 4:00 ferry from Anacortes, walking on, and we could all have dinner together at home on Crane Island. But there was lots to do for Yvonne and me first.

The day before, my attempt to staunch the leak from the guest bathroom toilet tank feed line had made it worse — unusable — so I reassembled the system, improving but not correcting the problem. I'd have to get a new feed line so after asking Yvonne whether she needed anything from Eastsound, I took the current feed line with me and crossed to Orcas, moored the *Huginn* and then drove our van north on Deer Harbor Road. At Channel Road, Terry's Taurus station wagon turned north ahead of me onto Deer Harbor Road. Since I'd already passed his house he was likely coming from the Cayou Quay Marina where he kept his restored wooden Canadian training boat, the likely origin of his trip north out of Deer Harbor. When I followed him into the lumber yard on Crow Valley Road twenty minutes later, I was certain he was on a boat repair mission. Inside I told him my surmise and he confirmed it. He couldn't work outside on his boat because of the rain (though by now it had stopped but sunshine didn't look imminent) so he would be working inside and needed painting supplies.

I took my toilet supply line to the plumbing department but couldn't find a match until the clerk showed me that the Fluidmaster Universal/FITS-ALL included three adaptors and so could connect to four different shut off valves. What a great idea! On the drive to the lumberyard I had also remembered I needed chain and bar oil and so picked up a gallon. Back home, the new feed line solved the leak problem — almost. I was reluctant to tighten the connection to the tank, worried I might crack the nylon. The toilet installation instructions were explicit in advising tightening by hand only. I'd have to check back from time to time to see if there was any dripping and tighten it further, if necessary.

Yvonne worked outside on her garden, making adjustments, and then began dinner preparations. The only area of the house now messy was my office and after taking care of some Crane Island Association Treasurer business, I put plumbing parts and saw chains in a sack and with the recycle and garbage in the dock cart towed it all to the back of the yard putting the former in my shop and the latter in the trash storage shed. In the afternoon permission came back from the University of Missouri to use an image of a painting by Lagrange of Devil's Island we'd use in the cover art for *The eNotated In the Penal Colony*. Nothing now stood in the way of publishing our sixth eNotated Classic.

At 4:30 Yvonne checked the Washington State Department of Transportation Vessel Watch Website. It showed that the *Elwah* was coming through Thatcher Pass so it was time to leave for the ferry landing. I parked the *Huginn* at the County dock just as the *Orcas Express* whale watching boat was leaving to return to its dock location in the Cayou Quay Marina in Deer Harbor. Yvonne had given me a list for the market: non-fat milk, "Naturally Nested" eggs, and a green carton of Greek Gods yogurt. Later when I unpacked the bag at home the yogurt was missing though I know I brought it to the cash register. Argh!

269: Susan, John, Andrew (not shown), James, and Keith

As the ferry closed on the ramp, James waved and I could see Keith next to him and soon all five were at hand and I was introduced to Keith's mother Susan, brother, Andrew, 15, and father, John. I described the sights as we cruised back to Crane and James filled in what I'd missed. Back at the house Yvonne and I took our guests on a tour of the grounds and then the house and they commented on the beauty of the island and the view. We heard about their Oregon adventure, that included river rafting, over a dinner of cauliflower white sauce over pasta and a salad from Yvonne's garden. John had caught a cold in Oregon and Andrew was fading after having gotten up early to make the drive north so the two of them retired while James and Keith filled us in on their visit to our Swedish relatives, me interrupting from time to time to explain to Susan who these people were and how we were related. Before 10:00 everyone was ready to go to bed. It was a pleasure to finally meet Keith's family and especially wonderful to see, hug, and talk with James and Keith. Our hearts were filled with love.

Two-hundred-seventy: Whales of July

"What is the good of your stars and trees, your sunrise and the wind, if they do not enter into our daily lives?" — E.M. Forster

There was talk of early rising the night before so I was at my MacBook Pro before 5:00 to get some work done before the socializing began. About 7:30 Yvonne came out of the bedroom to put the French toast casserole in the oven. It was close to 9:00 before everyone else made their appearances and by that time Yvonne and I were sitting at each end of the dining room table having breakfast talking about the day before and the day to unfold. Though cloudy the sky didn't suggest rain, a plus because we'd all be outdoors.

James reported he'd had one of his best sleeps in years but Susan reported that John felt worse than the day before and sported a rash that seemed ominous. Susan didn't feel well, nor did Andrew. Was medical attention available on Orcas Island? Yes, definitely. The Medical Center had a 10:05 opening but only for one. Susan said John would have the appointment and she'd take some of what he was prescribed. I got ready to take the couple to Orcas and then Eastsound but when he came out of the shower John said he would get by. It wouldn't be necessary to make a special trip to town.

After a leisurely breakfast, the French toast casserole supplemented with peaches and raspberries, we all made a circuit of the island, Yvonne, James, Keith, and I pointing to what we considered notable features of our Crane world — the fire engine and community center, the water tank, Dick and Nancy's rustic cabin, the site of the leak at well house #4, the osprey nest (with a noisy osprey on a nearby branch), an entrance to the nature preserve, a large banana slug (rushing, it seemed to me, across Circle Road) and then several more, the big leaf maple with mysteriously attacked, bark strips littering the ground below savaged branches, the airstrip (and warning sign), the moss-covered shelter roof, the remodeled cabin, and more. I was struck again at how much I knew about — or had experiences with and stories about — the Crane Island perimeter road.

270: Orcas sighted

We were due at the Deer Harbor Marina by 12:30 for whale watching and while Yvonne and Susan made sandwiches the rest of us got ready to go. As the *Huginn* cruised north toward Deer Harbor at slow speed, Yvonne pointed out crab pot floats and described the process of placement and retrieval. It was the first day of the summer crab season but because the day was so busy, Yvonne wouldn't have time to drop a pot so we wouldn't be able to treat our guests to fresh Dungeness crab. We moored the *Huginn* at the yellow-lined section of the Marina dock designated County dock while the others checked in with Deer Harbor Charters and then found an empty picnic table where we could eat our picnic lunch.

The *Squito* could carry 20 passengers and the whale-watching boat was nearly filled. Natalie would serve as our naturalist, a young woman Yvonne knew from the Garden Club and after introducing herself to all of us, she described the J, K, and L pods, the three groups that frequented the San Juan Islands (more than 80 orcas in total), as well as what is known about the daily lives of the orcas, in these waters mostly sustained by salmon. Perhaps because she knew Yvonne, Natalie gave us plenty of her time as we cruised south to Cattle Pass, between San Juan and Lopez Islands and the entry point to the Strait of Juan de Fucas and the Pacific Ocean, where we observed seals feeding on salmon or warming themselves in the muted sunlight.

Though the Pass was turbulent ("Angry water" Natalie said kayakers would describe it), the Strait was very calm, a good day to cross to Port Townsend on Admiralty Inlet, the head of Puget Sound and access point to Seattle, Tacoma, and the heavily populated areas of western Washington State. After observing a small Minke whale off American Camp on San Juan Island, the *Squito* headed west and south to take a position among half a dozen other whale watching boats scattered over a half mile wide area of the Strait where orcas seemed to be feeding and perhaps recreating as well. Whale watching boats, by regulation, were to maintain a 200 yard distance from the whales but with the engine turned off and the boat drifting, a number of times some of the orcas came a good deal closer, especially one trio — a mother with oldest and youngest sons. At one point the two year old rolled over on its belly to get a good look at us, presumably part of its ongoing education. John, Susan, and Andrew had never seen orcas living their daily lives and all off us were thrilled to observe these powerful and intelligent creatures.

Home just before five, Yvonne was surprised to find a stainless steel bowl of cooked crab in the refrigerator, left by Margaret for our enjoyment, and because Margaret was on Orcas then, Yvonne left her a thank-you voice mail. James made a fire in the steel hearth on the deck and we all sat in the late afternoon air — and sometimes sun — enjoying the crab in anticipation of a salmon dinner. Susan worked for Franklin-Covey and I was already a fan. She had described her role the day before, so today I asked John about his banking role in Atlanta and conversation drifted toward the more general topics of the economy and politics, and we discussed points of agreement, letting lie areas where we were likely to differ. John said that his views on social issues had become more liberal over the years but neither he nor Susan were certain that was true of their home, Atlanta or Southeast generally. Andrew had found one of grandma Opal's ukuleles and treated us to one of his songs and then we sang together "Somewhere Over the Rainbow" while listening to Israel "IZ" Kamakawiwo'ole's version.

James and Keith had made a DVD of their Europe trip and when the widescreen version of it proved too wide for our out of date television, James played it in 4x3 format from his MacBook Pro through the TV, stopping it whenever we had questions or comments, which was frequently, especially when seeing our Swedish relatives. What a pleasure! I was impressed at how much they'd done and how well, thinking back to my first trip to Europe in 1967. On the verge of drifting off, we vacated my office and retired to our various rooms, planning to reconvene for breakfast the next morning — with a plan to tour Orcas.

Two-hundred-seventy-one: Head in the Clouds

> *"At the still point of the turning world. Neither flesh nor fleshless;/Neither from nor towards; at the still point, there the dance is."* – T.S. Eliot

It had been raining most of the night, hard at times, and here and there patches of fog covered the water or the forests on Shaw and Orcas.

Having had to wait hours for everyone to get out of bed the day before I stayed in bed longer and when I did get up about 6:00 I put all the clean dishes away and then made a pot of oatmeal that would also serve Yvonne and anyone else with our tastes. Yvonne was in the kitchen not long after 8:00 and baked a sheet of drop biscuits which she and I began to eat after becoming impatient with the malingerers. Though John felt better, Susan felt worse and had been unable to sleep most of the night so she didn't make an appearance until 10:00. Andrew, dead to the world, put in about 13 hours, finally joining us at the dining room table about 11:00. The plan was to cruise over to Orcas, all get in the van, and then enjoy Rosario Resort and Moran State Park, stopping in Eastsound on the way back.

The minus tide was out and with seven people in the *Huginn* I was worried that we would get hung up in the mud just beyond the end of the Crane Island Community dock as Yvonne and I had a two years before, pushing ourselves forward with a boat hook and paddle until we cleared so I asked James and Andrew to move to the bow so the boat would be flat in the water and raised the drive unit as high as I could and have the engine still run. We made it and the boys clambered back to the cockpit and then into the cabin. We had found rain jackets for everyone who needed one, a colorful collection of yellow, blue, green, and red but now the rain began to abate. It wouldn't be an issue in any case.

Two-hundred-seventy-one: Head in the Clouds

On our way through Eastsound to Rosario, Yvonne asked me to turn off at Madrona so she could show everyone the new Food Bank building and then ten minutes later we were parked at the Moran mansion, only ten cars in the lot. The resort had a history of financial difficultly, in part because the tourist season was only nine or ten weeks long and efforts to attract off-season meetings hadn't ever been very successful. In August 1997 Yvonne, James, and I had taken the Victoria Clipper from Seattle to Rosario (it no longer makes a stop there) and stayed at the resort over a long weekend to look at property — the result of Yvonne's recommendation after being at Rosario in April with her childhood friend, Julie. By Sunday we'd made an offer on a house in Deer Harbor, closed in September, and came back in October to see what we'd bought — and suffered no buyer's remorse.

We've taken many visitors to Rosario to see the historic Moran mansion and the museum on the second floor, everyone having enjoyed the visit and the story of how Robert Moran, ship builder and Seattle Mayor had fallen ill and was advised by his doctor to withdraw to somewhere quiet and recuperate. That turned out to be Orcas Island and the advice must have been good because he lived another 40 years. The mansion has its own hydroelectric plant powered by water from Cascade Lake in Moran State Park, the first state park in Washington, and the result of the largesse of Moran.

The Grill restaurant at the Rosario marina was open and we all found something to eat before entering Moran State Park, buying a year pass, and then driving the road to the 2,400 foot summit, second highest island mountain in the lower 48. By the time we reached 1,000 feet we had entered a cloud and taking a chance we would rise above it, continued up — but were disappointed. On every other trip to the summit — by car or foot — we'd been greeted by 100-mile views. Today we couldn't see farther than 100 feet.

Two-hundred-seventy-one: Head in the Clouds

271: Rosario Falls in Moran State Park; Susan, Keith, John, Andrew

On the way down we pulled off the road at the Cascade Falls parking lot and walked the quarter mile to the Falls, and all of us were delighted to be in this special glen, the little falls 40 or 50 feet high, ferns and moss all around, crystal clear water passing below huge logs that had fallen across the stream. A few years before Keith had fallen off a moss-covered log that turned out to be more slippery than he'd expected, landing on his back in the water, discombobulated and wet but not hurt. None of us was willing to walk that log today.

Back in Eastsound we made a stop at Island Market and then Eastsound Instruments and Supply for guitar strings for Andrew — which John later installed — allowing Andrew to play and sing a few pieces while the group sat around the dinner table after the meal and while I cleaned up the kitchen. Because they had to be up before 6:00 the next morning to catch the early ferry, John, Susan, and Andrew disappeared while Yvonne and I talked with James and Keith about their Europe trip, especially their visit to what had been the Sachsenhausen concentration camp north of Berlin where thousands were murdered by the Nazis and then the Memorial to the Murdered Jews of Europe near the Brandenburg gate, a sculpture garden that, like Sachenhausen, caused the boys to feel existentially disoriented and profoundly moved. We hadn't had enough time to visit with James and Keith. James would be back in a few weeks for our family gathering, Borgfest, but Keith would be in Atlanta instead. We really enjoyed being with these remarkable young men.

Two-hundred-seventy-two: Fond Farewell

"Parting is such sweet sorrow that I shall say goodnight till it be morrow." – William Shakespeare

In order to be certain they'd make their 2:15 flight, John, Susan, and Andrew needed to catch the early ferry leaving Orcas Landing at 7:15 and arriving in Anacortes at 8:30 after stops at Shaw and Lopez. Because they were walking on there was no question of space on the ferry, which there would have been had they brought their rental car to Orcas. Our conservative plan was to leave the house at 6:15 and take the *Huginn* to the County dock at Orcas Landing and that meant they needed to get up by 5:30 or 5:45 at the latest. They could have breakfast at the Landing or on the ferry. James wanted coffee before leaving and made a pot. I woke Yvonne so she could say goodbye and we loaded the dock cart with whatever wasn't convenient to carry the 200 yards to the Crane Island Community Dock.

Fog covered Orcas east of the Landing and Blakely Island wasn't visible further on to the east. Since the fog was patchy and moving, I didn't think it would be a serious problem but I turned on the *Huggin's* GPS so I'd know where we were and where we were going, even if I could see. The water was calm; no other boats were about this early in the morning. As we headed through Pole Pass the fog began to move in from the south and by the time we reached Caldwell Point at the limits of the No Wake Zone, Crane Island wasn't visible, a half mile to the west but the course to the Landing was reasonably clear so I took the *Huginn* up on plane and we were soon moored at the County Dock and walked up to the Market where James and Keith took turns getting coffee and something to eat. And then the *Elwah* docked, disgorged a few cars and walk-ons and after hugs, the boys were aboard the ferry, on their way back to Atlanta and Los Angeles. We'd see James in two

Two-hundred-seventy-two: Fond Farewell

weeks for our Borgfest family gathering before he joined Keith having gone home to Atlanta for a visit and we'd see them both in the fall sometime in California. James would have his first dissertation committee meeting soon, a group of four UCLA professors who knew him well and he looked forward to the next step in his neuroscience PhD process.

Now returning to Crane I could see that thick fog about 100 feet high covered the water from Caldwell Point, perhaps to Pole Pass and beyond. The trip back would be slightly dicey. At the east end of the No Wake Zone I slowed the *Huginn*, dropped off plane, and cruised west at about six knots, the world invisible beyond a 50 foot radius of the *Huginn*. Here and there I could see some tree tops on the shore and that — with the map on the GPS screen showing my location and direction — gave me confidence — but were I to encounter another boat or log in the water all bets were off. Coming through Pole Pass was particularly nerve wracking. I could hear the MV *Evergreen State*'s warning blast as it moved east in Wasp Passage on the south side of Crane Island and then the answering toots of another boat sharing that space in the fog. Since foolish boaters abound one could be heading right for me in Pole Pass — though that was less likely at 7:00 in the morning than 7:00 in the evening. Home again, Yvonne called from the bedroom and wanted to hug me. She could see the fog and had been worried, not so much when we all left because she could hear us accelerate after passing Pole Pass going east so she knew we had good visibility there but she had worried about me getting back to the Crane Island Community Dock safely.

Our next set of guests would arrive Thursday and once they left it would be only a matter of days until the next group. It would be prudent to make a dump run even if not strictly necessary yet. Since the F150 was on Crane, I'd have to carry the trash and recycle in the van and the big cans wouldn't fit so I'd have to use large black contractor bags. While Yvonne caught up on her email, I filled the bags from the cans stored in the former privy and then carried them to the *Huginn* in the dock cart in two trips. Use of the bags made me more sensitive to weight than normal and I observed that the scores of magazines I would take to recycle after clearing out my basket in the living room were very heavy. Did I really need to subscribe to all these magazines? Could I get an electronic subscription that dispensed with the paper version? A new project. The tariff? $14.50 for two bags of garbage and four bags of recycle. The cans in the former privy were now empty. We could absorb the discards of another two groups of visitors.

272: A little fog coming through Pole Pass

I'd cut up and moved all of the six trees the arborist, John, had downed for us three weeks before; only a fifteen foot section, the bottom of the biggest tree remained. Margaret wanted a section to support her new bird bath, carved by an artisan from a boulder he found on a local beach so I called her and asked her to meet at the log with her instructions. The top of the log had a diameter of about 14", just right for her purposes so I trimmed the top and then made a cut 18" lower down, this time perpendicular to the trunk, unlike the trimming cut. She would put the slightly inclined cut at the bottom. She and I moved the 100 pound section to a spot near the 200 pound stone bird bath and I went back to the log to finish cutting it up. The stump end was wider than the trunk above it and the top end was supported by wood scraps so that most of the log was off the ground. I stuffed scraps here and there under the trunk and then began to cut it up, using wedges to hold the cuts open so the trunk as it sagged when the cut was nearly complete wouldn't bind the chain saw bar. The sawdust was thick wherever I'd made a cut. Four cart trips were sufficient to move the sections to the front yard firewood area. Now the way was clear to pull the sailboat out from its storage area and launch it at the beach next to the community dock. But not today.

Two-hundred-seventy-three: Crabby

"We can only be said to be alive in those moments when our hearts are conscious of our treasures." — Thornton Wilder

The sun had returned and Yvonne was off to Orcas for a number of errands but not before she dropped her crab pot in the waters of Deer Harbor several hundred yards off Chase and Mary's house. The season was three days old (it would last a month) and there fewer than a dozen floats visible where last year there were 50 at times. Margaret had already caught eighteen keepers (male and over six inches) off Double Island, around Caldwell Point in West Sound, sharing eight with Yvonne because only five can be kept per license. On her second day Margaret found eighteen crabs in her crowded trap, but returned ten to the water. The season looked promising, especially because so far the competition was low.

Leg cramps had woken me repeatedly during the night — perhaps because of the delicious chocolate pudding cake Yvonne had made and I had consumed while watching a movie — or because I had fallen off my regimen of Circle Road walks every other day. I took a fast walk, 40 minutes, noting the community water system tank level was at a satisfactory twelve feet. It felt good to exercise again and look for changes, signs of activity on the island — whether human or natural. Though Yvonne had seen stripped bark on the County Road on Stuart Island when we walked to Turn Point with our friends, I'd missed it. I saw no new cases this day. When we walked Circle Road with James, Keith, John, Susan, and Andrew, I'd shown them a stripped Big Leaf Maple branch across Circle Road from Jason and Theresa's and James had opined that birds strip bark all the time in this case perhaps to find insects — but he didn't have a specific suggestion.

Having spent the last few weeks on house work and socializing, I was eager to return to the *Penal Colony* project. We had permission to use the translation from Ian Johnston, an image of a Lagrange Devil's

Island painting from the University of Missouri, and Chris had completed the cover art work. My task was to make what I hoped were the final changes and corrections, create a Kindle/MOBI book version and provide it to Jens for review.

273: Approaching the house from Och's meadow

In the process of making changes and viewing the result, I found two bugs in my software — one I'd seen symptoms of. Kafka uses category rather than proper names to identify *In the Penal Colony* characters, for instance the Traveller (in Johnston's translation), someone who has come to this penal colony to observe and report, as he has for other colonies. In his eNotations Jens was concerned that he hadn't been consistent in capitalizing the category or social role names used as proper names, so I exported the eNotations and other text he'd written and did a search and (one by one) replace and then imported the text back into the database and then saw that since the import routine updates only what it considers changed text and since it didn't take case into account when deciding what had changed, the import routine didn't make the case changes, so I changed the compare to be case sensitive.

The second bug manifested itself in some eNotations where the text from the beginning of the paragraph as well as the passage being eNotated are shown as links pointing back to the primary text, bracketing the eNotation text. Jens and I had separately noticed that sometimes the links were justified, that is, stretched all the way across the line, unlike the eNotation text, which is formatted ragged right. I found I hadn't put any formatting commands into the routines that created the links so they were being formatted with the eReader's default format, that is justified. I was pleased to find and fix these bugs, a byproduct of putting a variety of books through the software. After fixing a number of content issues, I created a new MOBI version of the book and emailed it to Jens for review.

On her way home, Yvonne checked her crab pot, put the two keepers in six inches of water in a five gallon bucket, dropped the others back into the water, closed the pot and dropped it back in the water. After killing the crabs (one Dungeness and one Red) by removing their carapaces by holding all the legs in her two hands and then crashing the "nose" of the crab on a rock, she boiled the remains (four halves, each with muscle, three legs, and one pincher). After dinner she and I took the *Huginn* back out into Deer Harbor to retrieve the crab pot and any new keepers. We inspected six red and white crab pot floats before finding the one with her name on it. After finding it difficult to approach a float at the right distance — less than the length of the boat hook but at least three feet from the hull to prevent tangling the rope around the prop — I realized that I should be approaching the floats from starboard, where the helm was, rather than port. Of course. The pot had three crabs, two small females and one seven inch male that Yvonne pulled out of the trap and deposited into the five gallon bucket. The cockpit of *Huginn* was now strewn with seaweed and dabs of mud — and I briefly flashed on all the work I'd done recently to clean it. I'd just clean it again (and it wouldn't be difficult) before our next group of visitors, Thursday. Fresh, free crab was a treat we could provide our guests and family, even if I didn't partake. At 7:30 the warm sun in cool air was sinking toward the horizon, the water almost calm and sparkling here and there. A great season opener.

Two-hundred-seventy-four: Birthday Launch

"A boat is the closest thing to dreams that hands have ever made." — Robert N. Rose

A pervasive diaphanous fog left Orcas Island visible but indistinct. I was certain the fog would clear and not be an issue for our cruise to Friday Harbor in the afternoon to celebrate Yvonne's birthday with dinner at the Duck Soup Inn on San Juan Island. I collected her presents, including the hanging metal art work I bought at Crow Valley Pottery a few weeks before (after she pointed it out to me), and put them on the dining room table so she could admire and then open them after breakfast. A bit past 8:00 she came out of the bedroom looking droopy; the beginnings of a cold the day before were now the real thing. She was sick, having caught what John and Susan left during their visit (and which James reported from Los Angeles he had also caught). After some hesitation she agreed that we should defer the Duck Soup Inn until a time she would thoroughly enjoy it — and also minimize the risk of getting even sicker by taking it easy during the day — to be ready for the arrival of our friends from Boulder Thursday.

After fortifying herself with coffee, Yvonne began to open her presents, delighted with the small All-clad frying pan from Jen and James and the cards, gifts, and gift certificates friends and family had gotten for her. On her first July 19th in Boulder in 1979, no one had paid much attention to her birthday (no leadership from me), the result was tears, and I'd tried to do better over the years. She, on the other hand, remembered and made a fuss over everyone else's birthdays. Her 60th party, with family the year before in Walla Walla, WA and Moscow, ID was appreciated by Yvonne and enjoyed by all of us.

Two-hundred-seventy-four: Birthday Launch

274: Yvonne's birthday haul

With the day and evening now open, I checked online for the day's tides and found that high tide would be about 9:00 in the evening. That would give me the day to get the *Discovery*, our 20 foot Ranger daysailer, ready for launching. Yvonne was on board with the idea and she confirmed with Margaret that she'd be available to help.

I'd parked the F150 pickup in the lot near the community dock, so, taking a pair of long-handled pruning shears from the bag of Yvonne's garden tools, I walked across Och's meadow north of the house to the community dock and parking lot at Pole Pass. Returning home in our pickup, up Dock Road to Circle Road and then Eagle Lane, I'd trim low-hanging and road-intruding branches and bushes, something I'd been thinking about for months, anticipating towing the *Discovery* along these roads as well as becoming disturbed at the unkempt look of the neighborhood. As I drove under low-hanging branches, I stopped and climbed into the truck bed to reach and trim the branches, piling the cuttings off to the side of the road. More work than I had anticipated, the job took almost an hour and then the F150 was parked in the yard, its trailer hitch not far from the *Discovery*'s trailer tongue.

Since autumn I'd been watching the port side tire on the trailer the *Discovery* squatted on; it seemed to have a very slow leak and now I'd have to do something about it. I lifted my wheeled air compressor out of my shop and dragged it close to the yard power pole about twenty feet from the soft tire and then retrieved a tire pressure gauge from the pickup and measured the air pressure in the two tires. The port side tire read 15 pounds psi and the starboard (right) 40. I plugged in the compressor, let the pressure rise to about 80 and then filled and tested the soft tire several times until it reached 40 pounds. With the compressor available I decided to top up my compressed air carry can and did the same for the carry can from the community dock that I keep track of.

In the fall, when putting the *Discovery* away for the season, I covered the boat with two brown tarps, one very large and one small (over the bow pulpit and supine mast extending several feet beyond the bow), tying them together under the hull or to the trailer and I now removed them, shook them out, laid them each on the ground and folded and put them away in the storage tent. Then I took everything out of the boat, including the "cabin" contents under the forward deck and put it into the bed of the pickup, out of the way. Using a broom and a dust pan I swept all *Discovery* surfaces and considered that adequate though a washing would have been in order. I noticed that the jib in its bag and the dodger showed mold spots so I took them to the studio deck, laid the jib out in the sun, mixed some Simple Solution Oxy Charged Stain Remover and scrubbed the dodger and then the jib, later rinsing them and hanging them to dry from the deck railing. All in all it wasn't clear to me that it did much good. I probably should have given the solution more time.

I wanted to make sure the old four-horse two-stroke outboard was operational so I attached the fuel line from the portable tank that came with the boat, started the engine and shifted back and forth from forward to neutral to reverse. No problem, but I didn't want to run the engine more than a few seconds because I had no way to cool it. I'd been frustrated with the engine lift (that would hold the engine up out of the water when not in use) so I removed the engine and set it against the tool shed and then exercised the lift to understand exactly how it worked. I put the engine back and the lift acted up. Weight caused it to stick. I didn't like this particular lift but there wasn't anything to do about that until some future time.

With Yvonne's direction, I backed the F150 so that the ball on its hitch was adjacent to the receiver on the trailer tongue. When Yvonne and I couldn't easily lift the tongue to lay the receiver over the ball, I suggested she hang on the stern while I lifted. That worked. I towed the *Discovery* to the community dock and backed the trailer almost to the beach and then called Yvonne on my walkie-talkie. While I lifted the bottom of the now horizontal mast and slid it forward, Yvonne and Margaret, in the bed of the pickup, pulled it toward them until I could see that the foot of the mast would slide into its receptacle. Then they joined me on the deck of the *Discovery*, and while I pulled on the back stay they pushed the mast up and without much effort it was vertical. They held it while I fastened the back stay to its bar on the stern.

With the women aboard and giving me instructions, I backed the trailer and boat onto the beach and into the water. With the tires just shy of the water they paddled from the stern while I tried to push the bow backward to get the boat off the trailer, but without success, so I backed up another two feet, now with the tires in the water and with the additional buoyancy, the *Discovery* floated free and the women paddled it to the dock loading zone nearby where we tied it for later transfer to what had been its dock location the previous two summers. I'd move it the next day. The *Discovery* was launched for the 2011 boating season.

Two-hundred-seventy-five: Sail Ready

"Man cannot discover new oceans unless he has the courage to lose sight of the shore." — André Gide

Another cloudy July day when what we expected and wanted was sunshine. Though by afternoon the sun had made an appearance, it was through layers of clouds and intermittent. Where was summer? Farther east apparently, where much of the country was sweating through a persistent heat wave. Later in the day Yvonne reported that the forecast for the coming days weather in Deer Harbor had improved from rain to possible rain.

Our Colorado friends were due to arrive in Deer Harbor by Kenmore Air at 3:00 p.m. the next afternoon. Yvonne spent a good deal of the day meticulously planning our forays to Victoria and Vancouver with them, making choices about restaurants and activities and printing out maps and routes and by mid-afternoon took me through the itinerary so I'd be informed. Yvonne looked forward to the next two weeks, with friends and family, as the most fun of the year.

Jens had reviewed the near-final draft of the *Penal Colony* and rather than writing out instructions for corrections and changes emailed that he'd rather just talk them through on the telephone so I called him at 9:00. He had his notes and *Penal Colony* on his iPad. I had it on my iPad as well and also had the database software open on my Mac so I could make changes as we went along. Most of his desired changes were to the introduction. One issue was that the translator had used the British spelling, "Traveller," rather than "Traveler," and occasionally one of Jens' sentences would have both spellings, one as he quoted the Kafka translation and one as he wrote about travelers generally. He was concerned that the inconsistency would trouble some readers and I agreed but I pointed out that both he and the translator were consistent, using spellings in their writings that matched their contexts and it wouldn't make sense to change either one. The reader would just have to cope.

275: Wooden seagull perpetually trying to rise off the log

After we finished our call, I created a new MOBI/Kindle version of the book and emailed it back to him for a final look. He'd call or write if he saw a problem. Then I used the Amazon Kindle Digital Platform web service to initiate publishing for *The eNotated In the Penal Colony*, entered the title, authors, and other identifying information, uploaded the cover, the MOBI file, briefly reviewed a version of the book online, priced it, and sent it on its way. I let Jens know and then Chris, David, and Natasha. It was our sixth book and from a mechanics point of view the best yet. The second week in August I'd return to the project and bring the other five books up to date, putting them through the latest version of the software, making slight changes to the structure and any

Two-hundred-seventy-five: Sail Ready

needed corrections, a convenience of electronic books since there was no physical inventory that had to be accounted for.

After lunch I took the *Huginn* to Orcas and met Margaret in the lot. She pointed out that a VW neither one of us knew occupied two parking spaces in the lot, a problem now especially, when the lot was crowded. She'd write a note and tape it to the offending car. I then drove to the Post Office and Deer Harbor Marina, stopping to talk with Ken and Kate along the way, walking with their pooch, Cassie, south on Deer Harbor Road. It was Ken's birthday and I explained that Yvonne's had been the day before, about our recent visitors and visitors to come. We talked for five minutes and in that time no other car came north behind me on Deer Harbor Road. The Crane Island PO Box had a package that belonged in the UPS locker at the Orcas dock parking lot but had come via the USPS. Returning to the lot, I opened the locker to deposit the package and noticed a Fedex box for Margaret. She hadn't picked it up earlier, so I thought perhaps she wanted to return it. When I saw her later on the path across the meadow pulling her wagon to the dock, I told her about the package and she explained she'd been expecting something but at the Post Office. She'd look. She reminded me that while she was fishing on Vancouver Island, Viba would be cat sitting and conducting a silent retreat as she had done other times in the past. I reminded her that we'd be gone too so Viba would have all the quiet she wanted.

Though the *Discovery* was in the water and the mast stepped, it wasn't sail-ready. First, I had to move it from the red bull rail loading zone at the head of the float dock to the angled float dock. I was able to lower the engine into the water with little trouble after experimenting the day before on land. The engine started easily on the third pull and while I got used to the throttle and vagaries of steering the Ranger again, I took the boat out into Pole Pass and then back into the east side of our little marina, tying up securely and then mounting the rudder.

The jib and dodger were in the studio after being cleaned the day before. So on returning home, I took the jib out on the studio deck and folded it in a way that made sense to me after thinking about what it's like to raise the jib while out on the water. I'd need to find the three corners quickly, the head to raise, the tack with lines attached to work the trailing edge of the sail, and the clew to attach to the bow. The dodger, like a convertible top on a car, is made of waterproof fabric and flexible windows, and is intended to keep rain out of the cabin while still providing the helmsman visibility forward. As I installed the dodger I was reminded that it had been made for another Ranger. Some of the deck snaps were in the wrong location and it wasn't possible to button down the two rear corners simultaneously; the dodger was too small. I hung the boom on the mast and topping lift hanging from the backstay, then refolded the mainsail and draped the faded yellow sail cover over the sail and boom. The *Discovery* was ready to sail, perhaps in the next few days with our Boulder friends. The dodger, at least the outside, was a clean white, the aluminum mast black, the sail cover yellow, the deck white and the hull orange with a yellow water line stripe and bright red bottom. The Ranger, with the hull flaring up amidships looks like a shoe or slipper, light and fun. Painted on the stern, "Discovery/Crane Island" told a story of a beginning, an interlude elsewhere, and a return home, this time with Yvonne and me.

While I had worked on the *Discovery*, Margaret came by to ask whether I knew who owned the boat that had been moored at the community dock the week before, secured with only one line, amidships. She had added another line, written a note, and then taped it to the steering wheel but had no response for several days and then the runabout disappeared. She was seeing carelessness and lack of consideration on Crane Island common areas. And pot holes in the Orcas parking lot near Deer Harbor Road. I told her that Pat was in charge of roads and parking and Blair, the docks, and suggested she write them or Jason or me an email with her concerns and I'd see they were on the agenda for the upcoming Board meeting.

Yvonne and I ate the remaining chocolate pudding cake while enjoying Matt Damon and Emily Blount in *The Adjustment Bureau*, a very old story of fate and love in a newer Phillip K. Dick telling and then got into the hot tub, watching the little neighborhood raccoon begin his rounds in the twilight.

Two-hundred-seventy-six: Curb Your Enthusiasm

"The ornament of a house is the friends who frequent it." — Ralph Waldo Emerson

Again, rain overnight and just ending after 5:00 when I got up, not auspicious for the arrival of our Boulder friends by Kenmore float plane at 3:00. On the other hand, the so far moist and cool summer kept the fire danger low and Yvonne's garden happy without watering — and the rain was filing our two catchment tanks for use later when we might experience our usual summer drought.

Even before having breakfast, Yvonne took her crab pot out in the *Huginn* and dropped it in the water off Chase and Mary's house and then spent the morning and early afternoon prepping for dinner and Friday's breakfast. I put the *Discovery*'s trailer back where it belongs, moving it from what had been the driveway outside the fence south of the studio deck and Yvonne's vegetable garden where I had hosed off the saltwater from its dunking when we launched the *Discovery* two days before. Because I found that backing the trailer to its storage spot was going to take more time than I wanted to spend, I turned and then moved it by hand as far up the grade to the back of the yard as I could and then backed it with the pickup to finish the job. Last fall, with Margaret's help I had done what seemed too difficult today with an empty trailer — then with the sailboat aboard.

Dave had undertaken a process to convince the state to allow a water tap (from our community system) for each of the 64 lots — up from the 55 we were allowed now, something he discovered when doing research for the new long range plan the Board had been working on sporadically for the last three years but was determined to finish during the next. He had mailed me asking for detail pumping, metered usage, and unaccounted for statistics month by month for the last five years and

Two-hundred-seventy-six: Curb Your Enthusiasm

anything else that might be useful for making a case about the sufficiency of our system for more taps. Looking through my computer files I found I had only the last three years (having been in charge of the water system for only the last two) so I sent him what I had — the monthly meter reading and pumping reports from Gary as well as the annual month by month billing statements I provided the members and some year over year analysis I'd done and then wrote Gary about forwarding the two missing years to Dave and to me.

Over the last four years I'd dumped all the Crane related material into one computer folder and though it had some sub folders, the Crane material was a mess — redundancy, unneeded files, missing files — and knowing that I'd soon need to start the annual billing again and that I intended to restructure the bookkeeping process, it seemed an opportune time do do some housekeeping so I sat for more than an hour sorting and rearranging and deleting. Knowing also that I would soon be starting a next generation project with the eNotated Classics books and that I'd made a mess there as well by focusing on getting the books published for Kindle, ignoring housekeeping, I created some new folders for publishing the six extant books in EPUB format as well as further evolving the software. What a mess! I would be doing little with the eBook project in the next two weeks while we had company.

After I swept and vacuumed and Yvonne completed her meal preparations, we took the *Huginn* to the Deer Harbor Marina, parking it at the fuel dock and Yvonne went over to the Post Office and then to the Marina store while I pumped gas — not much over 20 gallons for $100 — the typical island surcharge adding $.75 or more per gallon for the cost of barging it out from the mainland. Though the sky was cloudy above and to the east, the west, over San Juan Island, was clear. The sun was coming. After moving the *Huginn* to the space identified as County dock, we walked to the far corner of the marina to wait for the incoming Kenmore flight. We were twenty minutes early and it was fifteen minutes late — as it turned out having stopped in Friday Harbor on San Juan Island before coming to Deer Harbor. The clouds had moved farther east, the water sparkled with a southwest breeze and the marina bustled, sail and power boats coming and going, some having come long distances, others, locals we knew.

276: Yvonne and Dean pull up the crabs

The Kenmore Beaver landed from the southeast and the pilot taxied it to the float plane dock, a dock with no piles stretching up from the water. The plane's port side wing would swing over the dock when it was being parked so there could be no vertical obstructions. The pilot, a smiling, blond young man in his mid-twenties jumped out and tied the port float to the dock and then greeted us, an outgoing woman passenger wearing iPod earbuds, and two other women there to see the landing. Barb was off first, then Dean, Tessa, and then Alan. After hugs all around they collected their baggage (they'd tried to keep it under 24

Two-hundred-seventy-six: Curb Your Enthusiasm

pounds but had averaged 27) and I noticed the lingering signs of a bike crash on Alan's face — a dark red patch under each eye. He gone over the handle bars of his new bike in Boulder after being stopped short by a curb he thought he would just ride up over. It was great to see their smiling faces.

After a stop for wine at the marina store, we boarded the *Huginn* and after some searching found the float to Yvonne's crab pot and while she pulled it up to the cockpit the others watched, then helped her bring it aboard, and then were excited to see a mass of crabs inside, eleven as it turned out, having entered the pot since about 9:00 a.m., attracted by the chicken, though protected by hardware cloth now half gone, bones dangling. Yvonne explained the culling process and Alan and Dean helped her remove crabs from the pot, toss the females and small males back into the water and the keepers into a five gallon bucket — that soon held the daily limit of five. The rest went into the water. Our Boulder city people were amazed.

Back home and after they put their things away, Yvonne led the group to the space between the house and cliff above the water to "murder" the crabs, demonstrating on one, in a state of high excitement because she was repelled by violence and killing — even of crabs — but knew that it was alright and was determined to do it. Dean and Alan then killed and cleaned two each, smashing the front tips of the shells against a big sharp rock to pull the top part of the shell off and instantly killing the crab. For the first time I watched the cleaning process and found it more complicated than I'd expected. In less than half an hour, Yvonne had cooked two of the crabs and we were all on the deck having crab and sangria — except for me — who didn't partake of either.

Since we were on the east side of the house, the deck was soon in shadow, so I built a small fire of sticks and charcoal that kept Dean, Alan, and I warm while the women went inside to prepare dinner. Yvonne's Mexican dinner was a big hit, cheese and then crab enchiladas covered in homemade green chili sauce with a salad and vegetables and what was left of the second pitcher of sangria. The women insisted on cleaning up and while I talked to Dean about his imminent retirement, Alan worked on a grant proposal due the next day. After being reluc-

Two-hundred-seventy-six: Curb Your Enthusiasm

tant to retire because he so much enjoyed being with patients he'd known for decades and families he'd treated for generations, Dean said he finally had no energy to give to the difficult patients, the ones that were so demanding, not because they objectively needed special treatment but because they seemed to need so much attention. Difficult patients had become Alan's curb and Dean had no interest in going over the handlebars.

And then they were all very tired, having gotten up about 4:30 to make an early flight at Denver International Airport and they retired to their respective quarters, this time Dean and Barb to the guest room, closed off from the rest of the house by another set of doors and Alan and Tessa to the bedroom in the attached studio, another quiet and private place. Yvonne and I dipped briefly in the hot tub and then after a little reading and drooping eyelids turned out the lights. How good to have our good friends in our good house.

Two-hundred-seventy-seven: Jones Island

"Life is like sailing. You can use any wind to go in any direction." — Robert Brault

 A cloudy morning that promised clearing but still a cool day and by 11:00 we were all aboard the *Huginn* bound for Jones Island. Earlier, Dean had helped me carry the Livingston dingy down the Raven Cove beach to the rising tide and launch it. I rowed the dingy out of the cove, along the small cliff our house sat on, past the meadow beach, along the breakwater that led out to the south side of Pole Pass and then through and to the left to the Crane Island Community dock. I moored the 8 foot boat behind the *Huginn*'s swim platform, put the oars into the *Huginn*'s cockpit, then found the 30 foot polyrope in the *Huginn* storage lockers and tied the dingy to the powerboat.
 Yvonne had made a picnic lunch and packed it into a covered basket, now sitting in the *Huginn*'s V-berth. With the two jump seats mounted on the engine compartment cover, and a life jacket for each passenger, our friends took their places, and Dean held the dingy against the port side hull, aft, so that it wouldn't interfere with my backing and turning the *Huginn*. Away from the dock, now on the flood tide entering Deer Harbor through Pole Pass, Dean let out all the slack on the Livingston's tow line and the two vessels crossed Deer Harbor toward the north side of Reef Island and the Orcas Spring Point shoreline across the way. Though most of the crab pot floats were much farther east, a few were close to Reef Island in the deeper water on the west side of an almost-island that came within 20 feet of the surface on the west side of Deer Harbor. We moved slowly, about 5.5 knots, or about 6 mph away from Crane and toward Jones Island. Even before we rounded Steep Point we could see the south shore of Jones Island, a Washington Marine State Park.

Two-hundred-seventy-seven: Jones Island

Jones has two mooring locations, the most protected, North Bay, facing Waldron Island and Canadian Saturna Island and served by a dock and six mooring buoys and the more exposed South Bay served by two mooring buoys facing San Juan Channel. Approaching the north bay, careful to avoid the reef marked by a big white buoy, we saw no obvious mooring opportunities. Dean pulled the Livingston against the *Huginn*'s port side to keep it out of the way and I made a pass to the left of the State Park dock, noticing that the only empty space had a 30 minute parking limit. Near the ramp from the pier the other side of the dock a small space was reserved for the Park ranger. The mooring buoys were all in use and a of handful boats were anchored, something I wasn't willing to risk, having been disappointed with the reliability of the *Huginn*'s anchor in the past.

We reversed course, leaving the little harbor and coasted south and then west to the south bay, picked the mooring buoy closest to the beach and once I edged up to it, Yvonne was able to hold its mooring line ring with our boat hook and then string the bow line, bringing it back to the cleat it started from. I gave her a second line to string on the same path — and we were safely moored. Because the *Huginn* doesn't have ready access to the bow along the cabin side, Yvonne had entered the bow area by crawling up through the hatch over the V-berth. Now we had to transfer our party to shore.

While Dean held the Livingston against the swim platform, I took my place on the Livingston folding seat appropriate for rowing and Barb and then Alan came aboard, Barb sitting on the rear seat and Alan in the stern. We had at least four inches of freeboard, not a problem unless someone bolted, even in water choppy with south wind waves and frequent boat wakes. I rowed back with an empty boat and rowed Tessa and Yvonne to the beach and then fetched Dean, who rowed us to shore. We picked up the Livingston and carried it past the high tide water line, parked it on a log and I tied it to a handy log.

277: Jones Island west shore trail

Walking west along the strand we climbed off the beach on a steep path and made our way to the nearby campsite 20 at the southwest corner of Jones Island facing Yellow Island and San Juan Passage. Yvonne had made us chicken salad sandwiches and pasta salad — with crab — and plain for me — but had forgotten forks so we made do with sesame corn chips. Then walking north along the cliffs we stopped a number of times to marvel at an almost horizontal madrona, a horizontal Garry oak that actually had grown down then up, a fenced Garry oak restoration plot, the radical difference between the climate of the southwest side of the island and just a few hundred feet inland, hundreds of visible trunks among a thousand or so downed in the 1989 storm (that dropped 167 trees on Crane), and a small cactus patch.

Dean's asthma acted up as we took the shortcut back to the north harbor from the Cascadia Marine Trail campsite on the west side and he and Alan walked to the County dock while the rest of us walked to the south beach looking at the thick moss, almost rain forest in the center of the island and the Adirondack shelters and orchard above the south cove. Tessa and Barb helped Yvonne and me launch the Livingston and I rowed us out to the *Huginn*, bobbing on its mooring buoy about 100 yards off shore. Yvonne pulled in the two mooring lines attaching the boat to the buoy and we made our way around the east side of the island to the County dock to pick up our friends, using the unoccupied ranger's dock location to park for a minute or two. I drove the *Huginn* leisurely back to Pole Pass, Yvonne was relaxed and sleepy in the afternoon sun.

Conversation focused on worries — especially about friends and family — the overriding question being whether one can actually do anything about many of these situations or even should, Alan and Tessa more interested in potential intervention than the rest of us. Yvonne explained her technique with niece Samantha of just being available, ready to respond should the opportunity arrive, facilitated by Facebook. Both Yvonne and I were skeptical about being able to change someone else and their life — that change had to come from the person, not be imposed (actually it couldn't be) from outside, but one could be present and supportive one way or another until or if help was requested.

As with the evening before and because we had to rise early the next day, the group broke up not long after 9:00 and Yvonne and I soaked briefly in the hot tub before reading for a few minutes.

Two-hundred-seventy-eight: Victoria

"High tea and fine living are meant to be shared with friends." — Henry James

    Barb and Dean were up by 5:30 but I woke Alan and Tessa and then Yvonne at 5:45 as per their instructions, a cool but sunny day in store. Dean reported to me he had seen six otters swim south outside our cove and was delighted to see them. By 6:15 we were all on our way with our luggage to the community dock house doors locked and the water turned off. I parked the *Huginn* on the inside of the outer finger since we'd be gone for more than 48 hours, put the cockpit seats inside the cabin and followed the others up the ramp to the parking lot. On the drive to the ferry landing, Dean, sitting shotgun, commented on how much further it was to drive to the ferry landing versus taking the *Huginn*. And it was, by water less than two miles, by road close to ten.

    We expected few cars in the inter-island queue and weren't disappointed. We had time enough to get coffee or tea at the Orcas Hotel and then would have to be ready to depart. Though the air was cool, the sun was pleasantly warm (I had seen "steam" rising from a drying roof as we drove to the ferry landing) so spent the 30 minute voyage on the *Hyack* to Friday Harbor, outside, above the car deck, first pointing out our house to the north at Pole Pass as we followed Wasp Passage on the south side of Crane. Because Yvonne and I had been across these waters so many times I could attach stories to many places in route — Temple's rocks off the southwest corner of Crane, site of boat crashes, then near McConnell Island, the low rocky island that had been the rue of the seven that had been injured recently in a midnight collision, then the rocks now at low tide just visible that had hung up the *Malibu* which then had to be lifted by crane onto a barge and then ferried to Seattle for repair, and the rocks of Shaw that had torn the skeg off the *Gumption* eight years before, marked on the charts I didn't consult, causing all of us picnic-bound some consternation when, after a loud scraping noise, I had opened the engine compartment and was greeted by water and smoke. (The exhaust line had become disconnected so I crawled into the hold and reconnected but *Gumption* would need a new skeg.)

278.1: Ferry rendezvous at Friday Harbor

Yvonne drove our van off the *Hyack* and dropped us at the Rocky Bay Cafe but because our group was fourth in the waiting line we agreed to meet Yvonne at the ferry landing, picking up food for all of us at King's Market. Dean got more coffee and we all got breakfast sandwiches or breakfast burritos and then some kind of pastry. We wouldn't starve. Yvonne left the van parked in lane 12, where she had been directed, and we walked to the head of the Spring Street pier, sitting on two facing benches in the warm July sunshine enjoying breakfast, the fresh air (Dean pointing out it was about as fresh as it could be anywhere in the US), and one another's company. Then the *Chelan* entered the harbor and we walked to the van, waiting to be directed aboard. Yvonne had given me the tickets and the vehicle manifest she'd filled out and I handed them to the attendant as I drove us aboard the *Chelan*, space having been reserved for us and the other twenty cars that came aboard at Friday Harbor, the rest of the ferry packed and quite different from what we'd seen in April and totally different from January perhaps eight years before when only three cars were aboard the Sidney by the Sea ferry.

The Canada customs line in Sidney moved fairly quickly and after I expertly answered the standard questions (Alan's appraisal), we drove past the marina to look and Yvonne and I described cruises there in our two *Simrishamn* sailboats and our *Gumption* trawler. We were soon in Victoria and found Marketa's B&B on Superior Street, not far from the Inner Harbor, the BC Parliament, and the Empress Hotel. Yvonne and I had never seen so many people in Victoria or the weather so pleasant, almost too warm, in the mid 70s. Buskers had gathered for a "convention" and were performing everywhere, flanked by the usual arts and crafts booths near the water. We were early for our high tea reservation at the Empress so after touring some of the waterfront we walked over to the provincial museum to see what we could learn about the Emily Carr exhibit, an early 20th century writer and artist Yvonne had come to know about and found interesting in part because she lived freely and independently among the First Nation people when that was considered scandalous.

High tea exceeded our expectations, more elaborate than it had been on the two occasions Yvonne and I had indulged in the past. The special Empress tea was wonderful (though I was dubious about having caffeine so late in the day) and the two three-layered serving trays contained six different kinds of sandwiches on the lowest level, scones on the next, and explicit near-candy on the top. We liked the pate (liver sausage) best. One table over, eight young women celebrated an engagement and one made her way to us looking for couples married more than twenty years, and that being the six of us asked for advice on successful marriages.

278.2: High tea at the Empress

We came up with "Don't go to sleep angry — talk it out" and Alan's "Keep sex interesting." After tea we looked at the lobby and then entered the Bengal Lounge. Tessa badly wanted salad and everyone but me wanted wine. Crossing to the harbor we investigated the Buskers' Fair and then took the water taxi to Fisherman's Wharf, houseboats and some shops, and then walked to our B&B where we sat in the sitting room and enjoyed the house port (except for me of course).

When we were in the sitting room, Marketa stuck her head in and confirmed, as Alan had guessed, that she was Czech, from Prague, as it turned out where James and Keith had recently visited, and because she needed to be present most of the time in her B&B rarely got back there. She'd been an exchange student, returned to Prague to pursue her painting and then courted by a Canadian had returned to Canada to marry him, then eventually divorced with a young son — who was now seventeen, in high school, and not very interested in his heritage. Marketa's paintings were everywhere in the B&B (seven rooms in all) and represented many painting styles, from abstract expressionism to cartoonish realism). By 9:30 we could hardly keep our eyes open.

Two-hundred-seventy-nine: Magic Garden

"The glory of gardening: hands in the dirt, head in the sun, heart with nature." — Alfred Austin

The day dawned clear and promised to be, for this area, hot — and we didn't mind. Now with our first breakfast at Marketa's B&B, we found the breakfast room at the back, south side of the the house, crowded with guests already in their places. Alan and Dean sat at one table, the rest of us with two young people, a young woman, Robin, who worked for the government trade department and her friend, a Frenchman, who worked in landscaping. Though she'd never been to the US, she idolized it, amazed that we'd come from Connecticut/Boston, Chicago, Denver, and Seattle, all cities she wanted to visit (She lived in Vancouver and had never been to Seattle?). We compared health-care and banking systems and talked about the EU currency and economy problems as well as the difficulties those countries had assimilating immigrants, something Canada and the US seemed better at doing. Why had he left France for Canada? Opportunity. A white and gray seagull appeared on the deck wall outside and we learned from the young woman serving us that it was "Gilbert" who had made daily visits to the B&B for the last nine years, his reward being the bacon, ham, sausage, and egg breakfast leftovers.

It was nearly 10:00 before we could tear ourselves away from the breakfast table, the time Yvonne thought we would already be at Butchart Gardens but even so we were among the first to arrive, the drive north easy on a Sunday morning. Barb had been to Butchart more than fifty years earlier with her mother, the Gardens and grounds smaller and less elaborate than they'd become. Visitors poured into the parking lot, a river of all ages, races, cultures, and languages, all happy to be alive on such a beautiful day and in a beautiful place. Many family groups included three generations, sometimes with only one representative of the oldest. As we came through the cedars and the view of the former quarry, now green and flower-clad, big smiles broke out on the faces of our friends. They had never seen anything like it — too stylized, Yvonne pointed out, for some — but overwhelmingly beautiful to all of us. Yvonne led the tour, explaining how the annuals are rotated seasonally from the Garden's greenhouses, and identifying what we were seeing, especially interesting to the women who did some though more modest gardening than Yvonne. We'd been to the Gardens in the spring with our son, Noah and his family, treated to swaths of daffodils and tulips but not the profusion of color we saw this day, some beds so colorful they were visually overwhelming. Everyone was interested in the story of the gardens — how when the quarry was abandoned, the wife of the owner, though an inexperienced gardener, was determined to make the space beautiful and invite the community to share it. The family project was now more than a century old and the business expertly run — at least evident in the way the grounds and shops were presented.

Coming through the Japanese Garden to the dock area where Yvonne and I had entered the Garden twice before after mooring the *Gumption*, we saw that Butchart was now offering Duffy Boat guided marine tours of the vicinity and since that seemed like a good idea to all of us we went aboard and then were driven south to Tod Inlet where I finally learned the origin of the pilings (the dock to export cement manufactured from the quarried limestone) and then north to Brentwood Bay where we learned more about how the ugly condo development had been allowed development (a mistake).

After lunch in the cafeteria and afternoon tea in the coffee shop we made our way back to Victoria and today our friends really noticed the dramatic snow-covered Olympics, above Port Angeles, twenty-five miles away, on the south side of the Straight of Juan de Luca, impressive, big water, with access to the Pacific at Point Flattery, seventy miles west.

Yvonne and I, like the others, I think, took a nap before getting ready for dinner, and we convened in the sitting room for wine, Yvonne

Two-hundred-seventy-nine: Magic Garden

having chilled the white in Marketa's refrigerator beforehand. Yvonne suggested we dine at the nearby Santiago, having examined the menu to the restaurant, arriving just before 6:00 and the later crowds, and were delighted to find much on the menu we'd enjoy, all at reasonable prices. Yvonne got prawns and I picked the chorizo, Alan and Dean sharing a big paella and all (but me off course) ordered the house sangria (Yvonne opting for the white rather than red.). The food was very good, done with a light touch, Yvonne explained, and our waitress, who made up for her slightness in stature with expansive gestures and friendliness, was a source of continuing bemusement. A round of port in the sitting room and then rest for the next day's travel.

279: Gorgeous Butchart Gardens

Two-hundred-eighty: Crossing the Straight

"Life is a series of crossings from one side to another." — David McCullough

 The breakfast room at Marketa's was filled again, this morning with young people, except for the six of us, all sitting at one table, unlike the day before, the advantage now of being able to talk with one another, the disadvantage being that we weren't meeting anyone new. Alan observed later than the young people seemed to have a harder time than we'd had striking up conversations with strangers, something, Robin, the day before said she admired about Americans. With a new menu, we all chose the Eggs Benedict except for Tessa who ordered the Florentine option. Gilbert, the seagull, had appeared on the railing outside and Marketa carried out a plate of leftover eggs and meat and though he was initially shy with all of us watching, he grabbed portions from the paper plate she eventually left on the railing, Alan and I taking photos of the this regular morning visitor. Both the morning before and this morning I'd noticed gulls and other birds seemingly on commuter runs not long after dawn, all flying from their night perches to their morning locations, each with different agendas above the Victoria trees, gulls alone and smaller birds often in pairs. We left the table at 9:30 meeting outside a few minutes later with our luggage, first having settled our accounts with Marketa and thanking her for her hospitality, though I forgot to return her keys and had to mail them back to Victoria from Vancouver when we arrived there in the afternoon. As I picked up Dean's small cloth-sided briefcase I noticed it was dripping water. Oh oh! Yvonne found a capless water bottle inside and Dean used one of the towels we keep in the car to dry it out. We stopped briefly outside the Royal BC Museum so Alan and Tessa could run in to pick up gifts

— a cloth loon and a cloth redwing blackbird that would make their characteristic cries when squeezed.

280.1: Marketa feeds Gilbert, the seagull

Leaving the museum not long after 10:00, we were at the Schwartz Bay BC Ferry terminal well before 11:00, picking up tickets at the paybooth for the reservation Yvonne had made before we'd left home for the noon sailing. We got out of the van briefly, Dean looking for an ATM that would honor his debit card, but were soon following the other cars onto the *Spirit of Vancouver* for the 11:00 sailing, a much larger ferry than any in the Washington State system and clearly designed for the bigger waters of the Straight of Georgia, built in Victoria in 1994, 548 feet long, with a capacity for 410 cars including 34 semis. The ferry headed west first around Piers Island, perhaps to avoid getting in the way of the smaller ferry crossing to nearby Fulton Harbor on Salt Spring Island, a place Yvonne and I with Boulder friends, Loren and Janelle, had cruised into once after coming from Brentwood Bay (and Butchart Gardens) and on our way to Ganges, the artist community and largest town on Salt Spring.

    Our van was parked on level four and we left Alan, seated on level six and working, to go outside and walk around the deck, eventually sitting at a table on the stern out of the wind — because of baffles — and watched and listened to a young naturalist begin her talk about octopi. I told any of our group nearby about Ganges as we approached Prevost Island and then we spotted two orcas fishing off Port Washington on North Pender Island. Cruising through Active Pass into the Straight of Georgia, I pointed out the little town of Mayne to Dean, where Yvonne and I had spent an afternoon on our way north to Montague Harbor, a wonderful anchorage, beach, walking, and kayaking area on Galliano Island. On the bow looking out into the Straight, I told Dean and now Tessa about the standing waves at the mouth of the Straight and what it was like in a small boat out on that big and often challenging water. The sky had been cloudy all morning and the BC coast we were headed for wasn't visible and we saw only one sailboat as we crossed, a blue-hulled, maybe 10 meter sailboat, it's northwest course taking it right up the Straight. I'd read that this part of the Straight of Georgia was affected by the nearby Fraser River, its current and the sandbars it created causing problems for small boats. And then we were at the Tsawwassen ferry terminal just north of Point Roberts, a US town on a peninsula separated from the rest of the US by Boundary Bay.

    We were soon on Route 99, the Canadian continuation of I-5 in the US, and then at the Museum of Anthropology Museum on the University of BC campus, on a point south and west of downtown Vancouver. After lunch in the coffee shop we spent the afternoon touring the museum, an occasion for those who hadn't been there to better understand Northwest Indian art and for me to pay special attention to the Bill Reid exhibits in and outside of the rotunda dedicated to his work, being struck again by his *Raven and the First Men* sculpture, a representation of the Haida Raven creation story. I looked closely at the jewelry he'd done and then at the canoe in the large pieces area and then at the long house and totem pole outside he'd done for the museum. In the Museum store I found a collection of his writings and happily bought it, looking forward to understanding how this mostly European had found his way back to his Haida roots and reconciled the artistic visions of the European and Northwest Indian traditions.

280:2 Bill Reid's Raven and the First Men

We were delighted to find that the modestly priced, century old, Sylvia Hotel was on Beach Avenue across the street from English Bay and the barges that had launched the fireworks we'd seen years before with Loren and Janelle and hundreds of thousands of Canadians. The seawall along the beach runs all the way around the Vancouver downtown, including a 5 1/2 mile section around Stanley Park, almost immediately adjacent to the hotel. After drinks in the hotel bar, we walked the short distance to the Raincity Grill, a restaurant we'd eaten at before. My halibut was good though Yvonne wasn't enthusiastic about the shrimp-linguini dish. Dean, Barb, and I faced Denham Street and so could watch the passersby, noticing that they were very casual, lacking the sense of style so characteristic of Seattle, and that none used a cell phone for talking or texting, instead talking to one another or paying attention to where they were and where they were going, again very different from Seattle where young people stare at their smart phones rather than the world around them.

Two-hundred-eighty-one: Off and On

> *"Tradition is not the worship of ashes, but the preservation of fire."* — *Gustav Mahler*

Meeting in the Sylvia Hotel Restaurant for breakfast we all ate too much, adding to the huge calorie count we'd been absorbing over the last few days. I shared an egg of my Jogger's breakfast with Yvonne and she moved two of the large blueberry pancakes from her plate to mine. Our server was cheerful and funny and we ate all we could but piles of toast went back to the kitchen for disposal. The tentative plan was to drive to Grouse Mountain, the nearby Vancouver ski area, ride the gondola and be treated to an expansive view of Vancouver, the Fraser River delta, and the Gulf and San Juan Islands to the west and south but the sky was overcast and some of us weren't so keen on driving and on leaving the city we hadn't yet really had a chance to see, so Yvonne floated the idea that we use the Vancouver Trolley service to both travel around the city, hear narrations about it, and get off, explore, and then get back on whenever we chose. The motion carried unanimously once our waitperson confirmed that her parents had done what we were now considering and greatly enjoyed it. Looking at the Trolley's website I found that we could order our tickets online and thereby get two days for the price of one, using the water taxi credit to take us to Granville Island the next day. Since we had no way to print anything the hotel staff did it for us and we were on our way.

The Trolleys (buses that look like trolleys) cover the Vancouver downtown in two routes, the red and blue, that intersect in several places, most notably at Canada Place, where all the tour buses congregate. The trolleys travel their routes all day long about twenty minutes apart. A Red stop on Beach Drive was close to the Sylvia but we weren't sure where and Yvonne collared a nice looking young man who pointed it out, happy to be of service. As we waited for the next trolley, we were visited by a bearded 60-something man who might have worked for the

Trolley company or was a volunteer for the city (we never found out) who explained how the Trolley system worked and then the Red Route trolley pulled up to the stop.

281: At the Floata for Dim Sum

We all enjoyed the driver's colorful commentary as he worked his way through the city and at Canada Place we changed to the Blue or east route, intending to stop in Chinatown, explore and have lunch. After walking up and down the Chinatown streets without being able to decide where to stop for a meal, Yvonne finally asked a young man in the store and without hesitating about a recommendation, he said "There" and pointed across and down the street. The Floata wasn't visible from the street and didn't cater to tourists. It served the Chinese of

Two-hundred-eighty-one: Off and On

the Vancouver area, for daily meals, and especially major occasions like weddings. We had never been in a place like it. The huge, high-ceilinged room could seat a thousand diners — with a large stage for the head table. We would have dim sum, steamed food, and each picked something from the menu as well as a serving of rice. First to come was a steamed broccoli and we all struggled to master it with our chop sticks.

Full from lunch but telling each other we'd be hungry again in an hour, we made our way to the Sun Yat Sen Garden and then adjacent Scholar's Garden (fee required) spending more than an hour at the site trying to understand the makings of a Chinese garden and comparing it to the very different presentation and feel of a Japanese garden like the one we'd seen at Butchart two days before. All the Chinese gardens we'd seen were dominated by human creations, were very substantial, heavy feeling. The Japanese gardens, on the other hand, blended any buildings into the landscape and had a much lighter sense.

On the way to Canada Place to return to the Red route I had a chance to talk to the driver about the riots following the Stanley Cup loss. He was embarrassed for Vancouver saying he really didn't understand why it had happened especially after the heady and good feeling times of the Winter Olympics. He offered that many people had come downtown the next day to help clean up and that everyone was determined that the perpetrators be made to pay, 800 or so already identified through what might potentially be hundreds of thousands of photos taken at the scene. It was clear to me that the people of Vancouver were very proud of their city, a beautiful, successful, and very diverse place.

The part of the Red route we hadn't yet traveled took us through and around Stanley Park, the huge beautiful forest within the city, and we got off to view the totem poles, one of which Bill Reid had been instrumental in having carved. The view south to the city across the bay was stunning, with float planes landing and taking off constantly, like Lake Union in Seattle, with the addition of a cruise ship berth, one of the Disney ships about to depart for points north. After an afternoon snack, we continued around the Park, seeing the cruise ship pass under

Lions Gate bridge and admired the lush and elegant forest on the island.

Yvonne had found a nearby Indian restaurant, Original Tandoori, and we spent the evening there, thoroughly enjoying the food from our almost private circular booth in the new and nearly deserted restaurant. From the first time I'd seen it many years before, I found Northwest Indian art inexplicably beautiful and powerful. What did everyone else think? They agreed. Where does its attractiveness come from? We didn't know but talked about the smoothness of the lines and the reuse of animal motifs. I wanted to know more so as Yvonne and I tried to stay awake reading for a while, I began to listen to Bill Reid, through his writings beginning in the 1950s.

Two-hundred-eighty-two: Crossing the Line

> *"Travel is fatal to prejudice, bigotry, and narrow-mindedness, and many of our people need it sorely on these accounts. Broad, wholesome, charitable views of men and things cannot be acquired by vegetating in one little corner of the earth all one's lifetime."* — Mark Twain

We woke to a cloudy sky that would burn off by midday as we left Vancouver dropping our friends at the airport on our way out of this attractive city but the first order of business was another breakfast in the Sylvia restaurant, everyone dubious about loading up again after our excessive consumption the day before. Yvonne got only a croissant though she ate some of my Denver omelet but Tessa dialed back to oatmeal for the morning. The plan was for me to drive the van to Granville Island and the others to walk to the Maritime Museum and then take False Creek Ferry to meet me.

We finished breakfast by 9:30 and were checked out not long after 10:00, though confusion about our bill took a while to resolve. I had checked out after asking whether the breakfast charges had been included, assured they were, and then was surprised that the bill was so low. I had brought the van up from the hotel's underground parking to the loading area and handed the paid bill to Yvonne who pointed out it wasn't ours. The young woman at the desk, perhaps a trainee had checked us out of the wrong room. A more experienced hand put things right and the total now was closer to what I estimated it might be.

As I turned onto Beach Drive, the others were already walking east and south toward the Maritime Museum about six blocks away and after I passed them I turned on to Pacific and then Burrard Street Bridge to cross False Creek, exiting on 2nd, driving into the Granville Island complex, finding covered parking and paying $9.50 to park the two and a half hours until 1:00 we'd be there. Two firms offer water taxi service to Granville Island from downtown Vancouver, the second called Aquabus and it took me a while to understand that they docked in two different places. By the time I reached the little blue ferry dock the others were sitting waiting for me next to the Granville Island Boatyard and not far from from the Granville Island Public Market, reminiscent of Seattle's Pike Place Public Market.

The women wanted to shop or at least spend time in the shops and because I found that enormously unsatisfying, I agreed to bring the men to the outdoor courtyard at the Market by noon. Alan, Dean, and I were now on our own recognizance and I took them back to the boatyard, a completely satisfying place, where, as it turned out, I used the ten or so power and sailboats parked on the hard as examples to lecture on boating design and maintenance. We looked at props, shafts, skegs, rudders, trim tabs, keels, hull shapes, bottom paint, swim platforms, and what interested them the most, zincs, after I showed them new zincs on the trim tabs of something that looked like a Nordic Tug, and talked about how the zinc is sacrificed to save the other metal on boats in saltwater. They were already using that knowledge with the women at lunch to challenge them about something they didn't know.

The Public Market was crowded though the women had found a table and chairs facing the courtyard where a guitarist was performing among pigeons, small children, and the parents who were trying, for the most part unsuccessfully, to keep the latter from touching the former. Still full from breakfast we ate reasonably lightly, enjoyed the sun and spectacle and then after looking briefly at the Emily Carr University of Art and Design, drove off Granville Island, found Granville Street southbound and headed for the airport.

From past experience we knew that Granville is slow going, Vancouver not having the massive freeways that destroy the aesthetics of a city and raise the decibel level while making for faster transit. Granville Street was under construction but we arrived at the airport by 2:00, two hours before they were to depart for Seattle and then Denver. We already missed them and there was talk about October in Boulder. Tessa and Alan, Barb and Dean were such good company and we had so much fun, beginning with pulling up Yvonne's crab pot right after picking them up from the Kenmore flight at the Deer Harbor Marina.

282: The Public Market on Granville Island

We found route 99 south and were soon waiting in line in the Peace Arch U.S. customs line, the boarder crossing taking about 30 minutes though almost instantaneous once we reached the booth. At Bellingham we exited I-5 at Sunset Drive looking for Trader Joe's and then when Yvonne remembered that it was on James and James was straight-ahead we quickly found the store and Yvonne shopped, stocking up especially on wine and beer while I napped. At Burlington we stopped at Costco and Yvonne bought more food for Borgfest, our family gathering, now only three days away, I had a retention filament added to my left hearing aid that had been lost (and was intended to keep the hearing aid from falling off and being lost) and bought a chicken caesar salad for Yvonne and a slice of pizza for me for dinner. We ate while we waited in the ferry line for the 7:20 and pulled into the Crane Island parking lot on Deer Harbor Road just before sunset in a clear sky and after taking two cartloads down to the dock and loading the *Huginn*, we crossed to Crane Island with a soft pink sky in the the northwest, the water calm and no other boats around. We could see Margaret's lights on and would hear how her fishing adventure had gone on Vancouver Island. The lights were on at Mike's though he and Evan were now in China at a gymnastics camp and probably Cindy and more family were now on Crane. The evening was warm by our standards, about 70. Summer was in full swing. I turned on the water at the meter and then went back to the dock to bring the rest of the groceries and wine to the house. With the first load, I'd noticed that a flock of about 30 Canada geese had flown noisily over the beach and then wheeled to the west, landing on the water about 100 yards off. Now from the head of the dock I could see that they were lined up drifting or paddling toward the rock that marks the south side of Pole Pass, completely quiet and not intending to land at the rock because the lead geese turned around and paddled back the way they'd come. In the failing light — it was almost night now — the geese were socializing and very much enjoying the evening. Were any now grown goslings we'd seen in the spring part of the group? I couldn't tell. The evening peace was palpable.

    We gratefully climbed into bed, me picking up Bill Reid's writings where I had left off in Anacortes and picking up some sense of the transformation he went through from a young man who didn't even know he had Indian relatives to becoming an accomplished rescuer of the Northwest Indian artistic tradition and master artist in his own right.

Two-hundred-eighty-three: Chipper

> *"Rest is not idleness, and to lie sometimes on the grass on a summer day listening to the murmur of water, or watching the clouds float across the sky, is hardly a waste of time."* — John Lubbock

The sun rose into an almost cloudless sky, the Salish Sea crinkled and sparkling. Walking Circle Road I noted that the tank level was just short of fourteen feet, the point at which it drains through the overflow pipe. Gary, with my encouragement was keeping the normal tank level higher this year to avoid running out of water when the population of the island suddenly, briefly, and unpredictably swells during the summer months. I saw no sign of anyone else on the island, but they were there, probably still in bed or enjoying their morning coffee.

In two days we'd convene the 2011 edition of Borgfest, our family gathering, and Yvonne and I would use the time to finish preparations. Because the ground was dry and some of her plantings wilting, Yvonne planned to water thoroughly and then ignore the garden for a week. Although she'd had problems the previous week getting water to flow from the 450 gallon tank at the corner of the house next to the deer fence, today the system worked as expected, perhaps because the level had risen sufficiently during rains more than a week before.

I worked briefly to drill out and then replace the frost free sillcock for the front garden. Sometime before we bought the house, someone had left a hose connected, the water inside had frozen and cracked the sillcock and it leaked. We'd made do by screwing on another valve and used that to turn the water off and on but because it was exposed, it needed to be covered in the winter, exactly what a frost free sillcock is intended to avoid. Two weeks before a plumber brought to Crane to help with lowering the closet flange in the guest bathroom so I could install a new toilet — on the floor rather than the 3 1/2" pedestal the previous toilet was mounted on — had added a cutoff valve to the supply line in the crawl space before it reached the defective sillcock and he and I had attempted to remove the existing, defective model but were unable to because it was tightly gripped by a decorative concrete border above the house foundation. He cut off the sillcock and today I'd try to drill out the copper pipe that passed through the three inches of concrete — but to no avail. I'd come back to this project and in the meantime Yvonne would have to run a hose from the back yard to the front yard to water.

283: Welcome!

The six trees we'd had felled, that I'd cut up and carted to the firewood area outside the deer fence in front, and the greenery Yvonne had burned, left two big piles of limbs back by the rain shelter and shops. I

Two-hundred-eighty-three: Chipper

rolled the chipper back from Margaret's yard and spent the rest of the morning feeding the sometimes hefty and long stripped limbs into the chipper that would accommodate a 3 1/2" diameter. The chipper is noisy and dangerous so I wore safety glasses and earmuffs. By noon I'd created a big pile of chips under the rain shelter that would have to be distributed by cart to paths that needed them.

I'd noticed that the two north side supports for the rain shelter (4" x 6" posts on adjustable steel supports embedded in concrete) seemed out of plumb and using a level I confirmed the observation. That side of the shelter was tilted slightly away from the east, the prevailing direction of the winter winds — which must have caused the problem — because from December through May the shelter had been walled with a tarp that protected the old kitchen cabinets before I moved them to my shop. I removed the lag screws securing the posts to the metal shoes and used a sledge hammer to tap them to put the feet under the heads and then put new screws through the holes in the shoes.

I filled our dock cart seven times, moving chips from the pile to the path south of the house, the path to the meadow and then from the gate in the deer fence to the south side of the lookout tower base where the boys and I would be working during Borgfest.

By 4:00 I was tired and found Yvonne on the couch in the living room reading. I put my MacBook Pro on my lap and began to work on a photo album with the intention of catching up before Borgfest but shortly after Yvonne closed her eyes for a little nap I did the same on the love seat.

Margaret had invited us for dinner to share the halibut she'd caught Monday off Ucluelet, BC, and Yvonne brought cauliflower and fresh baked chocolate chip cookies. Margaret told us about her fishing adventure and we recounted our Victoria and Vancouver adventures, leaving at twilight for the short walk home.

Two-hundred-eighty-four: Pictures

"Photography is the story I fail to put into words." - Destin Sparks

Especially because I wanted to put pictures of our Victoria-Vancouver trip online for our friends and also to catch up with a backlog of six photo albums, I was determined to use the day to catch up before being consumed full time with our family gathering, Borgfest, that would begin the next day, so I downloaded the 500 plus pictures I'd taken in the last ten days to iPhoto on my MacBook Pro, adding them to another 400 I'd taken since doing the last album a month before. I kept the image files in three places: the MacBook Pro hard drive, an external hard drive, and another hard drive that the Mac's Time Machine software used to do ongoing, automatic backups. The iPhoto database on the external drive contained 27,000 images in 32 gigabytes.

Beginning with the tree clearing project with John, the arborist, then the July 4th weekend, the Reid Harbor overnight, the James/Keith/Keith's family visit, the Food Bank new building opening, and the Victoria-Vancouver trip, I used the Mac iWeb software to create albums locally and then (free) CyberDuck software to transfer them to SiteTurn, the service that hosted our family website, in use since 2002. Many of the pictures I take aren't tied to a particular event so they don't go into an album, waiting patiently to be be included in something more general, such as sunrises, Crane scenes and so on. Each year I start a new home page for that year, adding links to albums as I post them and then at the end of the year making that page what amounts to an archive of the past year. Though any of a number of free online albums might make more sense, I like the idea of being in control of our family albums rather than depend on a service that could disappear with little warning. All in all perhaps 25% of the pictures Yvonne and I take end up in albums. Yvonne scanned the physical photos for 1978 through 1989 but I've yet to use them to make online albums but that's the goal

Two-hundred-eighty-four: Pictures

and 1990 through some of 2002, the year I began using a digital camera, have yet to be scanned. Then there are Yvonne's mother, Opal's albums, including pictures from the 1920s on.

About 9:00 Yvonne baited her crab pot with chicken and carted it to the dock, intending to drop it in the waters of Deer Harbor and hopefully increase her crab inventory for Borgfest and then when she returned continued the complicated process of getting ready for our family. As I worked intermittently on the photo albums, I talked to the Crane Island bookkeeper and then an associated CPA to get a sense of where the association's finances stood with respect to budget now that we were days away from our fiscal year end. I needed information in order to decide whether a deposit on an Orcas side dock repair should be written against the current or next fiscal year. If the association had a "profit," that is surplus greater than what we'd budgeted to move to reserves, the balance could be applied against current expenses. The association books are cash, not accrual based. By mid afternoon, after the CPA reported a favorable balance, I emailed the bookkeeper instructions for creating a dock repair deposit check and attached a scan of the contract with details and then sent an email off to Blair who was in charge of the docks and had negotiated with Waterfront Construction in Seattle that the signed contract and deposit payment would go out the next week.

In the afternoon Yvonne decided she needed a few more supplies so she left for the market at Orcas Landing and would pull up her crab pot on the way home. At about 4:00 she came in discouraged; she couldn't find her pot and was concerned that it had been stolen or had pulled its float under either because the water was too deep or because the line had fouled when she dropped the pot in the water. I volunteered to go look for it but she wanted to wait until after dinner.

For whatever reason our property contained many small stumps, left over from when someone had cut bushes and very small trees down and these stumps had been a continuing source of annoyance. They were hard to see and thus to avoid and both Yvonne and I had been tripped many times. Yvonne wanted them gone. Even if I were very careful I knew I'd probably ruin a saw chain by using it for this purpose so I began by using a hand saw but after doing three small stumps I found the work too difficult and too slow so I filled the gas and chain oil tanks on my Craftsman (Poulon) saw and stalked the yard looking for little trippers, finding and cutting about twenty down to the ground and by the time I'd done the last one the chain would barely cut but I had three new ones in reserve.

284: Dawn paddle-boarder

Yvonne thought we might want to put up the tent under the rain shelter (just a roof on four poles) — for James or for Jeni — so the remaining pile of chips there would have to be moved. I retrieved a small brown tarp from the storage tent and laid it just outside the rain shelter and shoveled most of the remaining chips on to it — having them on the tarp would make them easier to move later and then raked the rain shelter floor smooth.

After I'd cleaned up the dinner dishes Yvonne and I went to look for her crab pot. Mike's family was on the dock cleaning the crabs they'd caught and was sympathetic about our problem, offering crab if we needed it, but Yvonne declined, saying she had an adequate supply for right now in the freezer. I drove the *Huginn* back and forth among the pot floats, beginning some distance from where Yvonne had left hers — since she hadn't found it there. Perhaps it had drifted or become tangled with another line — but none of the floats we stopped to look at was hers — until we found ourselves in the area where she'd dropped it and there it was. She pulled it up and found one keeper, one small male and one female, and so dropped two back in the water and one in the five gallon bucket. We needed a better way of identifying her pot and in making sure she wasn't dropping it in water too deep. I suggested she use one of the *Huginn*'s extra fenders to supplement the typical red and white pot float and use the *Huginn*'s depth sounder and not drop her pot in water deeper than 55 feet. At home she put the 5 gallon bucket in the deck access guest bathroom so the local raccoon wouldn't get it, the raccoon having stolen all the chicken bait from the trap left on the deck the week before — paw prints visible as greasy marks on the deck.

Two-hundred-eighty-five: Flexibility

"We must let go of the life we have planned, so as to accept the one that is waiting for us." — Joseph Campbell

Son Eric and family had driven to San Francisco the day before and would take an early flight to SeaTac, arriving before 9:00, ride into the city on the light rail, meet daughter Jen at her apartment and sightsee at nearby Pike Place Market on the waterfront. Son James would arrive from LAX just before noon. I'd pick him up there, we'd go to Jen's, pick up that contingent and then all drive north to Anacortes. I'd need to be on the 7:15 ferry to be certain of meeting James on time. We'd be seeing son Noah and his family soon too, all arriving for our 2011 Borgfest family reunion.

The sky was overcast but that would burn off. At the Crane Island community dock the *Huginn* was covered with dew so I used the windshield wipers and then my hand to clear the window behind the helm. The tide was on its way out, to the southeast, through Pole Pass, the water teased up a bit by a breeze that promised a good day for sailing. I deposited two NetFlix DVDs at the Deer Harbor Post Office. No one about at the marina. No cars on the drive to the ferry landing until I got to Orcas Road. Near the ferry landing a few cars were parked along the road some distance from the parking lot because they hadn't been able to find a space earlier in the week. As usual I told the attendant at the waiting area I was bound for Anacortes and parked midway in the second row. There wouldn't be a huge crowd leaving Orcas on this ferry.

I'd already had an oatmeal breakfast at home. Now I wanted a cup of tea and so walked down to the Market and because they didn't have Awake I got a 12 oz. English Breakfast. Only a few people were in the store. The morning papers would arrive with the first ferry. Sitting in the van in line nursing my tea and listening to NPR Weekend Edition, I observed a dad with his 10 year-old towhead who he drew to himself from time to time as he carried on an extended conversation with

Two-hundred-eighty-five: Flexibility

someone in the driver's seat of the car in front of me, the boy watching and learning from his dad how to be a friendly adult man.

The drive to Seattle was uneventful, the traffic light, but when parked in the Radisson Hotel parking lot across the street from the Sea-Tac main terminal building and I turned on the cell phone to call Yvonne, she told me that Eric and family were delayed in San Francisco; their United Airlines flight had been canceled and rescheduled for the same flight the next day. After I picked James up, he and I would stay with Jeni and the three of us would pick up the other four in the morning and then drive to Anacortes for the ferry. Argh!

Soon James called to tell me he'd landed and then again when he reached the passenger pickup area. We picked up Jeni in front of her apartment building half an hour later and then drove Western to Ballard and then to the Paseo Caribbean Restaurant on Seaview near the huge Shilshoe Bay Marina. By now the sun had come out and the day was beautiful as Jeni and James waited in line to make their sandwich order. With their sandwiches in hand, we drove farther north to the Golden Gardens park and sat on a bench overlooking Puget Sound, the traffic in and out of the marina to the south and the crowd on the beach to the north. I called Yvonne to describe the scene and include her in the day's activities, knowing she was feeling lonesome and deprived of expected family.

After dropping Jeni for a downtown appointment, James and I took her Mac to the Apple store at University Village to look into getting a new battery and having the keyboard repaired. Because the computer was still covered by its Apple Care contract, the Geniuses at the store repaired what they could including supplying a new battery — all gratis — but it would have to be shipped to their repair center for a further repair they couldn't make in the store. After consulting with Jeni, we decided we'd buy an external drive at the store and then let her back up her hard drive with Time Machine before she shipped it to Apple for more free repair. I was impressed with Apple's helpfulness.

Two-hundred-eighty-five: Flexibility

285: Jeni, James at Golden Gardens in Ballard

Since the Sea Fair parade would start soon, James and I hustled back to the waterfront area and parked the van in the lot under Jen's building and the three of us walked up to the Public Market for Mexican food at El Puerco Lloron, an inexpensive, authentic seeming restaurant behind and below the market. Walking east on Pike we crossed 4th where the parade was imminent and a crowd was collecting and made our way to Pacific Place where we became part of the audience for Spielberg's "Cowboys & Aliens," a mixed genre film that I thoroughly enjoyed. On the way back to Jeni's we watched a little of the parade and soon were sleeping, James on the couch and me on a fold-up cot. The next day we'd make another try to pick up Eric, Kristin, Jackson, and Maddie.

Two-hundred-eighty-six: Back Home

"How often have I lain beneath rain on a strange roof, thinking of home." — William C. Faulkner

About 6:30 I left Jeni's apartment looking for tea and breakfast but the Tulley's downstairs was closed so I walked two blocks north on First Avenue to Starbucks and enjoyed my tea while reading the *Times* on line. Walking back to Jen's I was aware of the homeless sleeping in doorways under pieces of cardboard and searching trash cans for food and treasure, aware of an intermittent odor of urine. Neither Jen nor James was up yet so I woke them, took their breakfast orders and returned to Starbucks with list in hand, returned to the apartment building, dropped off the food and then took the van out of the garage and put it on the street.

While we were in route to SeaTac, Eric called Jeni's phone to report that he and his family were on the ground at SeaTac. We waited in the cell phone lot until they called telling us they had their luggage and we picked them up a few minutes later. Then we were on our way north on I-5 to Anacortes, the kids in car seats on either side of Kristin in the way-back seat, Jen and Eric in the middle seats and James and I in front. In Anacortes we stopped at the Market for wine and other supplies. The ferry landing was crowded and we were directed into the customs line for travelers coming from Canada, something I'd never seen before. Our destination on the *Hyack* was the galley and after lunch, Eric, Kristin, Jackson, and Maddie walked and ran all over the ferry, the sky finally clearing completely before we reached Orcas Landing. The Islands were beautiful.

Yvonne met us at the Crane dock and we were home with everything by about 2:30, the kids running all over the grounds in anticipation of big fun. Yvonne, Kristin, and Jackson left to pick up both Yvonne's and neighbor Margaret's crab pots over near Double Island. Margaret already had her quota of five and offered Yvonne whatever was in her second dropping. They came back with five keepers and Eric, dispatching and then cleaning them quickly, started the first two crabs boiling by about 4:00.

Granddaughter, Opal Ann, called from the ferry not long after 4:00; Noah, Natasha, Morgan, and Opal had driven on rather than walk on and would need to be picked up at the Orcas dock. We were all together before 6:00 enjoying crab and wine on the deck, shells thrown over the railing making the beginnings of a midden. I pictured it eight feet deep and shivered. Borgfest 2011 was underway.

After dinner James showed and narrated his Europe trip DVD to a packed house in my office. I picked up what I'd missed first time around. It was a great family sharing time, with vivid memories of trips together, especially the 1989 Europe trip when James was only three. Jackson fell asleep on the floor, Maddie having conked out not long after dinner.

Earlier Jeni had heard from her friend, DJ. He was on his way south from Vancouver and would try to make the 6:30 ferry — but because of the back up at the Peace Arch entry point he missed it by about fifteen minutes. The new plan was for me to take Jeni to Orcas about 9:30 and for her to drive to the ferry landing and pick up DJ while I waited in the *Huginn*. Darkness had almost fallen when we left for Orcas, each with a head lamp. While Jen drove the van to the ferry landing, I read a few more sections in the Bill Reid writings collection, fascinated by what he had to say about how Northwest art works, the challenges faced by the native people, the life of the Haida, saving old growth forest in the Queen Charlotte Islands and so on. I found him and his recaptured illustrated talks satisfying.

I had left the *Huginn*'s anchor light lit, so the pair could find their way down the ramp and finally heard a clomping on the aluminum. They boarded the *Huginn* and cast off and we headed for Pole Pass, the Milky Way our only illumination though I turned on the boat's headlight from time to time so as not to run over an invisible log. Approaching Pole Pass I saw two widely separated running lights, red to my right and green to my left and a white light above; a big boat was approaching the Pass but so slowly I was tempted to think that it was just sitting — though that wouldn't make sense. I saw other running lights behind it — which didn't make sense to me. They were too close to be separate boats and too far to be the same boat. After backing up I went forward again, not toward Pole Pass but outside and to the south of the mystery vessel — turning on the *Huginn*'s spotlight to see what I was facing — a large powerboat towing three sailboats; say what?

286: James video of their Europe trip. It was a hit!

Two days earlier in the morning off Bell Island I'd seen this same flotilla using our binoculars from the living room trying to figure out what was going on so, I wasn't totally surprised to see it now — but it still didn't make any sense — the power boat with three accompanying sailboats and the whole group coming through Pole Pass in the dark. By now it was nearly 11:00 and Yvonne had already fallen asleep and I was happy to join her. Jen and DJ would occupy the tent Yvonne had set up under the rain shelter. We'd see them in the morning.

Two-hundred-eighty-seven: Picnic

"We didn't realize we were making memories, we just knew we were having fun." — A.A. Milne

At about 6:30 a.m., Jackson, age six, appeared in the kitchen and climbed onto the high seat at the kitchen counter across from me and my oatmeal. He wanted some Marshmallow Pebbles in a cup — no milk — not my idea of breakfast, but what do I know. He had spent the night in the studio loft with Morgan, age ten, who would snooze until about 9:00. Jackson and I had a very nice conversation. He was much older now than when Yvonne and I had seen him a few months before in Los Osos. Then Kristin brought Maddie, age three, into the kitchen from the studio and returned there. Maddie opted for Marshmallow Pebbles as well, but in a bowl, with milk. Jackson, Maddie, and I sat at the dining room table eating breakfast while I peppered them with questions. Then Opal, age 6, joined us, choosing Cheerios from our standard alternatives. The three kids soon got into a conversation that led to activity outdoors — something new for this little group.

Yvonne came out of the bedroom to put her baked French toast dish into the oven, retreated, and then Natasha and Noah, who took off for a jog around the island. Soon everyone but Jeni and DJ were enjoying the French toast and when they were finished, Natasha and Morgan announced they would kayak the perimeter of Crane. Since the tide was flowing east through Pole Pass I recommended they head first south and then west, clockwise around the island. We pulled two paddle sets out of the tool shed and assembled them, designating Morgan the paddle and life jacket carrier and then Natasha and I each carried a kayak down the stairs to the beach ramp and then slid the kayaks one by one down the ramp and then laid them on the Raven Cove beach. I helped Morgan adjust the pedals on his kayak while Natasha got in into her blue kayak and pushed off at the water line, the tide halfway out, the beach gravel with a few larger rocks. Then I set the bow of Morgan's

Two-hundred-eighty-seven: Picnic

red and yellow kayak in the water, he got in and settled and I gave the kayak a push to launch him and pulled my camera out of its holster at my belt to take some pictures of the start of their trip, then climbed the ramp and stairs and walking to the house side of the cove took more pictures, the two of them now several hundred yards south.

We'd talked the day before about a logistically complicated trip to Jones Island but found more enthusiasm for a picnic on the "girls" beach at the west end of the island. By now Jeni and DJ were having breakfast and Yvonne and Kristin were making sandwiches and three bean salad for the picnic. DJ and I talked about his data mining consulting projects and the experience he had gained in that area at WaMu where he had confirmed that high customer satisfaction had a positive correlation with profitability but with the rest of his department lost his job when WaMu was taken over by the FDIC and sold to Chase, something Chase had wanted to do and managed to accomplish for a very small price tag. We went on to talk about the 2008 Crash and DJ filled in specifics I hadn't known.

When Natasha and Morgan hadn't returned from their Crane circumnavigation by 11:30, 90 minutes into their paddle, Noah and I became concerned and walked down to the community dock to take the *Huginn* out to look for them. But there they were, just off the beach revealed by the outgoing tide at the west side of the entry to the little harbor. It had been slow going through Wasp Passage where at times it was a struggle to keep from being carried backwards on the currents — with the help of the west wind. They were preparing to go through Pole Pass and come back to our cove but when I asked Natasha whether she thought the picnic kayakers should use the north or south route she said north — so the next group should launch from the community dock beach not our cove — and Natasha and Morgan paddled to the beach below the pier, now at low tide quite muddy, got out and we pulled their kayaks away from the water.

Yvonne and James would take the two singles and Jeni and DJ a double to the picnic beach at the west end of the island. I helped the four kayakers launch from the beach and then watched them out of sight while the others went on down Circle road towing our dock cart

Two-hundred-eighty-seven: Picnic

filled with picnic supplies. I'd given James a walkie-talkie and called him from Circle Road above the concrete barge ramp and below the north end of the airstrip and he answered promptly. They were almost below me and soon came in sight through the trees having come this far more or less at walking speed. By the time I reached the girls' farm the others were descending to the beach and the kayakers just coming into the beach, at low tide covered in a thick layer of green "sea lettuce." While Morgan especially and Jackson and Opal explored the rocks at either end of the beach, the women laid out a blanket on the coarse sand/fine gravel and we began to consume the sandwiches and salad — except for Morgan whose interest in the bull kelp, star fish, and other beach wonders was greater than his interest in food.

By 1:00 we were all ready to leave and Natasha took Opal in a single, Kristin took Maddie, and Eric took Jackson in the double and they turned south to take Wasp Passage back to our cove. Morgan quickly disappeared on the bicycle he'd ridden to the beach and the little bike Jackson had ridden was now in the dock cart with what was left of the picnic supplies. James was concerned about continuing to work on his dissertation proposal and took off for home while Yvonne, Noah, Jeni, DJ, and I took the south Circle Road route back to Eagle Lane, stopping along the way to look at the osprey nest (I saw an adult's wing unfold and extend over the edge of the big nest at the top of a dead fir). Passing the water tank I noted that the tank level was about 13 feet, a good level, about a foot short of overflow but allowing reserves for a higher summer population.

In the morning just as Eric and Yvonne were walking to the dock to take the *Huginn* to Double Island to pull her crab pot, Margaret called to say she pulled the pot earlier, along with her own, found them both empty and moved them farther from shore. I walked quickly to the dock and caught Eric's attention just as they were pulling away from the dock. They came back with five keepers — Yvonne's pot had collected twelve crabs in two hours — and in the late afternoon Eric cooked up a platter of crab cakes for dinner.

287: Picnic at the west end of Crane

Most of the afternoon the four kids were either in the hot tub or running around the backyard playing zombie, having fun without often crying and mostly self-sufficient, the first time that had happened on Crane and a development Yvonne and I and I think everyone else applauded (and I toasted at dinner).

Two-hundred-eighty-eight: Departures

"The children are now working as if I did not exist." —
Maria Montessori

Kristin needed to make her way back to Los Osos so she could go back to work. Eric would stay with the kids through the end of the week. When it proved impossible to make a reservation on the airporter from the Anacortes ferry landing to SeaTac and the Kenmore Eastsound (land to Boeing field) and Deer Harbor (water to Lake Union) flights would arrive too late, the only practical alternative was for Eric to take our van and drive her to the airport so we left the house and I ferried them to Orcas and they were on their way by 6:30 a.m. an hour before the early ferry left. Having spent three hours during the night thinking about the house retention topic Eric had raised and we'd discussed at dinner the night before, I didn't make it out of the bedroom until Eric and Kristin were almost ready to leave, Jackson eating breakfast and Maddie telling Kristin she didn't want her to leave — though in a cheerful way I thought. Yvonne made an appearance to say goodbye to Kristin and left the bedroom door open so the kids could find her if need be. I told Kristin I thought we'd see them in October.

Back home, I paid attention to the kids and emptied the dishwasher, a daily occurrence with a dozen or so of us under one roof, and soon Yvonne was frying Swedish pancakes in two pans, adding to a stack wrapped in foil in the oven until the batter bowl was empty and then fried a pound of turkey bacon. Jackson and Maddie were served pancakes and I showed them how to butter the pancakes, roll them, and then top them with jam or syrup. Soon everyone but Jeni and DJ, still in their tent in the rain shelter, was enjoying Yvonne's Swedish pancakes, and then Jeni and then DJ appeared, the rest of us having generously left them six pancakes.

288.1: Cousins

Noah and Natasha wanted to take Morgan to the Eastsound skate park and Jeni wanted to take DJ to the top of Mt. Constitution so I suggested Noah take the *Huginn* to Orcas and they all go together in their Highlander — and they did — while James worked on his dissertation proposal, Yvonne went back to bed for a while, and the three youngest kids played inside and then outside, undetectable currents carrying them in one direction and then another at a rapid pace.

It was warm on Crane, perhaps 70 and perhaps 80 in Eastsound, Jeni reported later, the sky cloudy in the morning but mostly cleared by noon. The group returned from Orcas mid-afternoon about the time Yvonne had wrestled Maddie down for a nap in our bed and while James worked on a grilled chicken, sesame noodle dinner, I talked with Jeni and DJ, especially about Afghan history — to the present — and Afghan cuisine — which DJ described as the best in the world — and having influenced food preparation and tastes both east and west along the Old Silk and Spices route. About 4:30 I took him to the ferry landing in the *Huginn*, Jeni along for the ride and to say goodbye and while I

Two-hundred-eighty-eight: Departures

waited in the boat, they saw and talked to Eric as he drove the van off the ferry returning from Seattle. Jeni and I then boated back to the Orcas dock and waited for Eric to park in the lot and walk down to the dock — with the items Yvonne had asked him to pick up at the market.

Stu and Liz, in their 22' SeaSport, were helping Howard and CeAnn, in their aluminum skiff, carry a small refrigerator back to their house, the two couples neighbors and I introduced them to Jeni. Back home while Morgan listened to his iPod, Jackson and the two girls played hard outside, the games now being for Jackson to tow the dock cart up our driveway (up the mountain Jackson said) having one of the girls jump in and then run the cart down the driveway as fast a possible, without, of course, crashing or falling. Jackson had fallen only once, the day before, and then on the small bicycle racing down the mountain sustaining only a small scratch. Overwrought American parents would probably be appalled at the danger rather than appreciative of the joy and schooling the adventure entailed. Mike had called for some help with his boat. It would be picked up from the dock but the keys needed to be brought from his house and put into a boot in a storage locker under the cockpit floor so I did that and confirmed by telephone that it was ready.

James' supper was a great success, the kids all looking for seconds, and when we were done the group walked next door to Margaret's to help her move her trailer out of her driveway. Once Yvonne's chocolate chip cookies were out of the oven, we could begin the meeting Morgan had convened to make construction plans for the look-out/fort that we'd begun two years before, the last time Borgfest had convened on the island (the year before it having coincided with the celebration of Yvonne's birthday in eastern Washington). Yvonne had supplied Morgan with a flip chart, and easel, and a black marker, making a rendering of the current state of the fort on the pad as a starting point. Morgan, age 11, ran a good meeting, though the adults continually tried to take it off topic with their various humorous suggestions (or so they thought).

288.2: Morgan leads discussion on tomorrow's building project

The plans were extensive and optimistic and would play out over the next two days. With my eyes slamming shut, I finally convinced Yvonne to come to bed and the young people, the kids asleep some time before, could continue their reconnecting and bonding, or so we hoped. Yvonne and I whispered to each other in the dark how wonderful they all were and how happy we were and then slipped off to the land of Nod.

Two-hundred-eighty-nine: The Fort

"The creation of something new is not accomplished by the intellect but by the play instinct acting from inner necessity. The creative mind plays with the objects it loves." — Carl Jung

James was booked on an afternoon flight to Atlanta to meet Keith and stay with Keith's family until retuning to Los Angeles on Sunday, where he would get back to his lab work and continue writing his dissertation proposal, a draft due in less than a week, so he reserved a seat on the Anacortes/SeaTac shuttle and would need to take the early ferry, leaving the house by 6:30. A glorious morning, the water flat, I parked the *Huginn* at the county dock just as the *Hyak* pulled in. He'd stop at the Market for breakfast, coffee, and something to take for lunch and that was the only food he had, as it turned out, until he reached Atlanta, about 12 hours later while we were eating dinner on the deck, because Airtrans carried no food, not even for sale.

Eric likes to make pancakes and had purchased blueberries the day before so he could use them for this morning's flapjacks. While he kept two griddles going, Yvonne cooked up a pound of turkey breakfast sausage. It was nearly 10:00 before we all left the dining room table, Morgan very eager for us to start the next stage of construction on the fort/lookout tower. First, we carried all the wood I'd stored under the south house deck, 2 x 4s and 2 x 6s already stained a cordovan brown that we hadn't used when flooring the main platform and building the upper platform between two madronas and one fir. Then we scoured my shop for tools and fasteners we'd need, Eric disappointed to find only a handful of the 3" nails we wanted to use for framing. Noah insisted that the construction site be equipped with a boom box — or something that would play music. Once the extension cords were in place we could talk about the building plan, the wood it would require and what I'd have to get at the lumberyard to supplement what was on hand. By 11:00 the plan and therefore needs were clear. Noah, Eric, and Morgan would start the construction and I'd go to the lumberyard to fetch four 8' 2x 4s and 14 angle brackets to make a ladder for access to the upper deck from the lower, 20 10' 2 x 4s for framing (the room on the lower deck would be five feet high) and thirteen 8' 2 x 6s to finish the upper platform and to make rafters for the roof of the five by eight foot room on the nine by eight foot deck.

The Orcas heat surprised me, perhaps eight or ten degrees warmer than our shaded construction site on Crane. After stopping at the Post Office to make a deposit and to pick up the mail, I followed a very slow silver KIA SUV out of Deer Harbor along Deer Harbor Road and then Crow Valley Road to the lumber yard. With the pickup truck on Crane I'd have to use the van to carry lumber to the Orcas parking lot for transfer to the *Huginn* and since I thought the roof rack was too fragile, the lumber would have to go inside the van and it took me a while to figure out how to do that, including trying but not succeeding in removing one of the center row captain's chairs. the load ended up sticking out beyond the end of the vehicle so the back door wouldn't close but I used some bungee cords to tie the boards together so they wouldn't be likely to slip out and to hold down the rear gate. I used the Orcas dock cart to move the lumber to the *Huginn*, requiring four loads and since the tide was out the ramp was steep and the boards encouraged by gravity wanted to escape the cart and plunge into the Salish Sea.

I towed one load to the house and then encouraged the others to come and get the remainder. By 2:30 the lumber was stacked and ready for use and Noah and Eric continued with the upper deck and lower framing while I installed lag screws through the lower plates to securely hold the feet of the walls to the deck. Morgan had found a piece of scrap plywood and begged Noah to cut him a sword. Then Morgan wanted to sand the splinters off and I pulled a palm oscillating sander out of my collection of brightwork refinishing tools and showed him the power outlet pole in the yard and how to use the sander. Once Jackson saw Morgan's sword he wanted one as well and found a plywood scrap Noah then cut with my Bosch jigsaw, which he admired, and then Jackson did some sanding. The boys now each had his own sword and they drifted away from the fort project, dueling without injury for the next hour.

Looking at Eric's framing Noah was concerned that the house on the deck might be too small, with inadequate space for four cousins to sleep overnight. We also needed to decide on a door size and its location — so rather than be faced with a recall task we asked Yvonne to come to the site for a consultation. The plan had her approval. Yvonne brought out beers for Eric and Noah and lemon flavored water for me. Before we quit for the day and put the tools under the deck to avoid the danger of overnight dew (which wouldn't be likely to happen this time of year), Eric took a picture of our progress with his cell phone and sent it to Kristin.

289.2: Closely attended

Jeni made up a batch of artichoke dip and served it with pita chips and corn chips, with wine, and Natasha prepared pizza dough and fixings, first making a pizza for the kids on the grill on the deck and then one at a time for the adults who chose their toppings, put them on a plate and put it on the deck railing for Natasha. I was surprised that it was possible to make pizza on a grill. It was good, the late afternoon warm, and we sat on the deck for some time, the kids in the hot tub, then out, looking for something more to do. Natasha and I continued our conversation on the deck talking first about the prospects for the planet given the eventual decline of the petroleum-based economy and then about when and how parents should direct/meddle in the lives of their children — after age six or so — my position being as little as possible consistent with reasonable safety and the respect of others. Opal had asked a willing Yvonne to bring the wig and costume tub to the liv-

Two-hundred-eighty-nine: The Fort

ing room and soon Opal, Maddie, Yvonne, and then Eric appeared on the deck in outrageous attire. And then we were all in the living room dancing and trying one wig after another, and the one bizarre mask that Maddie found a bit frightening, Jeni, with her new camera, and me taking lots of pictures and some video.

I could see the setting sun reflected in the trees and rocks of Bell Island and suggested we move the party to the dock to watch the sun go down and we got there a few minutes before it dipped behind Orcas. Then Morgan announced he wanted to take a dip in the water off the end of the pier, something we'd all talked about for some time but couldn't actually bring ourselves to do (the water being 50 degrees), so I recommended he don a life jacket from the *Huginn*. With Noah ready to pull him out (there was no ladder) and Jeni and I with cameras recording video, Morgan ran off the end of the dock, hooted at the overwhelming sensation of cold, Noah pulled him out, and then Morgan was running down the dock to get to the hot tub as quickly as he could. Yvonne had made oatmeal raisin cookies and the adults sat in the living room clearing a plate and sipping port. Natasha saw my Bill Reid book, we talked about Northwest art and then I found Reid's "Raven Steals the Light" story. I'd see whether the kids would sit through a reading the next day.

Two-hundred-ninety: Hornets

"Nature is often hidden, sometimes overcome, but seldom extinguished." — Francis Bacon

The morning was warm enough, in the sun on the deck, to have breakfast outdoors and Yvonne made another batch of Swedish pancakes, Morgan the last to appear but the yellow jackets, hornets actually, showed up quickly, attracted, probably by the bacon and sausage, and their presence was annoying and slightly threatening to those like Noah who were allergic to their stings though he wasn't to bees. I retrieved two fly swatters from the broom closet in the kitchen and smacked the hornets whenever they landed, usually on or around food. Maddie had eaten little of the pancake on her plate on the kids table and was now roaming around the deck so I didn't hesitate taking out one hornet that had landed in her food. The hornets appeared one at a time and I dispatched them as I able but their flying was so random, rather than purposeful the way a house fly would be, that it was hard to find swatting opportunities. Maybe that was an adaptive trait but they weren't getting any food either so random flying couldn't be one. It wasn't obvious where they had come from, usually a nest in the ground or sometimes inside a wall if the right sized opening is available. I encouraged Morgan to look for the nest because he'd been successful in the past spotting them, at our house on Cayou Valley Road in Deer Harbor and here on Crane. Two years before we'd found a nest inside the skirting around the hot tub — accessed via the pull holes in the doors — and in the ground in Yvonne's planting area below the deck to the east toward the water. The year before the hornets had established a nest in the wall of the studio, entering through a hole left from an antenna mounting. In all the cases I sprayed the nests with hornet poison, some concoction of citric acid I think, the first time only after I'd dressed myself head to toe in a hooded paper jump suit and goggles. It wasn't necessary. I'd been stung in the past a few times but it was only slightly annoying.

290.1: Warm enough for breakfast on the deck

Eric, Noah, Morgan, and I went out to the fort construction site, Noah focusing on the upper deck and staining and Eric on the "house" framing. I began picking up sticks and branches fallen over the last four years on this northeastern part of our property and other parts that we'd never cleaned up. This activity turned into a project and I recruited Morgan to help once I began to cut dead limbs from trees and some live ones that blocked the deer path along the cove just north of our property — at the foot of the meadow we cross on our way to the community dock. We rarely came to this area but the rocky bank afforded views of Orcas, Bell, and Shaw and it occurred to me it would make a nice spot for a lunch picnic, so that's what we did, Yvonne and Jeni making chicken salad sandwiches. The tide was out so the rocks and in some places beach were drying in the noon sun and Morgan, with Jackson tagging along, walked along the rocks usually covered by water and climbed up the bank to our picnic area. Opal and Maddie stayed on the blanket with the adults, not risk takers like Morgan and Jackson. I was pleased that we'd in effect claimed this area and though we'd owned it for four and a half years finally took possession of it. The narrow deer trail right along the rocky cliff led along the east side of the house to the south and through the trees along the south side of the meadow in the other direction. It was a place I imagined old-enough young children would enjoy exploring.

290.2: Picnic lunch just north of the house

After lunch, and back at work outside, Jeni came to tell us that Yvonne had been stung by a hornet that had slipped under her foot as she lifted it from a flip-flop and then attacked her as the put weight on her foot and set her heel down. Jeni and Natasha had put baking soda paste on the sole of her right foot and wound it with an Ace bandage and administered Benedryl. I found Yvonne in the bedroom with Maddie encouraging the three year old to take a nap. The hornet sting did not turn into a problem.

Jeni had decided to take the Clipper from Friday Harbor back to Seattle since the price was about the same as the Shuttle but the travel time shorter and its destination in Seattle, the waterfront convenient to her apartment. Since the Inter Island ferry didn't have coordinating times it made sense to take her to Friday Harbor in the *Huginn* — and besides Yvonne wanted to stop at King's Market in Friday Harbor to pick up more groceries — so we left the Crane dock about 3:00 for Jeni's Clipper 4:00 departure. Until we entered San Juan Channel the water was reasonably calm but then became choppy — from the south wind and boat wakes. We tied up at the county dock and I hugged Jen goodbye and she and Yvonne walked up the ramp to the pier, Jen bound for the Spring Street dock and Yvonne for Kings the next block up. I had taken Bill Reid's writings to read but soon started to doze in the warm cabin and gave myself up to it — and then Yvonne was back with two small bags of groceries and we slipped the mooring lines. Friday Harbor was very busy, with boats of all sizes, from inflatable dinghies to 50 foot sloops, going into and coming out of the marina or to the fuel dock. Yvonne and I talked about how fortunate it was that Eastsound was so far from the ferry dock — walking off and then on to the ferry again — for a day trip, for instance, wouldn't work. You need a car to get from the landing to town. San Juan channel was choppier than when we'd come south but the trip back would be mostly with the wind and waves. I followed a big powerboat for a while but it was too slow so I slowed down and turned left to go over the wake and the bow turned up to 30 degrees and stayed there. The boat was riding the back of the big powerboat's wake. Yvonne didn't like that at all. I pushed the throttle forward and we were soon over the hump heading north at 22 knots. Coming in to Wasp Passage and then around the west and north side of Crane, the water, in the lee of the wind, was flat and a pleasure to ride across.

290.3: Noah can't resist

Back at the community dock Natasha was sitting on the rocks above the water while the four kids crawled over them and from time to time waded. The tide was at just the right level — a broad sandy beach without the mud or seaweed that appears at low tide. Morgan did some jumps into the water and then Noah appeared and did several including one from the pier ten feet above the water.

Eric and Noah had made great progress on the fort/lookout tower, using up all the relevant wood, though we were long on 2 x 4s and short on 2 x 6s — which we had decided after I had gone to the lumberyard to use for the ceiling/upper deck. Noah had covered most of the raw wood with opaque cordovan acrylic Cabot stain and I picked up a brush to help finish the job. The in-tree, triangular-spaced deck was covered and just needed the 2 x 6 edges trimmed. The framing and rafters for the "house" on the lower deck were done but the walls were open.

290.4: Evening campfire

When it began to get dark Yvonne herded everyone outside to the fire pit outside the rain shelter, carrying a bag of marshmallows and three metal wienie roasting sticks. We pulled the benches and chairs out of the rain shelter and arranged them upwind around the fire pit, with twigs and branches already piled and ready to be ignited. Burn piles were forbidden by the Fire Marshall this time of year but 2' by 2' campfires were still permitted (until the fire danger became extreme). I took used motor oil from the tool shed and a gasoline can and poured half a cup of the former and just a little of the latter on the tinder and then dropped a match on it. Poof! The campfire was ready for marshmallow roasting within a few minutes. The roasting wands proved too short — the user had to be too close to the fire — so several of us found appropriate dead branches and used them for the roasting.

My first attempt came back from the fire black and I couldn't figure out what to do with the husk over the now liquidy center so I pulled it off the stick with my fingers and then couldn't get the sticky mess off my fingers. Yvonne wanted us to sing campfire songs so I led "Bingo," the repetitive song in which claps are successively substituted for letters. Then Yvonne performed *By the Sea* as she remembered it from an 8th grade talent show with her friend Julie. Opal and Morgan liked playing "Which is Better" (or "Which is Worse") and we spent about 30 minutes thinking of close to gross or absurd choice sets — such as "Which is worse, forgetting to wear your pants to school or forgetting which class you're in?" all the adults — and Morgan — remembering dreams with those themes. When it was almost dark I led the group in Taps, at least the lyrics I more or less remembered from Boy Scouts and then we trooped back to the house and I returned to the fire pit with a five gallon water bucket and poured it over the coals remaining from the fire. Day was done and the sun was gone.

Two-hundred-ninety-one: Sailing

"Twenty years from now you will be more disappointed by the things you didn't do than by the ones you did do. So throw off the bowlines. Sail away from the safe harbor. Catch the trade winds in your sails. Explore. Dream. Discover." — Mark Twain

Natasha was obligated to work Saturday so the young family, reluctantly I think for Morgan and Opal, left Crane mid morning to take the 12:05 ferry to Anacortes and then drive the 150 miles home, avoiding the shorter route via the Edmonds-Kingston ferry because it would likely have a lengthy wait time because of the traffic across Puget Sound to the Olympic Peninsula, but before they left we had a leisurely breakfast of scrambled eggs (prepared by Eric) and turkey sausage and turkey bacon, sitting around the dining room table, the sky overcast, and cool wind coming across the Salish Sea.

Noah and family were ready before 10:00 and everyone walked them to the community dock, their luggage in our dock cart. Then goodbyes and I took them across to Orcas and helped carry their luggage up to the parking lot, Morgan with two plywood swords, both made by Noah, one repaired with Gorilla glue after Morgan smashed it one time too many on a stump. Noah had made two for Jackson as well and for two days one or both of the swords were at hand — and often part of sword fights with blows that never landed on one of the boys. Noah had cut out the swords and then the boys had used one of my sanders to remove splinters.

Margaret was on the Orcas dock and helped move luggage to the parking lot. As Noah and Natasha were loading their Highlander, a car pulled into the lot and two carpenters joined Margaret and they headed down the ramp to her boat.

Two-hundred-ninety-one: Sailing

291.1: Morgan, Opal, Maddie, Jackson in front of Corrina's mural leaning against the half-finished Borgian fort

When I was back on the dock, Rupert and Rachel had come in on their C-Dory to drop off Rupert so he could bring his replacement Suzuki over by barge as part of a complex barge run that included a truck with new double-pane windows for Margaret and the installers' tools. Josh would use our F150 to pick up the tools at the north side ramp and bring the tools to Margaret's. The wind was fresh from the southeast and Rachel wasn't enthusiastic about taking the C-Dory back to Crane, since it would be her first solo trip. I offered to take her and then bring Rupert back to Orcas to pick up his boat after he had arrived back on Crane with his new car. I knew that Rachel, a film director, was working on an iPad app to facilitate the movie making process and we talked about her progress, now at a working prototype stage which had received an enthusiastic reception from people in the industry. She had

Two-hundred-ninety-one: Sailing

an angel investor lined up who was eager to invest but she wanted to make another pass through the prototype with a UI (user interface) expert before she began using other people's money. She said that Rupert, a director who had a CBC documentary miniseries soon underway, provided guidance that represented the business interests of film making.

291.2: Opal and Morgan

After lunch Eric returned to the project site to build the ladder to the upper deck and Maddie took a nap with Yvonne and in a while I moved the unused lumber to its designated place under the deck, putting scraps as spacers between layers so that it would dry and not warp. About 3:00 Jackson and Maddie put on their life vests and we walked down to the dock and put them on the 20' Ranger *Discovery*. Eric and I dropped the dodger out of the way and he and Yvonne removed the sail cover. I lowered the outboard, got it started, and we were on our way passing to the west of Pole Pass and northwest across Deer Harbor to get out of the lee of the island to we'd have some wind. Eric raised the mainsail and I turned off the engine and then realized the topping lift was holding the boom and that I'd forgotten to attach the pulley system to the boom.

291.3: Noah and Natasha

After I'd put things right we began to sail, fast enough to be satisfying. We wouldn't raise the jib since our goal was especially for the kids to be on the water, sailing. Jackson soon took himself down to the open cabin and laid down on some life vests and was soon asleep.

Two-hundred-ninety-one: Sailing

Maddie didn't seem to realize that she was supposed to be excited about sailing by being terrified or exhilarated. After sailing away from and then back toward Pole Pass with many tacks in the process, I started the motor and Eric dropped the mainsail and he and Yvonne wrapped the sail back and forth over the boom and then secured it with sail ties. Three teenage girls in an inflatable were in the *Discovery*'s space at the community dock but then rowed out away from it as I got close. The wind was blowing briskly through Pole Pass and over the breakwater but when I managed to bring the stern to the dock Eric grabbed a line and leapt ashore. He used a second line to pull the sailboat parallel to the dock and he and Yvonne tied it up. The kids had come back to life and were beginning to whoop and holler.

Eric grilled turkey burgers outside and Yvonne doctored some brown beans. Everyone had a good appetite. After the kids were in bed Eric, Yvonne, and I talked about the possibility of Eric and some of his friends buying us out of the Crane property when we were ready to leave. We'd look more into that possibility in the future.

Two-hundred-ninety-two: Swarms

"Patience is bitter, but its fruit is sweet." — Jean-Jacques Rousseau

Eric, Maddie, and Jackson came into the kitchen from the studio about 6:45, Maddie carrying Minnie Mouse and her Baba (blanket) and Jackson his plywood sword. By 7:10 we were out the door, their luggage in our dock cart heading for the community dock — on the way to the Orcas ferry landing for the 8:50 Anacortes ferry. Yvonne, up early to take us across to Orcas led the way with the kids in their yellow and red and blue and green jackets. Once on Orcas Yvonne hustled the kids up the ramp and Eric and I took the luggage, storing it in the rear of the van. Yvonne had put the Captain Crunch and Fruity Pebbles boxes in a plastic bag with allotted portions already in sandwich bags. Yvonne took the *Huginn* back to Crane Island where she started doing laundry — all the bedding and towels for thirteen people — and quit when she'd done five loads — though there was more to do.

We parked in the first row of the waiting area — at the landing more than an hour before departure — and cars poured in after us. As we crossed the rocks that make up part of the path from the gate to the hotel deck, I noticed that chairs were being set up in the grassy yard for an afternoon wedding and that brought back a flood of memories from Tim and Kelly's wedding the year before. The Orcas Hotel Coffee Shop was crowded but I found a table at the south windows while Eric found food for himself and the kids (coffee and cherry danish; peach yogurt, a blueberry muffin, and apple juice) and then I ordered a cup of Tazo Awake tea.

292: Eric, Yvonne, Maddie, Jackson

Wisps of fog hung over Harney Channel separating Shaw from Orcas Island and consolidated into dense fog as the *Hyak* plowed eastward through Thatcher Pass to Rosario Straight, a not uncommon pattern in the San Juans. I told Eric about how years back I had seen three or four power boats following the ferry east through the fog to Anacortes, happy to be out of the ferry's way and letting it run interference for them. That same trip I'd seen two small power boats huddled around the Thatcher Pass channel marker buoy east of the pass, as the ferry passed close by, waiting in a safe place for the fog to lift.

Maddie slept the whole way to Seattle and Jackson was quiet, dozing once in a while, I think, while Eric, an aerospace engineering professor, and I talked about the evolution of his thinking on departmental process and teaching methodology at CalPoly over the last four years.

Two-hundred-ninety-two: Swarms

He was determined to do more for the students and the university than was possible through traditional approaches.

We found a parking place on Western Avenue across the street from Jeni's apartment building and took the kids and baggage up the windowed elevator to her floor. I'd forgotten that they hadn't yet seen Jeni's place and they found it very interesting, especially when hearing about the swimming pool. Kristin had wanted the kids to see the Space Needle so I drove them to the entrance off Broad, gave them hugs, and drove to I-5 and headed north toward the Burlington turnoff for Anacortes. Within minutes almost, Eric had taken pictures of the kids at the Space Needle with his cell phone and posted them on the internet.

Though I arrived at the Anacortes Ferry Landing two hours before the 4:00 departure of the Shaw-Orcas ferry, lanes 3, the Orcas loading lanes were already filled and I was diverted to lanes 5, the fourth car from the head of the lane. I'd get on the ferry but somewhere behind me as the overflow lanes filled drivers would have to wait for 7:20 ferry.

Though everyone had to wait hours in most cases, I saw no grumpiness among the travelers, only smiles, conversation, dog walking, food fetching, and some Frisbee playing among the thousands of drive on and walk on passengers. The sun was warm but the air — a cool 73 degrees. The *Hyak* was docked on the left and the *Elwah* on the right, white and green twins, characteristic Washington State ferries with a tall center tunnel that could accommodate high trucks if need be and two layers of auto only lanes on either side, topped by two passenger levels. The silhouettes of walk-on passengers moved along the loading bridge to enter the *Hyak* at the level of the lower passenger deck while the lighted sign at the head of the loading lanes told us that propane tanks needed to be shut off, that drivers shouldn't use cell phones while loading, that food was available at the Cheesecake Cafe at the landing or in galleys on some of the boats. Shaw cars boarded the *Hyak* first since they would unload first and then trucks and cars with trailers and then the two lanes labeled 3 and the two labeled 5 — until the *Hyak* was full. The sky, almost cloudless except for cloud banks over the Cascades and especially around Mt Baker, the dormant volcano, to the northeast, was an intense blue as was the water reflecting it on a crinkly surface created by a noticeable southwest breeze. A lone sloop sailed west through Guemes Channel to pass south of Cypress Island and then through Thatcher Pass into the San Juans. On the *Hyak* half the passengers on the second level were out on the deck surrounding the cabin, sitting in the sunshine or standing at the rail to have their pictures taken or to look out at the water that stretched unbroken across Rosario Straight and the Straight of Juan de Fuca to the Olympic Peninsula. A ten year old girl in a violet jacket with long golden hair that blew in the breeze leaned over the rail and then returned to her parents and younger brother sitting on a bench against the cabin wall in the sun. Most young boys seemed to have crew cuts, buzz cuts, short hair that reminded me of the 1950s.

Parked in the Orcas lot, crowded for the last several weeks, I carried the two car seats down to the dock where Yvonne would soon pick me up. As we cruised west toward Pole Pass she told me about Roger's memorial service — that I'd missed because of my chauffeuring. Perhaps two hundred people had attended the service and reception, and though too religious for her taste, Yvonne had appreciated the chance to acknowledge this friend and his widow Joan. The house was picked up, clean, and quiet again, its normal state and over dinner we reviewed the fun we'd had over the last week, for me the most ever.

After dinner Yvonne and I walked Circle Road around the island. Near the community center six teenagers drove by in a green Gator at a reasonable speed and we said hello. The tank was at 11 feet. I'd have to write Gary an email. We talked the whole time about the last three weeks and our plethora of visitors, tired from hosting but happy with the experience. When we turned off Circle Road on to Dock Road a quarter mile from our house we encountered the teenagers again, smiled, and gave them the thumbs up. Some Cranians had complained about irresponsible young drivers at an annual meeting but these weren't. They were good kids.

Two-hundred-ninety-three: Day of Rest

"The best and most beautiful things in the world cannot be seen or even touched - they must be felt with the heart." — Helen Keller

Having nothing pressing to do, nothing that couldn't wait and still outside my normal daily routine, I didn't get out of bed until after six and didn't start my morning walk around Crane until half-past seven. It was clear the summer was hastening on. The grass growing up in the crown of Eagle Lane, the road that connects the four houses in our neighborhood with Circle Road, the former barely wide enough for one car with salal, ocean spray, and young firs crowding in and the latter a wide one lane packed gravel road, looked worn out, from lack of water and walkers.

Turning left on to Circle Road I took another look at the four dead windfalls just off the road thinking about when I'd slice them up and take them home in the bed of my pickup while it was still on the island and then at the community hall/fire station I stepped back off the road so I could clearly see the cracked tree across the road leaning on its neighbor and noticed that it was cracked in two place, the lowest about 30 feet up and at a second place five feet higher on the leaning, almost disconnected section. In spite of what John, the arborist, had told me in June it wasn't obvious this was something we Cranians could do for ourselves.

Stepping back on the road I saw a bearded man in his forties I didn't recognize carrying a light jacket turn off Circle Road toward what had been Bob and Nancy's farm. Was he staying there or avoiding me? The tank was now down to ten and a half feet, leaving about 7500 gallons above the fire reserve. Gary would be coming to Crane today to add time to the pumps. The island was crowded with people, that is to say, there were probably 40 on our 250 acres and mostly invisible to one another unless on the roads or at the docks. It was the high season on

Crane, August usually warm and sunny, and the time most likely for people to return to their vacation homes.

293: Spring rains grow tall grass

Just over the hill and at the base of the airstrip I stopped to look closely at the now idle little farm. Because the spring rains had extended into early July, the grass had grown very tall, five feet at least in many places, and now it had turned a yellow tan. The dark gray posts that held up the deer fencing were buried in gold and years earlier would have been cut by now by a horse drawn mower and stacked in the hayloft in the big yellow barn. Here and there in the golden field perfectly formed dark green Christmas tree firs towered over the grass.

Two-hundred-ninety-three: Day of Rest

The field, cleared a century ago with great effort, would be forest again without a mowing every few years.

Yvonne was up now having breakfast and reading yesterday's *Seattle Times* and told me she was taking the day off; she was worn out after the intensity of the last month. She would stay indoors today, lie on the couch and read about how Eleanor Roosevelt had been a transformative first lady. Because she'd been complaining my hair was too long I let her cut it, but not as short as she had the previous time and then we talked about the possibility of a fall trip in Washington, Oregon, California, maybe Arizona, and Colorado to see friends, family, and places we hadn't been. That lead to talking about our van and her concern that because it had so many miles on it the van might break and leave us stranded some place. And we talked about our future on Crane, how long we would stay and where we would live, covering some of the same ground we had with Eric, who wanted to find a way, with friends perhaps, to eventually buy us out and keep the Crane property in the family, if only partly.

I spent the afternoon creating an online album of Borgfest 2011, our family gathering over the last week, picking about 150 pictures out of the 500 I'd taken, using iWeb, adding captions, posting it to our family Website, and then writing everyone that it was ready for viewing. Earlier in the day Noah had written everyone a sweet note of love and appreciation and later James, Jeni, Eric, and Natasha added to the thread. The photos included a beautiful shot of the three youngest working together with an iPad and pairs and groupings of adults engaged in conversation, really together for a time.

During the past two days Yvonne and I had talked about conversation, when it's great and when it's not, who does it and who doesn't, and what it is, agreeing that it requires interest in one another, especially relative to really understanding where the other person is coming from and always speaking to that point, creating a bridge between minds or souls. Much interaction is parallel monologues or free association where good conversation is a cooperative creation of something that didn't exist before and can be savored together. We had that with our family and a few other people but in our experience it was unusual.

Two-hundred-ninety-three: Day of Rest

My pattern is to find or remember an interest or concern with the other person and then raise it as a starting point, to come back to it, deepen it, explore it, see where it moved — but I found that process almost never reciprocated. Others could embellish, expand upon what was in their minds but had little interest really in what was in someone else's. Noah had explicitly referred to insightful conversation in his thank you note and we'd talked with Eric about conversation as well.

Later in the hot tub Yvonne talked about how she felt a little blue, as her mother described it when visiting family left, and temporarily without much motivation to jump back into her busy life of volunteering, socializing, and taking care of her garden and the house. I felt that too in a way. For almost a month we'd dropped our routine for one that was intensely social, with family and old friends, and had felt enriched by it in a way our routine hadn't and couldn't. At least for right now we were feeling an openness and perhaps desire for change. A door had been opened and we were looking through it and we might find ourselves questioning what had seemed obvious before. Or maybe we needed this day off or perhaps a longer sabbath, as Yvonne said, to get her mojo back.

Two-hundred-ninety-four: Comparisons

"We are all in the gutter, but some of us are looking at the stars." - Oscar Wilde

Yvonne spent the morning catching up, especially with Food Bank tasks because the Board would meet the next day. One job was to bring the Food Bank website up to date , referring to the completed and in-use new building rather than it being under construction. Because the Food Bank iWeb source files were on my MacBook Pro that had died some months earlier, I had to download the finished HTML home page file from the website, open it with KompoZer, and then let Yvonne modify the text data, then upload it back to the site. Very clumsy. Sometime in the future I'd either need to recreate the project on my other MacBook Pro or set up the Food Bank site with a free blogging service.

Though not eager to leave Crane this day, after lunch Yvonne went over to Orcas to see to the grounds at the Post Office and Community Club. She liked to be seen weeding since she thought that might make other Deer Harbor residents feel guilty — and though they might not volunteer to help with groundskeeping they might with something else. As it turned out Laurie saw her and said hello and Eric as well, who had done much to clean up the grounds in the first place and who commented encouragingly that maintenance was much easier than it had been and she agreed. At the Deer Harbor Community Club the new septic system had resulted in the addition of two boulders on either side of the septic tank lid to protect the tank from someone parking on top of it but the functional boulders conflicted with the rest of the landscaping. She'd have to think about what to do.

Later at home she watered her front garden; the typical August drought was very hard on some of her plantings and the 450 gallon catchment tank was exhausted. Crane water was supposed to be used for domestic purposes only; she was considering digging up some of what she'd planted and giving it away. In a winter month we use about

1800 gallons of water or about 60 gallons per day. In July we'd used four times that amount — partly because of having visitors and partly because Yvonne had done watering. Because Crane Island encourages water conservation, the rate per gallon changes with usage; $.03 per gallon to 3000 gallons in a month, $.05 per gallon between 3000 and 4500 gallons per month and $.10 per gallon over 4500 gallons. Our water for July had cost about $240 and as it turned out just over $1000 for the year — August through July, not exorbitant in comparison with some communities on Orcas but much higher than what typical household water costs on the mainland.

294: Kayaks at rest

Overall, Crane Islanders would pay just under $9400 for their use of 273,000 gallons of water in the fiscal year just ended. Our annual water bill was second highest for the island though the winner didn't live on the island and was here only occasionally but then in entertainment mode. Besides paying for water usage — annually, in arrears, members had to pay a $100 meter fee as well as $700 dues, annually, in advance, as well as fees for moorage and so on.

The window installers at Margaret's had made progress over the weekend installing all the lower level windows and were ready to work on the upstairs and needed extension ladders, so at Margaret's request I carried over two. By replacing the single with double pane windows, Margaret intended to make her cabin more livable in winter in anticipation of living on Crane year around beginning in about eleven months. She had electric heat and a wood stove but being conservation-minded tried not to use much of either and as a consequence was too cold in the winter. Presumably the new windows would allow her to be comfortable without using more energy.

I spent the day mostly on Crane Island accounting and water matters in anticipation of a Board meeting the coming Saturday and the annual members meeting a week after that. At the Board meeting I would suggest reconsidering doubling the meter fee to $200, something the Board had decided to do after the coming year's budget suggested we wouldn't be able to make our normal reserves deposit in August 2012 but the current year was ending with a surplus — we hadn't been able to complete or even start a number of projects — and I suspected that would be true for the coming year as well. We could stick with the budget we'd sent to the members for consideration before voting on it at the annual meeting and know that revenues would be lower and be very confident that expenses would be even more so.

As part of our effort to create a new long term plan — the operating plan was twelve years old — we needed to understand our water usage better and be able to document it to the State so we could expand the potential number of users — and Dave needed historic usage and pumping information and I looked through both my paper and electronic files to find what he needed — but was only partly successful. It would be desirable to find meter reading source documents and put everything into a database, or at least spreadsheets. A big job.

Two-hundred-ninety-four: Comparisons

James called from Los Angeles and we talked about his experience in an Atlanta suburb with Keith's family a few days after leaving Crane, very aware of the differences in housing and lifestyle. The Atlanta houses were huge, all pretty much the same, and much less expensive than houses that big would be in Seattle or the San Juans. They locked their doors even when in the house. We locked our doors only when we'd be gone overnight. In Atlanta, much of the time it was too hot to go outdoors so everyone stayed inside except to play golf or go to a pool. We could be outdoors year round. Huge box stores bordered the residential area making shopping convenient — by car. We had limited shopping that took about 25 minutes to reach and better shopping was hours away. James liked LA city life and Crane country life but not suburban life very much.

After a hot tub soak, Yvonne took the iPad to bed and looked at condos for sale in Seattle — just to see what was on the market — thinking about the future — and some nice ones downtown were much less expensive than they'd been.

Two-hundred-ninety-five: People

"The art of conversation is the art of hearing as well as of being heard." — William Hazlitt

Judith and Barbara were already walking down the ramp to the float when I approached the Orcas dock. They were early and so was I. The breeze out of the southeast and the clouds had kept the day cool, in the low 60s — in August — and both were wearing jackets. I hadn't seen Barbara in two years perhaps and had forgotten her folksy warmth. I was nice to see both of them.

Entering the house, Judith said her first order of business was to see the IKEA kitchen so Yvonne took them both on a tour and I added details when it seemed relevant. Besides curiosity and a desire to praise our work, they had a practical reason to know more about the kitchen project — they had just bought a 30 year old house in Portland near Lewis and Clark where they both taught, had furnished it from IKEA, and now wanted to update the kitchen.

Dinner conversation over halibut veracruz and 18-hour no-knead bread focused for a time on the Food Bank, in transition over the last two years from a casual, ad hoc organization founded by a now elderly couple to a more structured organization with a building and active board and feeding more people. Yvonne, its secretary, had attended the Board meeting earlier in the day during which Larry, Board president and operations manager had announced he would resign in October, not unexpected but now definite and requiring the Board to find a volunteer replacement for this demanding position. The question we discussed was what the duties of the Food Bank Board should be and the related question of whether it was really needed or whether the organization just needed an operational component. Yvonne thought the Board should provide guidance, planning, policy, fund raising, taking the longer view rather than the just-get-through-the-day view. Judith, who had been my colleague on the Library Board, suggested that different organizations need different kinds of boards, some active and that meet frequently and some, like the Food Bank, she suspected, that would have little to do once the transition had been completed. My sense was that boards are responsible for the continuity and persistence of organizations, having a different role than volunteers or even paid staff that may come and go and that taxing and regulatory bodies may insist on boards so as to have people to hold accountable. Barbara thought the Food Bank Board needed to protect the organization via insurance, maintaining food service health standards, and so on. Yvonne, who was trying to bring a level of professionalism to the Food Bank Board and so at every meeting asked about the budget — only to get blank stares — assured Barbara she wasn't feeling overwhelmed by all the ideas being put forth and that it helped her sort out what was important for the organization.

Barbara was very interested in whether the Food Bank did any means or need testing, asking what would happen if she, or anyone else who had the funds to feed themselves came to the organization and asked for food. Yvonne answered that the group's policy was to give food to anyone who asked — no matter what. But what about free riders? It's better to have a few free riders than make life even more difficult for people who are already embarrassed about having to ask for food and the means testing process would be time consuming and expensive. Better to let the people who ask for food sort themselves out.

The discussion of the Food Bank Board and non-profit volunteer boards generally led us to discuss homeowner association boards, infamous across the country for fostering bad feelings, fights, and sometimes property sales. Barbara and Judith had their stories about the Spring Point homeowners association and in particular one member who created trouble by insisting that no one cut any trees down even if that meant having 25 small sick trees rather than 12 big healthy ones. Though the Crane Island Association experienced friction in the past there was little today in part because most of the members and the board in particular had made comity a top priority, higher than rule following, though that didn't mean rules were ignored.

295: Life finds a way

Two CIA members had expressed unhappiness with the fact that the Crane Board had collected all the known policies together, discarded some, added some, and rewritten some and that I expected the discussion at the coming annual meeting to be protracted and unproductive, and we talked about techniques for leading such meetings by doing active listening or what James called reflecting. Rules, guidance, suggestions are important for Crane because leaving people to their uninformed good intentions might lead to results even they wouldn't want. But the insistence on strict rule following doesn't make sense either on Crane since it is blind to nuance, context, and comity. And it is often the anarchists regarding their own behavior who want to impose rules on others, something I'd seen on Crane.

Two-hundred-ninety-six: Girdled Branches Mystery

> *"Every particular in nature, a leaf, a drop, a crystal, a moment of time is related to the whole, and partakes of the perfection of the whole."* — Ralph Waldo Emerson

Something caught my attention outside in the near dark early dawn in the cove below our house. Unlike the last few days the water was calm and smooth everywhere except where the rocky bank on the other side of the cove met the receding tide. Ripples broadcast the recent entry or exit of something from the Salish Sea and then I saw movement, a mink, barely visible was climbing the bank over layers of seaweed, a different kind at each remove from the average water level — none above, rockweed right below and then sea lettuce below that with Green ribbon even lower and less tolerant of exposure. I couldn't see the mink top the bank; perhaps it had entered a crack in the rock above the high tide line. I assumed it must have been fishing in the darkness.

Again the day was cool and overcast, summer nowhere evident as I crossed to Orcas in the *Huginn*, mooring at the almost empty dock, most of the boats usually there now at the Crane community dock or private docks on the island. On both sides of Deer Harbor Road in the vicinity of the Post Office and the marina temporary No Parking signs announced restrictions for the next day between 5 a.m. and 9 a.m. I'd heard from Judith the evening before at dinner that the house vacated by Dennis and Candy when they moved to Oregon and bought by neighbors Bob and Phyllis was to be moved to Eastsound and donated to OPAL, a group focused on creating permanently affordable housing on Orcas. Nickel Brothers would do the move as they had other buildings on Orcas including some imported to Orcas from other places in the Puget Sound or Vancouver Island area, notably one next door to

Dennis and Candy's house and three that Ken and Kate had Nickel's bring from Canada, unload at North Beach and move by truck to a nearby five acre parcel they had subdivided for the three houses, which they'd improve and in one case enlarge. House moving was a rare but not unusual sight on Orcas, simpler than some other locations because much of the utility infrastructure had been buried years ago to mitigate the need for repairs due to falling trees and branches and because there were no overhead bridges, traffic lights, or other infrastructure that clutters urban or even suburban areas.

296: Osprey nest above Circle Road

I parked in Howard's driveway and he came out to wave me into the house. Because Sheila was gone to a niece's wedding on the East

Coast, the Greybeards were meeting in the house rather than the little "honeymoon cottage" inside the garden fence on the hillside above the house, David and Brian also in attendance. I'd missed a few weeks because of guests and was happy to again be part of this regular Wednesday morning gathering, Howard handing me a mug of strong, hot tea. Howard and Sheila provide prodigious amounts of bird seed to the local population and sometimes, reluctantly, to acrobatic red squirrels, and are great observers of avian life, something always going on at the edge of the deck outside their dining area. David asked about a swallow couple at the feeder and that prompted Howard to describe how some of the birds were suffering from a kind of conjunctivitis, the eye swelling until it burst, pointing to his pellet gun leaning against the wall and how he had dispatched one recently to end its suffering. Coming into the house I'd noticed that an extension to the house was under construction at the north end, the closet, I assumed, that Howard had talked about adding. He was surprised and a little worried that I'd noticed it since he hadn't filed for a building permit and was worried others might notice the new construction and report him — something I assured him wouldn't happen, the wall of the small addition already painted to match the house, and I opined that because the extension was airborne, that is without a foundation, there was no need to report it. He wasn't expanding the footprint of the house. The San Juan Islands were replete with owner built, non-permit-carrying property improvements, in part because the County was notoriously slow in reviewing requests for permits and often denying them or insisting on costly and what seemed to be unnecessary modifications. The State of Washington had recently created new building restrictions for wetlands and anything near water, the rules being so onerous when applied to the San Juan Islands that it would be almost impossible to build or improve anywhere and that hearings were being held to call for special treatment for the islands good intentions, that is the protection of habitat and the appearance of coastline having run amuck here where enforcement would make it impossible for all but the wealthiest to live.

Though the three big open fields on Crane, once belonging to small working farms, hadn't been mowed and were covered with yellowing

Two-hundred-ninety-six: Girdled Branches Mystery

five foot high grasses, on Orcas, "farms" along Deer Harbor Road near Pole Pass and all through Crow Valley west of Orcas Road to the foot of Turtleback mountain, bundles of hay lay in the fields waiting to be picked up and stored or sold. The rampant green growth of May and June had ceased, like the sun in its trek north, and was now beginning to withdraw, the green ripening to yellow.

In the late afternoon while Yvonne attended a Deer Harbor Community Cub Board meeting at Bev and Dave's — that included wine tasting in anticipation of a Club fundraiser in a few weeks — I did my my island peregrination, content to see the tank at twelve feet, and noticing that branches in some big leaf maples had turned brown, others yellowing, something I'd seen in prior years but didn't know the cause of. It wasn't anticipation of October; it was girdled branches, caused by who knows what, though likely a bird, and who knows why but probably connected with a search for food or perhaps nesting material. Most trees were untouched but some had been significantly damaged, the tree's normal shape distorted over time by the unexplained parasitic action.

Two-hundred-ninety-seven: Home Improvement

"Every accomplishment starts with the decision to try." — Gail Devers

After all our guests were gone on Sunday, the water in the hot tub looked cloudy, sand and dirt on the seats and floor. I added some chlorine, shock, and brought the PH level down but that didn't do much good, nor did another treatment two days later. I hadn't changed the water in more than a year and it had been fine but now it wasn't. I was reluctant to use more community water both because it's a shared resource we try to conserve and because all the guests and Yvonne's watering would put us in the five or even ten cents per gallon water billing category.

I had let the tub cool overnight by turning off the power and leaving the lid open. Did Yvonne want me to fill her pond with some of the water? Yes — so I let the hose draining the tank empty onto the rocks lining the pond until the level reached the bottom of the snow lantern and then let the rest run into the salal close to the bank. She didn't want the chlorinated water anywhere near her garden.

After wiping down the fiberglass sides of the hot tub and sponging out the remaining water, sand, and dirt, I took the door off the little pump house under the deck in order to remove and clean the filter and noticed that the concrete floor needed sweeping. Rats had gotten into it over the last winter and though I'd put metal screening over their entrance the floor was still littered with their dried dung. I didn't want to use a broom we used in the house but I had a whisk broom in the *Huginn* I could press into service.

As I walked onto the dock, I noticed that a Northwest Indian canoe with ten paddlers had come through Pole Pass heading west, on what mission I couldn't tell. How long had it been since that had happened?

Two-hundred-ninety-seven: Home Improvement

Since we had recently seen canoes off Jones Island and taken a close look in the Museum of Anthropology in Vancouver — and because I'd been studying Bill Reid's writing and work — I watched the canoe until it disappeared out of sight behind a point. Then I began noticing the dragon flies working the dock area, remembering how in Concord, Massachusetts one summer morning outside our house, I'd watched a dragonfly sitting on a lilac branch and was surprised to see that it could move its head separately from its body. Above the dragonflies, swallows wheeled and turned this way and that and I squinted to look for the insects they were seeing and pursuing, occasionally two the same one. I could see one flying insect. They could see hundreds, maybe thousands.

Then I looked more closely at what was growing out of the top of one of the wooden pilings. I'd taken a picture the previous summer of salal taking root in the piling. Now it was dead and an 18" high cedar had taken its place, looking just like cedars and firs and occasionally alders and maples grow from rotting stumps, nurse trees of a sort.

While fetching the whisk broom from the *Huginn*'s cabin, my adjustable oil filter wrench caught my eye. Unscrewing and screwing on the spa water filter container had always been problematic. Perhaps this wrench would help so I took it along and walked across Dock Road toward the break in the split rail fence and the path across the meadow to our house in the trees and was startled to hear my name spoken. It was Dan and Jan; they'd been there all the time and I'd walked right by not seeing them. Their puppy had grown. We talked about the weather — where was the summer — and the upcoming Board meeting — Dan was a Board member — but spent the most time talking about how having a house on Crane was time and money consuming — that in retirement our lives were focused on projects rather than, as Jan said, fun. I didn't tell them that projects were my fun.

Crossing the now golden meadow I noticed that dragonflies were on patrol a foot or two above the high grass and swallows criss-crossed the air twenty feet above them. About 100 feet up a turkey buzzard hung in a circle, its eye on something midway up the field I couldn't see.

Two-hundred-ninety-seven: Home Improvement

Before we had bought the house in the fall of 2006 someone had left a hose attached to a frost-free sillcock and the freezing water had damaged the sillcock in a way I hadn't been able to repair; even when turned off it dripped. The temporary fix had been to screw on a brass valve that a hose could be connected to, using that valve rather than the sillcock valve to turn the water off. The downside was that the sillcock was always filled with water and so could freeze in the winter, potentially causing a disastrous leak so we'd covered it with a foam cover over winter. But it needed to be fixed — so when I had a plumber out to work on lowering a closet flange to install a new toilet I asked him to install the new frost-free sillcock I'd bought more than a year before. He managed to cut the old sillcock from its water supply in the crawl space and put in a shut off valve but couldn't remove the old sillcock because it was imbedded in a 12" high, 3" thick concrete apron that runs along the lower edge of the house below the cedar siding and above the foundation. He cut the faucet off but couldn't get the copper tube that ran through the concrete out. I had tried drilling it out to no avail and now had borrowed Howard's Bosch rotating hammer drill and bought a 1" diameter masonry bit to use with it and went to work on it while Yvonne worked nearby weeding and thinning her garden in the afternoon sunshine. The bit kept coming loose so I got a big Cummins drill I had picked up at a garage sale years before and after an hour managed to remove all of the old frost-free but the new one wouldn't fit through the hole.

 I didn't much like working in the crawl space. It was reasonably clean, the black plastic over the dirt and rock floor probably less than six years old but in most places the floor joists were less than three feet from the floor, waste water pipes hung down here and there converging on the outflow to the septic tank, the line I had to insert a new "T" into two years before when I added a toilet and sink to the shower room off the back porch. Fiberglass installation hung down here and there and was wound around hot and cold water PVC supply pipes further adding to the crowded feeling. I had left a halogen light and 100' extension cord in the crawl space following that project, using it subsequently for a clean up and check I'd done the summer before and the

Two-hundred-ninety-seven: Home Improvement

plumber had used it to illuminate his recent work. Crawling the 70 feet to the sillcock location was hard on the knees as they encountered rocks under the plastic sheeting.

297: Water feature

After crawling in to enlarge the hole from the inside I found I didn't have enough room to work; a floor joist was in the way so I crawled back outside and walked around the far corner of the house and worked on the hole until I could pass the shaft of the sillcock through the concrete apron. But how would I fasten the sillcock to the concrete? I tried drilling pilot holes in the concrete for masonry screws but got nowhere. I found an eight inch long piece of 1 x 4 cedar under

Two-hundred-ninety-seven: Home Improvement

my shop/shed and took it, along with the 22 calibre stud driver I'd bought at a yard sale but never used back to the house, drilled a 1" hole in the cedar, put the sillcock shaft through it and through the concrete apron and then nailed the cedar scrap to the concrete with the stud driver and then screwed the sillcock flange to the cedar. Back in the crawl space I cut down a right angle assembly I'd scavenged from a yard standpipe and used it to connect the sillcock to the water supply valve in the crawl space. I'd let the glue dry overnight before turning the water on.

After a spaghetti dinner and a walk around the island, Yvonne made fresh peach cobbler and we savored it as we watched John Stewart skewer a hypocritical Fox News woman commentator. The hot tub felt good, the water now clean, though the chlorine had precipitated ferric iron out of the water. I'd have to adjust the PH again. Then further along in a Thomas Hardy biography until my drooping eyelids made it impossible to see the page.

Two-hundred-ninety-eight: Leaks

"We are all apprentices in a craft where no one ever becomes a master." — Ernest Hemingway

Pink and gray clouds waited over Orcas to the northwest and Blakely almost straight east was almost invisible in low clouds, a very weak blue overhead and a gentle southeast breeze put goose bumps on the water except where it was out of the wind in our cove and instead a slight rocking prevailed. The outgoing tide through Pole Pass was visible as a river flowing across standing water to the southeast and then south and then west through Wasp Passage bound for the Straight of Juan de Fuca and the Pacific. Pink clouds had turned a burning gold and the sun finally appeared above Caldwell Point on Orcas. It would be a beautiful day.

By 8:00 the hint of fog in the east had covered Harney Passage and was moving through Pole Pass into Deer Harbor and through the trees behind the house, our regular doe and two fawns unconcerned as they nibbled their way around the yard outside the deer fence, tasting, chewing, moving on. By 6:50 I could no longer see Orcas two hundred yards away and that's where I'd need to go soon but I was certain the fog would dissipate or drift elsewhere — or, in a pinch I could use the Furuno GPS system in the *Huginn* to make an instrument crossing and docking on Orcas. When I finally left the house about twenty minutes before nine, Pole Pass was mostly clear but fog covered the two marinas in Deer Harbor and climbed the palisade where David and Maxine lived and where we'd be having our meeting in a few minutes. With fog blocking their view they'd wonder whether I was going to make the meeting until I actually appeared.

298: On our way to the potluck, Yvonne carrying brownies

Jens and Chris were already sitting with David at the dining room table, Chris having walked from his house a mile away. After Chris and then I told boating lost-in-the-fog stories, we picked up the six pages of notes I'd written two days before and discussed our financial position, sales, expected royalties, the need for better accounting and sales tracking, the status of ten book projects, ideas for ten more, what we'd learned from the most recent preparation and publishing process, the need to publish the six books with Barnes & Noble, Jens' intention to experiment with the two eNotated Kafka books in his fall class at Wellesley beginning in a few weeks, the desire to support student Kafka annotation for Jens' class, the attractive business extension of providing academic libraries with classics — annotated and not, that Natasha simply didn't have time to do marketing for us, the important function of reviews, and the possibility of having Dick lead marketing and join our group. By 11:30 I found myself worn out by having talked — explained — so much and after stopping at the Post Office was home by noon eating lunch.

Yvonne had eaten earlier and was reclining in her comfortable chair on the studio deck in the August sunshine, expecting soon to be asleep. And I was soon on my back on the living room couch with my eyes closed. And then I wanted to do something physical and useful. Yvonne was in the kitchen preparing brownies for the Deer Harbor Community Club potluck that evening and I told her I'd be in the crawl space turning on the water for the frost free sillcock I'd installed the day before. Adequate time had passed for the glue to dry but would it leak? I'd seen a very small leak the day before where the plumber had screwed the shut off valve I wanted in the line to the feed end of the PVC water line. Yvonne stood by outside and after I opened the shut off valve in the crawl space opened the sillcock outside. There were no leaks at the glued joints but water was leaking from both ends of the open shut off valve. I put pipe dope on the screw on joint I'd added and tightened it thoroughly I thought — but it leaked worse that the one the plumber had done. No good. I turned off the shut off valve. I'd need to take out the valve and just run straight glued-together pipe to the sillcock but I didn't have any more splice pieces. It would have to wait.

I moved all the remaining scraps of wood from the lookout tower project area and then applied cordovan acrylic stain to any visible bare wood, especially the top decking Eric had trimmed and the upper deck access ladder he'd built the day before I drove him and his kids to Seattle.

Margaret's three-man window removal and installation crew had left her house the day before after six days of work, including over the weekend. We wanted to see the final product so she invited us over for a look. A few details remained unfinished, for instance the interior varnishing, but it looked good and solid, and being double rather than single pane windows would make a positive contribution to her comfort in cold weather as well as reduce heating effort and costs. But she need some 1/2" trim and none of the lumber yards carried it. What about Dan? He had a complete shop on his property on Crane, was a skilled cabinet maker, and probably could help. Back home again I saw his pickup drive into Margaret's driveway. Good!

Howard had started the grill on the lawn behind the Deer Harbor Community Club early so it was almost ready to accommodate fish, steaks, burgers, and whatever else attendees would soon be cooking on it. I returned Howard's rotary hammer drill to his pickup and asked Bob whether he'd like to look at the new septic field installed two weeks before. He would. The rear parking lot was almost empty but the cars started to pull in, deftly using the new space the septic project grading had made available. While Bob waited in the lot - at 80 he wasn't eager to climb the slippery earthen grade I nearly lost my balance on. I followed the excavation path north and then east through the woods for about 100 feet and then found the new drain field, three laterals each about 35 feet long, more capacity than we needed. Why? Eric later told me that the county requires new septic systems to have a "three bedroom" capacity — even though this building had only one toilet and no bedrooms. The extra capacity was valuable and the system, costing about $13,000, wouldn't have been much less expensive with smaller capacity.

Sitting between Clay and Steve at dinner, I talked with Steve about our son Eric and CalPoly's aerospace engineering department, having given him a substantial brochure about the senior projects Yvonne and I had seen in the spring, and suggested he get a tour of the department from Eric next time he and Pam passed through SLO, certain he'd find the changes interesting, now 46 years after his graduation from the department. Clay had spent the summer working on his trawler, enjoying the bustle and minor drama of the marina, something I'd done over a period of ten years and also enjoyed. His big project was to apply Cetol, a varnish-like product to his boat. I'd used a traditional teak oil/linseed oil varnish on the Simrishamn's brightwork, and there was plenty of it on the traditional Baltic pilothouse sailboat we'd had for four years and then sold. But then I thought again about the exact language Clay had used. Had he said he was applying the Cetol to his teak deck? He had. I told him that I'd never heard of anyone varnishing a teak deck. Teak stands up well to sun and the elements and its natural gray is attractive and functional, not something to cover. Beside coating the teak could make it slippery; left natural weathered teak provides good footing even when wet. He said he finished one of three decks. As we drove to the Orcas dock I told Yvonne about the exchange and was concerned Clay had ruined his deck. But maybe I was wrong. I'd have to ask Howard, Chris, and Brian. They knew much more about it than I did. The east wind carried the *Huginn* through Pole Pass and because the dock was so full of Crainians coming to the Island to take advantage of what was now recognizable as summer, we had to park on the west side rather than our normal east side mooring. What a difference from January.

Two-hundred-ninety-nine: Book Sale

"A committee is a group of people who individually can do nothing, but as a group decide that nothing can be done." — Fred Allen

All was quiet as I walked up Eagle Lane through the encroaching forest to Circle Road and then left a hundred yards around a bend until the community center was visible. No vehicles; no sign of anyone there to attend this last Board meeting before the annual members meeting in a week. I walked through the open garage door past the island fire engine and opened the door into the meeting and social area and found Martha, association Secretary arranging tables and benches. After we greeted one another, I went back into the garage section of the building, took the conference call speaker phone out of the cabinet it's stored in and began to set it up. By that time Dan and Pat had appeared; we had a quorum. I set up the phone connecting it to the phone jack in the garage area via a long cord and then called the 800 dial-in number Martha had, as usual, arranged and the voices of Dave and Blair were added to our conversations. and then we could hear the sound of Jason's Gator. We could begin the meeting.

In my Treasurer's capacity, I reported that the fiscal year had ended more successfully that I had projected in early July. Water billings would be about the same as the previous year instead of nine percent lower. I'd been able to pay the Orcas dock repair bill before the end of the fiscal year out of "profit" not needed for deposit into reserves. These and other good news items made it unnecessary to raise member fees for the next year so I'd recast the budget and handed it out to those present. This wasn't the budget that had been sent to the membership in July, what they expected to vote on at the Annual Meeting in a week. Since I thought it would be confusing to switch budgets and since the bottom line was the same and since the prior budget hadn't even hinted that we were raising the flat water meter fee, I suggested we just stick with the budget we'd sent out, not raise the fee, and use this new budget as our informal guideline for the year. And the kerfuffle began.

First Martha said we needed to raise the meter fee so that the water system would be self-supporting, what we had all heard was a state rule though none of us knew for certain. I pointed out that then we'd need to reduce the dues, because we didn't need the extra money and altogether it would be difficult to explain this to the membership at the meeting and further that we would be doing a long term plan over the coming year and that would tell us what we needed to do about fees. She was adamant. Jason pointed out we had considered raising fees, first general dues, because we thought we needed more revenue and then decided to raise the meter fee instead and the meter fee change was due to a need for revenue and a convenient way to do it not because we were trying to make water self-supporting. And on it went. Dave said the state had a rule but we could interpret it any way we chose as long as what we did overall made sense. Martha countered that it wasn't fair to in effect use dues money to support the water system to make up the $7000 difference between revenue and expense. I pointed out that property owners without meters benefitted from the water system being available. Without it, their lots would be almost worthless. They were seeing appreciation because the island had a water system and were in fact riding on the coat tails of those of us who used and paid for most of the system. If they didn't help pay for the system through dues then it would only be fair to charge some significant fee, perhaps $20,000, to get a meter once they chose to build. Martha changed her mind.

299: Hummingbird feeder

Two-hundred-ninety-nine: Book Sale

Now the question was what to do with this new budget document and everyone, except me, felt it should be introduced at the meeting even though it wasn't what had been sent out. Martha found the relevant paragraph in the association CC&Rs. I didn't see the point of making last minute changes that had no practical consequences to the membership but the others, perhaps worried that word would get out that the budget the members had approved wasn't the real one, insisted I present the revised budget for approval. They had a point. That's what I would do.

A few road areas had pot holes so we'd budgeted for repair for the coming year but Martha suggested that perhaps we should bring in a barge of gravel and redo all the roads as had happened more than ten years before. Pat, the Roads chair, with an excavating business said several times he'd walked the roads and except for the pot hole areas, the roads were in good shape and didn't need work. I agreed. The last road project had cost $18,000 apparently. Today it might cost twice that, the only benefit being that it would look more cared for (but on the other hand less rustic). Pat would look into the costs of an island-wide road project but would focus in the coming year on the potholes, for which we had a budget.

The meeting ended peacefully by about 11:30 and when everyone was outside and Martha and Jason were having a conversation about recruiting three new members for the Board to replace those going off, I pointed out the broken fir, right across Circle Road, the top half, about 30 feet, leaning against a neighboring tree and subject to falling at an inopportune time, perhaps on a passerby. We talked about how to pull the top down and Dan, Pat, and I agreed to meet the next day, Sunday, at 10:00 to do the job.

After lunch Yvonne and I walked to the now very crowded community dock and crossed to Orcas, stopping on the way to Eastsound at the Deer Harbor Post Office. The marina was full and people were everywhere. After parking on Prune Alley, Yvonne walked to North Beach Road and through the park to the Library Faire while I walked to the hardware store to pick up some one inch PVC splices, cleaner and glue, so that I could remove the cut-off valve in front of the frost-free

Two-hundred-ninety-nine: Book Sale

sillcock that was leaking and replace it with straight-through piping. Once the material was in the car I walked to the park grounds and reported for duty at the cashier station for the Friends of the Library book sale, something I'd done for several years both during and after being a Library Board Trustee. Shoppers crowded around tables stacked with books, hardcover fiction here, literature there, and history someplace else. At $1 per paperback and $2 per hardcover (3 for $2 and 3 for $5) the books, some culled from Library shelves and most donated by serious island readers, were attractive to purchasers and arm load after arm load came to me and the other cashiers for purchase. And then at 2:00 the prices were cut in half, increasing the rate of sales and then just before 3:00 I helped announce that a box of books now cost $1.00 (better to get rid of them than to have to clean up and dispose of them), and buying surged again. Just after 3:00, when the sale was to end for the day, I couldn't help myself, grabbed a box, abandoned my post and went first to the Biography table, then Literature and Poetry, and then Philosophy and Religion, finding a plethora of good books I wanted but didn't need, filling my box to overflowing and then out of extreme generosity paid $2 instead of $1 dollar, and told by Friends' organizer, Pierrette that I could go, carried my heavy box to the Market parking lot where Yvonne had parked so she could do some shopping there. Later, back at the dock parking lot and seeing the box of books in the back of the van, Yvonne hinted, no said, that I was crazy. Irrationally acquisitive about good, nearly free books, certainly. Yvonne likes to check books out of the Library. Much more sensible.

    Yvonne grilled salmon on the deck grill and used olive oil in some way. It was delicious. And then peach cobbler (fresh Robert's peaches from the Columbia Valley). After dinner, the film, *Cedar Rapids*, an amusing look at the life of an insurance agent coming of age, a world I knew well from having provided that community technology and understanding about it for many years.

Three-hundred: A Dangerous Situation

"There are no shortcuts to any place worth going." - Beverly Sills

The community water tank remained steady at 13 feet even with 30 more people temporarily on the island, an indication that Gary had set the pump timers perfectly. As I walked Circle Road along the north side of the island, the road now dusty because we'd had no rain at all in several weeks, I noticed slug tracks, curlicues coming from one side of the road, making a loop or two and then exiting back where they came from, not random but purposeful in some way. Someone had deposited shovels full of gravel and soil here and there on Cabot and Cynthia's driveway — with what purpose?

The *Huginn*'s gas tank was less than a quarter full — and Yvonne wanted the *Sunday Seattle Times* to savor over coffee little by little for the next three days so just past nine we walked to the community dock and boarded the *Huginn,* moored on the west side of the main dock (because of the August high season). Few crab pots were evident in Deer Harbor and Yvonne explained that the word on the water was that Deer Harbor was fished (or crabbed?) out and activity had shifted to West Sound. The Deer Harbor Marina was bustling, nearly all the slips filled and half a dozen boats anchored out and as I swung the *Huginn* around to dock starboard side at the fuel dock, a young man, working there for the summer approached to help with the gas. Yvonne and I tied up the boat and she headed for the ramp and the Marina store and while the young man swiped my credit card at the pay station, I retrieved the fuel key from under the seat and unscrewed the fuel cap on the stern and then began filling the tank from the hose he offered me after returning my credit card. Yvonne wanted me to spend not more than $100 so at just over 21 gallons I handed him back the hose, screwed the cap back on, returned the cap key to its hiding place and got out to move the *Huginn* away from the fueling area, closer to the ramp to the store and saw Yvonne returning with the newspaper.

After she put the paper on the seat in the *Huginn*'s cabin, we walked up the ramp and then down the other side to the long-term moorage area, turning left at the first finger to look at Clay's boat, a Grand Banks-style trawler, to look at what he'd done with the teak decks. The boat had a heavy teak rail on stainless steel stanchions like the Nauticat pilothouse we'd sold a year before and he'd clearly spent a great deal of time removing varnish and then sanding all the brightwork and decks — a big job. With some finish sanding and a good varnish the boat would look elegant. But what about the deck he said he'd already coated with Cetol, a kind of varnish? The boat had three deck levels; the main deck that circled the cabin, a raised deck aft over the stateroom, and a deck on the fly bridge, accessible by ladder from the stateroom roof deck. It was the stateroom roof deck he'd varnished and though it looked nice enough, he'd made it impervious to water and slippery when wet. Later in the day I emailed Howard, Chris, and Brian, all old salts, about varnishing teak decks, wanting to be certain before I wrote Clay to strongly advise him not to varnish the other decks.

As soon as were home, I walked quickly to the Crane Island community center to meet Dan, Pat, and it turned out Pat's teenage son Tennyson, to cut down the broken tree across the road. Dan had driven his tractor, at one time owned by Dean, former owner of our house, and Pat had brought a fishing rod, a slingshot, and several hundred feet of 3/8" line he bought for crab pots. The plan was to shoot a lead weight tied to fishing line over the top part of the tree, attach the rope, and then pull it up over the tree and down the other side. The slingshot belonged to Pat's teenage daughter, Pat surprised that she had wanted one when he found she had bought it with her own money, and when Tennyson's shots failed to clear the top of the tree Pat took over, with Tennyson handling the fishing rod with plenty of slack already drawn from the reel. Branches from nearby firs made it difficult to get a clear shot over the top part of the broken fir leaning on its neighbor so Pat, Tennyson, and I walked off Circle Road into the trees so Pat could make his shots from the other side. After one small mishap, the lead weight hitting my arm as Pat pulled it down when it landed on a live branch rather than going over the trunk, Pat succeeded in crossing the trunk and lowering the weight down the other side. He then tied the fish line to the rope and while Tennyson handled the rope, Pat reeled in the line from the other side of the trunk in the trees. And then the 40 lb. test line broke.

300: Bicycle run amok

I asked Tennyson if he liked to climb trees. He did. Why don't you tie the rope around yourself, climb the sturdy neighboring tree, and then tie the rope to the broken trunk where it leans against the tree you're on? Tennyson was climbing and almost out of sight in seconds and I played out the rope as he dragged it up the tree behind him, struggling through the branches that grew profusely beginning eight feet above the ground. Then he secured the line and climbed safely down.

Dan had brought a pulley and some nylon webbing and he and Pat fastened the pulley to a large cedar farther from the road and then dragged the remaining rope back to the road and attached it to the hitch on the front of the tractor. Three of us watched from the road while Dan slowly backed up the tractor and four branches on the supporting tree broke in succession as the rope pulled taut — and then the upper, broken part of the tree we wanted to remove pulled away from its supporting neighbor and crashed to the ground. Dan and Pat each powered-up their STHIL chainsaws and cut the fallen trunk in sections and then Dan downed the standing section of the trunk and he and Pat cut it in manageable sections and we all moved branches and trunk off the road to a space behind the row of bordering firs.

Preparing to leave, Pat asked me if I'd like some firewood. I would. He was in the process of building a house at the other end of the island, delayed because of the business downturn, and he was concerned that the Douglas fir trunks that had been lying on the ground would be useless as firewood by the time he was in a position to burn them. Later I drove my F150 to his construction site and visited with him and with Doug, whose house was already complete, and whose wife was the daughter of Bob and Sue in Deer Harbor. Pat would pull out six or eight logs from the pile using his excavator and leave them where they'd be easy to get at. Thanks. I'd be back some time in the next few weeks and he'd be gone back to Seattle.

I now had the PVC splice pieces I'd need to finish the frost-free sillcock replacement in the crawl space so I told Yvonne I was turning off the water and then made my way to the other end of the house in that unpleasant space. I cut out the shut off valve that leaked at each end and replaced it with a section of PVC. The directions said to wait two hours before pressurizing the system so while Yvonne surfed the web with the iPad, I read a Thomas Hardy biography. Waking up after dozing in my chair I found Yvonne outside and told her I'd need her help testing my plumbing work. I gave her a walkie talkie and took the other one with me into the crawl space while she waited near the in-house shut off valve in the studio pantry only a few feet away. At my direction she turned on the water — no leaks — so she turned on the outside faucet. No leaks. She could now again water her front garden and the new sillcock was again operating as a frost free device. Good. I took the tools and plumbing supplies out of the crawlspace and put them away in my shop, leaving the halogen light, on a long extension cord that came back to the crawl space door and electrical outlet nearby inside, for certain future use.

Three-hundred-one: Rules and Goals

"Rules are for the obedience of fools and the guidance of wise men." — Harry Day

For the first time in days, maybe weeks, no wind disturbed the pre-dawn Salish Sea extending east from the rocky shore below and twenty feet east of the house, it resembling liquid mercury more than water. Blakely Island was barely visible as a dark hulking mass behind Harney Chanel, the tide slack, some pink visible in the northeast sky. A beautiful day in store.

The mail at the Deer Harbor Post Office included thank you notes from Barb and Tessa and an unexpected agricultural present from Dean we'd have to figure out what to do with.

I hadn't yet received the year-end "compilation" (un-audited financial reports) from the accountants to be presented to the membership at the annual meeting in less than a week. They were late. On Saturday I explained to the Board that the budget we'd sent out to the membership was no longer quite appropriate because the year-end totals were better than my projections which in part meant we wouldn't need to raise water meter fees. I had suggested we just stick with the budget we'd sent out for member approval but practically speaking work with a different one during the year. They objected, saying they wanted to present the new one I'd worked on and I explained that I had more work to do on it. Martha said she'd need it by Wednesday. I spent a good deal of time going through each line item adjusting items to actual when I knew they'd be the same this coming year ending up with a reserve contribution identical to the tentative revised budget I showed the Board Saturday and then sending it to Jason and Martha — for her to distribute at the members' meeting next Saturday for consideration and approval.

Three-hundred-one: Rules and Goals

301: Buck at dawn

Back came an email from Martha — no way. We'd have to distribute an exact copy of what the Board had approved Saturday (even though only four of the other six at the meeting had seen it). Martha was very concerned that we follow whatever rules seemed to be applicable in any situation. My tendency was to be concerned about what we needed to accomplish, seeing the rules as guidance, and not absolute. These philosophical differences dominated island governance and human interaction, the people with business backgrounds seeming to focus more on goals and those without more on rules. On the other hand, the rules-oriented people seemed more casual about spending money and the goals people on saving and making do. The Board had done a long range plan in 1999, hiring a firm that specialized in such things and paying a non-trivial fee. The plan recommended annual or bi-annual review, not surprising because the consultants might benefit financially from what from my point of view were likely unnecessary and unproductive efforts. Martha was adamant that we begin to do the reviews on a regular basis — that is, follow the rule — and spend money. I had said I thought we could do it ourselves and I encouraged Dave to express his opinion because he'd been on the last long range plan committee and was the lead for the new effort. When at the Saturday morning meeting we had talked about repairing potholes in the island roads, having put $2000 into the new budget for the purpose, Martha suggested that we look at a total overhaul of the roads, continuing to propose that even after Pat, who was Roads chair and because of his excavating business more knowledgable than any of the rest of us said that the roads were in very good shape and didn't need more than pothole repair. Martha, it was evident, liked the idea of attractive, new, clean gravel everywhere even if functionally unnecessary and costing $25,000.

Joyce and Larry were walking down the ramp at the Orcas dock as I pulled in to pick them up in the sunny late afternoon, the wind still calm as I'd come to expect island summer days to be. On the way over to Crane a fishing boat preceded the *Huginn* through Pole Pass, moving not faster than six knots but creating a big wake that I steered over, into, and through, bigger than I would have expected in part perhaps because it was full of fish and riding low in the water. At home the sun was shining on the deck through the space in the trees where we'd cleared some tall Douglas firs, so Yvonne had arranged the deck table for appetizers and the four of us sat in the sun and talked about their new Tucson winter home, when they'd be there, and the projects they had in mind. A few weeks before we'd had dinner with another rainbirds couple who had a house in Tubac, just south of Tuscon who also wintered in the sun. Maybe we'd visit sometime. Besides access to sun, Joyce and Larry had another reason to get away from Orcas; as long as they were on the Island, people would be after them about Food Bank operations issues even after a manager replaced Larry in October. In a sense, they had to leave Orcas part time in order to retire, his life, especially, having become busier and more stressful, with less free time, after he had retired from Island Market and accepted the responsibility of bringing the Food Bank through a transition from ad hoc and casual to organized and more formal — in its own new building.

Three-hundred-two: New Car

"Our battered suitcases were piled on the sidewalk again; we had longer ways to go. But no matter, the road is life." — Jack Kerouac

Yvonne and I walked into the Orcas Hotel coffee shop about 7:45 a.m., our van parked in lane 1 of the vehicle waiting area for the 8:50 ferry to Anacortes to go car shopping in Burlington. With 128,000 miles on the odometer, Yvonne was worried the van would fail us driving cross country, in Arizona, for instance. I'd been resisting the idea of a new car but was attracted to the idea of getting something that would use half the gas our van did.

The coffee shop was crowded but Yvonne snagged us a table while I got her an eight oz low fat latte and a twelve oz Awake tea for me. Three blueberry muffins waited in the day-old basket but Yvonne wasn't interested and I'd already had my daily oatmeal at home. More than 100 years old, the hotel has a comfortable slightly worn out feeling, authentic, real in some way that newer places lack. Yvonne would say it's real. We talked about the Saturday Crane Board meeting and the collision of what amounted to different philosophies of life, an example of democratic process in action, a good thing, and then walked down the outside stairs and then across the road to the market to buy the *Seattle Times*.

The sun was bright overhead even when the ferry ran into fog coming through Thatcher Pass into the Rosario Straight area limiting visibility on all sides. Driving off the ferry in Anacortes I could see that the fog occupied only the center of Guemes Channel probably over colder water that had come in from the Pacific through the Straight of Juan de Fuca. Mount Baker, to the northeast in the Cascades glowed white under a covering of unmelted snow. Yvonne said she'd read that Paradise, on the flanks of Mt. Rainier, a jumping off place for hiking where Noah and Natasha had worked the summer between sophomore and junior years at Western Washington in Bellingham, was still covered in 40 feet of snow, something that discouraged visitors and had never been seen since measurement had begun there.

302: Goodbye

As we entered the Skagit Ford showroom, Joe, who we'd never met but had made an appointment with, greeted us as we came in. We wanted to look at a 2012 Ford Focus Hatchback. We'd had a number of Fords over the years and I'd read positive reviews of this small car with European origins that was a pleasure to drive and had very good mileage compared to the competition. I'd seen an attractive small white hatchback parked next to our van on the MV *Yakima* and asked Yvonne if she knew the make. She thought I was joking and smiled when she told me it was a Focus. Hmm.

The test drive was successful, the car quiet and responsive, though much smaller than what we'd been used to in three generations of Ford vans. Yvonne had thought we might want to look elsewhere as well, for instance at a Mazda 5, but I didn't since its mileage was unimpressive, so we began the interminable purchase process with Joe, ever polite and helpful — seemingly disinterested in whether we actually bought a car from him. As far as I could tell the process was highly choreographed with half a dozen steps. First we "built" the car we wanted, on-line, with Joe's help. Since they'd sold their last hatchback in the morning (so we were told), he checked for relevant inventory in the Seattle area and found two that might be relevant that he could trade his remaining Focus for. We decided on the gray model — which established the purchase price to negotiate from. Then he had the van appraised to establish a trade-in value and since we said we were interested in financing because of low rates came back from the credit manager with a ridiculous monthly payment. I told him I was insulted, he asked whether we'd be willing to make a down payment, we would and he soon returned with something much more reasonable but not quite good enough. The next step was the credit manager himself who told us he could provide a better interest rate (3.65%) and then tried to sell us a variety of what amounted to insurance policies, one being a 100,000 mile everything except what normally wears out, like tires, package. When we resisted, he dropped the price and it was attractive enough that we added that to the tab, eager to reduce the risk of possible high repair bills down the road. We wouldn't know whether we'd made a good decision until about five years in the future. Joe had taken the initiative to have the car delivered that afternoon and Yvonne and I left to pick up a few things at Costco and something to eat while we waited for the 7:20 ferry back to Orcas. Joe called Yvonne's cell phone about 4:30 to say the car would be ready by 5:00. I'd put the possessions we'd had in the van in a Costco bag while Yvonne shopped at Kohl's, so vacating the van and moving everything to the Focus was simple. Joe programmed our iPad to interact with the new car's Synch system,

Three-hundred-two: New Car

something Microsoft had developed, but because Yvonne's cell phone didn't have bluetooth wasn't able to make the car recognize it.

Back on Orcas and driving Deer Harbor Road to the Crane parking lot on Orcas I was very pleased with the way the new car handled. It would be a pleasure to drive and reminded me, in the best possible way, of the sports cars I had in my 20's and then the Saabs I'd had in my 50's. Grandma and Grandpa had moved from a van (Yvonne was mourning its leaving our lives because of everything that had been associated with it) to something that could be described as a practical, reasonably inexpensive sports car, from staid to sporty, a stretch but maybe. We expected to drive the new car to the ocean and be with Noah, Natasha, and the kids in late September, then to Portland and Ashland, then to Los Osos to see Eric, Kristin, and the family, on to Los Angeles to see James and Keith and then to Colorado, visiting what we hadn't yet seen on the way, and then my family in Colorado Springs and our friends in Boulder, perhaps three weeks overall. Yvonne felt better having a new car to do it in. I felt better that we'd burn half the gas along the way and save $400 or so.

Three-hundred-three: Keeping an Eye Out

> *"The art of seeing is forgetting the name of the thing one sees."* — Christian Morgenstern

I began my morning walk before sunrise, clear, and not a ripple on the Salish Sea. The community water tank level was a bit over thirteen feet, having gained a few inches over Monday's level, the island transient population lower than on the weekend. Crossing the meadow back to the house from the dock area, the newly risen sun causing everything its light struck to glow, I hurried home to get my camera and started taking pictures from both sides of the meadow, east across the water toward Blakely shrouded in fog, the early ferry from Anacortes on its way to Orcas in Harney Channel and then from the community dock, the smooth water, at slack tide, reflecting the firs, madronas, and willows along the beach and rocky shore, both alive and long dead. A magic time.

Crossing to Orcas, a seal surfaced ahead of the *Huginn* and looked at me before gracefully diving, perhaps the same harbor seal I'd seen perched on the rock off the beach west of the Crane dock that dries at low tide, the seal taking the shape of a shallow "U" with head and tail raised, necessary since the rock was only big enough to support its midsection.

I suspected that Howard was hosting the Greybeards in the house rather than the honeymoon cottage, a shed in the garden, because Sheila was still on the East Coast at a family gathering, but maybe she was home again so I checked the cottage first — no they were in the house. David and Howard were talking about the Flashman novels by George MacDonald Fraser, in particular about a two man cricket match, while Brian listened, the tea water heating on the stove. Knowing almost nothing about cricket, I asked Howard, an Englishman, for an explanation, and we spent the next hour, Howard and then with Chris, also an Englishman, who arrived a few minutes later, describing and demonstrating, at times with Howard's cricket bat, this complicated, charming, and to me bizarrely arbitrary game that Abner Doubleday replaced with baseball in America.

303: Early morning fog at the marina

Then David had to leave for an acupuncture appointment and then Chris, with Lynn for their weekly volunteer session at the Orcas library and Brian, Howard, and I talked about Clay and his application of Cetol varnish to the teak deck of his trawler, agreeing that at the least it would make the deck slippery so later I followed up by sending Clay an email with a link to a practical website about the care of brightwork and

Three-hundred-three: Keeping an Eye Out

decks, congratulating him on how hard he'd worked, explaining that I wasn't trying to be bossy, but suggesting he might want to do more research more before applying Cetol to the two larger decks he had yet to cover.

Since it wasn't yet 10:00, Pat's substitute at the Post Office hadn't distributed all the mail but I took what was there, including a book box from Amazon containing *Northwest Coast Indian Art: An Analysis of Form* by Bill Holm that had been referenced in *Solitary Raven: The Essential Writings of Bill Reid*, edited by Robert Bringhurst and went back to Crane, arriving I realized, without my backpack containing my MacBook Pro and two biographies of Thomas Hardy, too distracted, I assumed, by the fact I was driving a new car, conscious of and pleased with its reaction to Deer Harbor Road. Greeting Yvonne at work on Food Bank tasks in the studio, she asked whether I had brought the *Seattle Times* and *Islands' Sounder*. Oops. Another sign of distraction. I promised to return at lunch time to pick up the papers and the rest of the mail.

At the Orcas Dock, Martha had just returned to her inflatable with a female friend and was cordial and congratulatory about all the work I was doing as Crane Treasurer. Ok, thanks. Our Post Office box was full and a fifth proxy in the Crane Island box. In the parking lot I saw Bob, who in response to my question about what was new said that he had recently fallen on and injured his shoulder while he and Sue wrestled with a kayak on their beach almost across from the marina and then he told me about an ongoing saga with a mysterious group who had called him earlier, telling him he had won $395,000 and a new Land Rover/ Range Rover and would get the prize as soon as he wired $2000 in handling fees. After calling the Better Business Bureau and then being referred to a fraud investigating agency, he had played along with the grifters to gather more information. Then Cal asked about our new car, ever vigilant about all traffic on lower Deer Harbor Road, offering that it was too small, and it certainly was compared to his Buick, and I noticed the SUV and pickup parked on either side of it. The Focus looked like a toy compared to typical American vehicles. As I took the mail and

Three-hundred-three: Keeping an Eye Out

my backpack out of the Focus parked at the head of the dock, Tom came up the ramp and we exchanged greetings, no more.

Three-hundred-four: Disappearing View

"Perspective is worth 80 IQ points." — Alan Kay

Since Saturday would be the Crane Island Association Annual Meeting and I was Treasurer and Water System Committee Chair, I would be making two reports and wasn't prepared for either. The members had been sent a proposed budget created before year end but the Board had voted to replace it with a more accurate one that had the virtue of not requiring any increase in dues or service fee rates. I would need to report on the past year's financial picture and the new, improved budget for the coming year and the assumptions and plans that lay behind it.

Having observed one full fiscal year as Treasurer, I now felt reasonably comfortable with the Association's accounting but I wanted to make sure I hadn't overlooked anything as well as understand the five year revenue trend I suspected was downhill at the same time some expenses had risen. I also wanted to be certain that I covered the water front accurately. I couldn't do either with my personal records. I'd need to incorporate information from the twin storage tub Association Treasurer archive as well as the two folders I'd been given by the former water chair. Almost a year before I'd goner through the Treasurer archive while I was home alone, Yvonne in Seattle, and I spread the file folders all over the living room floor. Rather than clarify, the process had confused me to the point I thought my brain was malfunctioning (and it probably was). But now I knew more and was able to discard two feet of irrelevant, unnecessary, and duplicate material, including old insurance policies the agent would have and partial year financial statements that were important at the time they were printed but not now. I was able to find year-end financial statements back to 2002, several years of members billings, a hodgepodge of Board meeting minutes, and member directed water system reports. The living room was again a mess but I didn't blink when Yvonne pointed out that she would soon be picking up the Deer Harbor women's walking group for a Crane circuit and that they'd come into the house at some point.

304: Japanese maples in the front yard

I wrote a financial report draft that pointed to healthy cash reserves, more than $400,000, but showed that dues and fees revenues were down 7% and interest returns down 17% from 2008 levels. One important project of the coming fiscal year was to get a handle on what our reserves should be both currently and over the next decade and then what dues and fee structure was required to create adequate income for current expenses and as contribution to reserves. At the next Annual Meeting the Board would present its findings.

I then began to write the water report summary and was interrupted by James whose morning email contained a response to comments by New York Times readers to an article explaining how addiction was a physical condition, a kind of disease, not of choice or weak will, who refused to accept the conclusion, arguing instead for a kind of Cartesian dualism that saw mind and choice as independent of the brain. James wanted to talk about the complaints his primary advisors had about his dissertation proposal draft. He explained that initially the focus was to be on the risk-taking and addiction in rats, not just behavior but the underlying genetics of it, but because one of his advisors had a clinical orientation she had suggested that the research also include human subjects but then complained that she wasn't happy with the way James suggested including them. It looked like a clear case of scope-creep to me and I suggested James try to convince her that his original focus was a big enough project and suggest that he could work with her on research outside of but related to his rat/addiction/risk-taking paper. He thought that might work and hung up to go see her.

We were to drive to Sylvia and Gordon's with Sue and Al but he, a realtor, was tied up with now rare clients so Yvonne and I went on without them and they caught up later. The house, on the north side of Orcas, was perched on a rock with a view of the Straight of Georgia and faraway Vancouver to the north but the view was beginning to disappear behind quickly growing Douglas firs that belonged to the property owner below, a problem we'd had with our house on Cayou Valley Road in Deer Harbor and one reason, though minor, we were eager to move to Crane and be right on the water.

Gordon and Sylvia had almost just returned from Germany and would be going back soon and stay until mid-October in their condo in Bavaria, comfortable there in Sylvia's native land. Neither Al nor I were optimistic about the US economy and local real estate in particular. Gordon showed off his new MacBook Air. It was 10:30 before we were back in the Crane parking lot and made our way in the light of the rising half-moon down the ramp and into the *Huginn,* crossing to Crane on calm waters and walking home across the meadow, the way so familiar that even though the path was cast in moon shadow we made our way quickly and confidently through the trees, and home.

Three-hundred-five: Success

"What you get by achieving your goals is not as important as what you become by achieving your goals." — Henry David Thoreau

About three in the morning I woke up thirsty and still feeling too full from Sylvia's rich late dinner the night before and saw glowing white everywhere I looked outdoors; the moon was illuminating a dense fog that made it almost impossible to see across our cove to the trees on the other side. The fog persisted through most of the morning, beginning to break up about 10:30, patches of the world emerging here and there until by 11:00 Crane and its surrounding water was visible, an island of clarity in a foggy world.

Margaret called: she and her contractor Josh needed to bring a big window from the Orcas parking lot I'd seen sitting on the roof of her Passat to substitute for one that was too small for her purposes in the addition she'd had built five or six years before. Could I help? Of course. The way from the Crane dock to the Orcas dock was clear of fog. The brightly colored August world covered over in some places, land and water, was incredibly beautiful, something I'd never seen the likes of before.

Margaret backed her car into the center of the lower parking lot and she and I untied the ropes holding the new window to two by fours tied to the roof rack and then waited for Josh, expected any moment, to help us slide the 80 pound wood window down to the ground, basking in the morning sun that promised the best summer day yet this season. Josh parked on the level above and we soon had the window on the ground and then upright in the old agri-fab dock cart with the front panel removed. Josh, at the front, held the window to keep it from falling over and Margaret and I each had one hand on the cart handle and the other on the window and we took it slowly down the ramp to the dock and parked the cart next to the *Huginn*. It wasn't much trouble to slide the window into the cockpit, setting it on the engine compartment cover and sliding it back against the transom. Josh and Margaret held it so it wouldn't fall over while I drove the boat slowly to the Crane dock. There we put it aboard another agri-fab cart and wheeled it to the head of the dock where I'd already backed up my pickup near the dock. Sliding the big window into the bed, we then laid it at an angle and Margaret climbed into the bed to watch it while Josh and I rode in the cab the half-mile, Dock Road to Circle Road to Eagle Lane and then down our shared driveway and then into her driveway, very slowly between the crowding trees, almost to the house where she'd been staining trim. What had seemed to me potentially difficult turned out to be easy, though time consuming, because we'd had wheeled devices that made carrying unnecessary.

When I walked into the house, Yvonne was on the phone — with James. How did his meeting go with Lara, his advisor, I wanted to know? and she replied that James wanted to talk with me about it. Was there a problem? Rather than tell me the outcome, he fed me details about the meeting process — he suggested that his dissertation be scaled back to what he had originally intended, rats, risk, and addiction, with a genetic component, abandoning any attempt to extend it to also cover human subjects, in the interests of practicality. She was reluctant to give up on a human dimension, coming from a clinical orientation, suggesting one idea after another, none adequate after a short discussion. Acknowledging that the goal was James' success she blessed the return to the original plan and then David, another advisor, back from a vacation in Morocco did as well. James would rewrite his proposal and have it ready for his two principal advisors on Tuesday and the proposal meeting with two more on Friday. He was happy and so was I. His only real concern was that his research, attempting to find a correlation between risk taking and addiction would come up with a null result. It would be a year before he'd know. I pointed out that science worked that way and in any case he could just spend longer working on his PhD. He acknowledged that it wasn't uncommon for graduate students. Later Yvonne and I received an email, James delighted that his second paper as primary author had been accepted for publication. Excellent!

305: Underway on the Discovery

I continued to work on my water report for the next day's Crane Association Annual meeting and Gary, our water system manager, called saying he'd been contacted by several homeowners about the new Cross Connect Policy, suspicious that the water committee or Board had made up some arbitrary new rule just to harass them. I was surprised — and then on reconsideration not. Gary and I talked about water quality testing (he'd cover that at the meeting) and brown water (I'd talk about why it occurs) and then I'd talk a bit about the plan to add a float switch to the tank that could control the #5 and #6 well pumps. Yvonne handed me a note while I was talking to Gary: she and I were going sailing at 3:00. A beautiful, warm (72 degrees), sunny day with a light wind out of the west.

Only the second sailing occasion this summer, we exited the Crane marina just west of Pole Pass and motored past the southern-most no wake buoy just north of Crane and I raised the mainsail while Yvonne steered and then let the ancient four horsepower, two stroke outboard die. We were sailing. I pulled the jib back from the cabin and with some trouble raised it and we were sailing faster. We spent the next 90 minutes tacking back and forth across Deer Harbor, from Spring Point on the north to Crane on the south, usually slowly but sometimes at a clip, watching all manner of boating activity around us, often too fast and too reckless for our tastes, occasional wakes lifting the stern three feet — but I didn't care and neither did the *Discovery*.

While I folded the jib on the Crane dock, Yvonne went home to grill some halibut, potatoes, and carrots, that she later served with a caesar's salad. Delicious. I talked with Blair, who was on the dock with his daughter-in-law's father about the next day's members' meeting and his role as harbor master or dock steward while they got ready to take his crab pot out and drop it in West Sound off Double Island. Then Brooks and Gretchen docked with a load of groceries for guests the coming week and I helped move them to the head of the dock, Gretchen compromised by a lung condition. Just after dinner and after she'd taken Josh back to Orcas, Margaret yoohooed outside the kitchen door and then came in to offer Yvonne two fresh crabs and Yvonne accepted. Very tired, especially because I'd only slept from midnight to 3:00 the night before, I was asleep just after 10:00 but not before Yvonne, who melted into the bed. The ibuprofen had done me some good, the rib I'd apparently cracked raising the *Discovery*'s outboard bracket two weeks before having become successively more sore now fading from my attention.

Three-hundred-six: Memories

"The heart has its reasons which reason knows nothing of."
— Blaise Pascal

After almost eight hours sleep after having taken ibuprofen the night before to reduce the ache of a cracked rib, I felt rested and strong. The sky was a striking orange and I got out of bed to photograph it but by the time I was outside and had changed the CoolPix's settings, the orange had faded a bit, the pictures not capturing what I'd just seen. When I'd finished breakfast, the sun had just risen, streaming into our cove, into the yard, and on the rain shelter, and two shops 70 yards away. I'd finished breakfast and was washing out the pot I cooked my oatmeal in, when I saw something move outside, a buck, as it turned out, drinking at Yvonne's pond outside the deer fencing. Perhaps hearing me somehow (or reading my mind?), he lifted his head and stared at me through the kitchen window, persisting for the minute or so I stared back, until going to get my camera at the other end of the kitchen. The bucks antlers were reddish, the velvet on each dangling from its base, now beginning the process of dying as bone to be shed this coming winter and regrown in the spring. Finishing his drinking, the buck moved into the nearby salal and began to browse and I noticed two nearby does. Harem building. In the early evening Yvonne and I noticed two fawns just off Eagle Lane, not far from the house, now perhaps on their own.

At 9:00 the Crane Island Association Board of Trustees would host a meeting to introduce and discuss the complete collection of policies we'd edited, that not having been done for perhaps twenty years. Our intention was to bring clarity to what was often cited and often incorrectly, without a definitive source and had had negative responses from several Association members who had commented in emails they'd circulated that we already had too many rules and rather than add or change them we should be dispensing with them so in order to avoid a very long and contentious afternoon annual meeting, we'd scheduled this morning session for discussion and editing. This early meeting was surprisingly well attended and for the most part the questions and suggestions germane and helpful. The member who had expressed his doubts about rules didn't attend but was represented by his neighbor. During the two hour session the wording was slightly changed on three policies and a few more were identified as being controversial.

After this first meeting and as I walked down Eagle Lane and then turned downhill on the driveway we shared with Margaret, I felt the world, what I saw become intensely visible or hyper-real accompanied by a feeling of joy that almost made me cry at the beauty of it.

After lunch I joined Yvonne on our little bluff facing the water — very busy for the last four or five weeks with power and sailboats cruising to or from Canada and now, on the weekend, day trippers in open powerboats they'd put in the water from trailers on the mainland. The sky was intensely blue viewed through the madrona leaves, hanging on branches whose growth had fractured the thin bark now drying orange, hanging in pieces with new, green bark underneath. This was the first time this summer I'd sat and enjoyed the view from this beautiful spot though the three youngest grandchildren had come back to it over and over again when visiting a few weeks before.

I made handout copies of the outlines of the Treasurer and Water System reports I'd make to the members and walked back to the community building, Yvonne on the phone with Jeni and to come later. The room was packed, the sliding door open to the outside, with the nine member Board in front, four at a picnic table and the rest sitting in a hodgepodge of old metal folding chairs, green plastic patio chairs, and wooden benches. Gary and Wilma were sitting in the back, Gary available to answer questions about the water system I couldn't. Yvonne appeared after about half an hour and sat in the back of the room near the door. Discussion of the policy document went well, raising fewer questions than at the morning meeting and area by area the policies were voted on and unanimously accepted, the second step in a three year planning process (the first a survey, the last, to come, a ten year needs analysis and a funding plan).

306: Crane Island Association Annual Meeting

After three hours, half the group had drifted off but those remaining stayed to see Dan demonstrate the compressed air foam system on the island fire and rescue vehicle (an outfitted Ford Expedition), the only real controversy having been related to the Fire and Safety area and generated by Nancy who among other things thought Crane should have a fire bell or siren people could come to the community center to activate, not satisfied that we were connected to the county 911 system.

We walked home with Margaret and Moonie the cat came out to meet her. Moonie's health had improved over the last two days as he responded to his vet's treatment for the recurrence of a stomach problem that nearly killed him before Christmas in Ohio. As we passed Samantha's grave, Yvonne blew her a kiss, our little black dog now gone exactly a year, and missed every day.

The late afternoon sun still shown on the deck near the hot tub, present because John had felled six trees for us in June and we, with Tim's help for three, had cut down another six in the winter and spring. I brought chairs and a little table and Yvonne cheese and crackers and we sat in the sun talking about the day, the next, and plans for a trip east and south in October. After dinner but before a movie (*Beautiful Kate*), Yvonne and I walked around the island, counterclockwise, seeing no one else though perhaps 50 people were now on the island. Hearing an osprey's insistent chirping I saw it at the top of a dead tree at the intersection of Circle and Rocky Road and almost as soon as I pointed it out to Yvonne and she saw it, the fish eagle took flight south, some important business at hand.

Right now some of my high school classmates were gathering at a Chicago area country club for our 50th reunion and I'd chosen not to attend, without regret so far, imagining myself there and balancing that against costs and responsibilities, I couldn't make it work even though some friends and relatives had recommended that I go.

Though the association's annual cycle would begin again and though I had lots to do — with annual billing coming up and in taking the bookkeeping back from the accounting firm we used — the intense focus on the annual meeting was over and I felt myself relax a bit. Now I could return to the ebook business and my long list of to-dos.

Three-hundred-seven: See It Through

"Nothing is particularly hard if you divide it into small jobs." — Henry Ford

Late morning while I was completing the editing of the reports I'd made to the members and the Crane Island Annual Meeting attendees in preparation for sending to Martha, sister Julie called back after missing me earlier, now on her front porch, the traffic noise from north Nevada Street in Colorado Springs audible over the phone, and she described the lightning strike on the tree in the parkway the night before, a simultaneous flash and crash, fortunately with minor damage. During the course of our conversation clouds formed to the west, toward Pike's Peak, in the clear blue sky, another thunderstorm approaching perhaps, common in Colorado but very rare in the San Jan Islands, only a handful of occasions I'm aware of over the last decade. The scaffolding ex-husband, Karl, had recently stored in basement had infected the house with roaches that she and son, Cooper, were fighting, uncommon in the west and in our experience non-existent in the islands. With the price of gold increasing almost daily, the store where Julie's daughter, Phoebe, worked continued to be very busy, with a steady line of people, some selling and some buying, the gold jewelry going to Denver to be melted down into ingots for resale, the precious stones going into the caldron as well since it was too much trouble to remove them.

Yvonne spent the morning baking and I carried the mocha brownies and pesto puff pastries in a Costco bag to the dock on our way to Bev's for the Food Bank volunteer recognition party, encountering Cabot on the beach at the community dock, in a life vest, preparing to launch his kayak on the beach while Martha and Stuart, his neighbors on Crane, offered advice and encouragement.

Three-hundred-seven: See It Through

307: August sunset colors eastern sky

We would make our way to the Doe Bay area, on the east side of Orcas, more than 25 miles from the Crane parking lot on Deer Harbor Road, less than half that as the raven flies because we'd have to drive north and east to get around the top of East Sound and then south and east to get to Bev's, passing through Moran State Park and along Cascade Lake and then through Olga.

Having never seen Bev's house before I was struck with its open Northwest architecture and its setting, in a cove on a beautiful beach facing the Cascades, with mountainous Lummi Island to the left, Sinclair Island straight ahead, and Cypress just visible to the right around the point that sheltered the beach, a bit of Guemes Island behind it, and the Anacortes Ferry Landing out of sight south of that. The beach, with two mooring buoys close to shore, a runabout tied to one and a dingy to the other, was covered with smooth, two inch diameter pebbles to the mid-tide water line and fine gravel above the pebbles. Half a dozen groomed big cedars and Douglas firs stood a bit back from the beach surrounded by salal and then green lawn closer to the house, perhaps 75 feet from the water.

What was especially striking about the house, roughly an H shape, was the see-though central room, with huge sliding glass doors making the walls on both the land (entry) side and the water side, so that approaching the house you could see straight through it to the water, islands, and mountains on the other side. A deer fenced courtyard with a concrete central area and wood decking transition along the house walls, blooming lavender at the gate being visited by mason bees and potted flowers, some on wheels, on the decking to the left.

The central section of the house, turned perpendicular to the entrance, had a big skylight that straddled the peak of the roof, somewhat smaller than the one in our living room ceiling, a huge stone fireplace wall to the right and a big kitchen to the left, with a bamboo floor and Douglas fir trim visually warming the big space.

Looking up at the skylight I saw a humming bird struggling unsuccessfully to get out. It had run into a glass door and then flown into the house, Bev said, and she had little hope for it. Did she have something long I could hold up for it to sit on? She did, extendable to twelve feet or so. She gave me a wash cloth I draped over the top and then I found a stool near the back door, stood on it, raised the pole under the hummingbird, it fluttered aboard, and then sat exhausted on the washcloth while I lowered the pole, carried it outside, and leaned it gently against a wood pile, letting the little bird decide when to fly away. Ten minutes later when I checked back it was gone.

Twenty-seven volunteers, board members, and spouses attended the Food Bank volunteer recognition party, enjoying the setting, the house, and one another, with wine and appetizers, then stuffed shells, salad, and bread, followed by brownies and ice cream consumed when people paused to let others talk. I met some of the Food Bank volunteers, knew others from other organizations, and saw some new faces, talking about boating, the future of oil, children and grandchildren, and the Food Bank.

Three-hundred-seven: See It Through

When the others were leaving, Bev invited Joyce and Larry and their daughter Debbie, who had helped with the serving, and Yvonne and me to stay for a glass of wine and we talked more about family, Orcas, and the development of Bev's house, a process, in stages that had taken almost 50 years, the most recent and most dramatic being the big room and kitchen done in 2003, five years before her husband died.

Yvonne and I crossed to Crane after sunset, in wind that had come up presaging a change in the weather. A hot tub soak, reading, and lights out and I continued to think about the entirely satisfying design of Bev's house, a northwest style with Native American traces — for instance the four huge poles — as well as the use of naturally finished indigenous woods — and masonry that matched the colors of the rock exposed on the beach — a big open space like a longhouse but bright and open while being warm in look and fact (with radiant heating in the floors). What a pleasure that someone went to the trouble and expense to create such beauty and then share it with others.

Three-hundred-eight: The Good Rain

"The sound of rain needs no translation." — Alan Watts

    Though it had been predicted and the morning sky was gray, not with the thin low clouds that would burn off by late morning, but substantial, weather clouds, I was pleased to see rain on the big living room skylight that sat across the ridge line for half the room. The two "rain barrels," one 75 gallons and the other 450, were all but empty and Yvonne had been watering her front and back gardens every few days, a Japanese maple having already lost its leaves because of the dryness and the currant bush next to the hot tub turning yellow two months before its time.

    The good rain peppered the decks outside and big drops falling from the eaves visible through the living room windows continued the process of eroding the opaque stain on the deck, exposing the wood in a gray line across the brown Yvonne had put down two years before.

    By 10:00 Yvonne had decided she wouldn't go to Eastsound for some minor shopping, the rain having dampened her enthusiasm, and she took up her regular position on the couch, recumbent with a new novel, legs covered with a thin throw, the house a little cooler because of the rain on the roof. Later in the afternoon after a nap she recruited me for a walk around the island, the rain hesitating and intermittent and the empty white five gallon bucket Yvonne used for carrying crabs now with a half-inch of water in the bottom. Not enough rain to cure the drought but enough that Yvonne wouldn't have to water for a few days, something I looked forward to because using well water was expensive and prohibited for irrigation by policies the Crane Island Association had just affirmed at its Annual Meeting two days before.

308: Pat had logs to share

Leaving Eagle Lane we turned left on Circle Road and as we approached the Community Center I saw that the folded ping pong table and a picnic table had been left outside on the grass behind the building, removed to make way for seating for the Annual Meeting. Both tables belonged inside. I pulled open the big sliding door that opened the meeting room to the outside and Yvonne and I stacked the green plastic patio chairs and folded and leaned against the wall ancient metal card table chairs, certainly at least 60 or 70 years old, with a complex design I'd never seen anywhere else. The ping pong table was clumsy to carry and it wobbled as we set it down on the concrete floor, one castor missing for some time, making one leg shorter.

The banner from last year's 50th anniversary party hung above the spinet piano, the gift of someone who probably didn't want to carry it off the island, and it had sustained a series of injuries over the years, one leg missing and the other cracked, the stringing visible because part of the face of the piano had been removed by person or persons unknown.

Near the turnoff for Rocky Road a doe and fawn stared out at us from the border of the Nature Preserve absolutely frozen and therefore invisible — except for some ear wiggles. The island was quiet, the drops now coming from trees rather than the sky, the grass bordering the roads already looking greener, perked up after looking old and stressed for many weeks. As we came through the gap in the split rail fence from the parking area at the community dock to cross the meadow to our house I spied a small garter snake I'd seen occasionally enjoying itself in the sun and held Yvonne's arm so she wouldn't step on it as it slithered into the high yellow grass bordering the path.

Kelly had written from Paris with a link to a blog written from the point of view of baby Noah reporting on and showing what their emerging life was like in the city that would be their home for the next few years, scenes in the photographs bringing back memories of the three times Yvonne and I had visited the City of Light over the years.

As part of her campaign to make her house more energy efficient and comfortable, Margaret had bought a new kitchen door and it was sitting in her boat waiting for transfer to the house. Josh, who would install it, and I carried it to our pickup I'd moved to the dock area and then drove it to Margaret's house and unloaded it on the back deck where Josh could pull the old one out and put the new one in. In appreciation, Margaret brought over some homemade chicken soup and Yvonne made her take some mocha brownies left over from the Food Bank volunteer appreciation party the day before. Yvonne made tomato-garlic pasta for dinner with a salad from her raised bed garden and zucchini from Larry and Joyce's — with slices of a baguette that had been warmed in the oven. Delicious!

The sky showed signs of blue here and there among the evening clouds. Perhaps the August sunshine would return in the morning.

Three-hundred-nine: They're Back

"The impediment to action advances action. What stands in the way becomes the way." — Marcus Aurelius

Midmorning Yvonne left for Eastsound and I continued working on creating a new version of *The eNotated Sailing Alone Around the World*, a combination of interacting software and database changes, more complicated than I had anticipated, when I saw our pest control provider put down his equipment at the head of the front walk and approach the house to discuss his quarterly visit to prevent carpenter ant infestation, something that had apparently happened with the previous owners and which had required substantial efforts to reverse. He had provided us some sugar ant poison three months back and wanted to know whether it was working for us, sugar ants being harmless and very tiny but which when they come upon something they like, generally sweet, they mount a considerable effort to have it, traveling long distances in two-way lines from their nest. In May and earlier we'd experienced successive campaigns at various places on the kitchen counters and though I continued to see the little ants on the floor here and there occasionally I assumed they were outliers, explorers randomly wandering the territory looking for treasure they could report on and bring the rest of their siblings to but I never again observed the concerted action we saw on the counters. Our pest control provider was pleased, telling me this new treatment was much better than anything they'd had to work with before.

In the late afternoon, when Yvonne was making dinner, slightly cooked summer vegetables with parmesan cheese, I decided to fix myself an Italian soda with blackberry syrup and plain water, not fizzy, and as I pulled the bottle from the top shelf of the cabinet that held another five flavors as well as our small liquor collection (port, vodka, Grand Marnier), I noticed sugar ants on the bottle and on my hand. They'd crawled up the wall out of sight and were feasting on the sugar

Three-hundred-nine: They're Back

under the edges of the bottle cap that had dried there from drips left from pouring. I took all the bottles out and cleaned them, leaving them on the counter by the sink temporarily and Yvonne filled and set an ant trap on top of the cabinet where they seemed to be entering from who knows where. Later in the evening I saw a dozen ants making their way in both directions along the floor trim in the guest bath, neither their origin nor destination evident or even which was in what direction, but since the bathroom backed up to the kitchen wall with the anty cabinet, what I was seeing might be a section of their supply train. Yvonne put down poison on two scraps of paper along their route on the floor and they were soon crowded around the edges of it feasting on what we hoped they would carry back to the nest and feed their queen.

The day had turned sunny, yesterday's rain clouds gone, their remnants emptying over the Cascades before reaching eastern Washington, and the tourists were everywhere in a bustling Eastsound. Next Tuesday, the fifth in the month, the Orcas Unitarians were responsible for the Food Bank lunch in the Community Church basement, next door to the new Food Bank distribution building, and Yvonne wanted to talk to Barbara about how many people to expect so as to recruit the right number of Unitarian suppliers. Lunch numbers were down from what they'd been at the beginning of the summer in part because of the change in how the Food Bank did its Tuesday distribution, more or less simultaneous with the church basement lunch, a coordinated but separate effort from the Food Bank itself. When the distribution and the lunch were held in the same place, the church basement, Food Bank customers would come earlier to sign in and get a queue number and then wait a half hour or more before being called to pick up their food bag which the Food Bank staff had been assembling in the next room and while they waited they had coffee or often lunch. Now, with the new building and streamlined procedures, there was no waiting and they "shopped," picking what they wanted from the shelves and counters rather than take a bag that the staff had had to prepare and likely contained items they didn't want or need. Because the Food Bank customers no longer had to wait they didn't wait and because they didn't wait for their Food Bank food they were less inclined to stop for lunch as well. Yvonne thought the Tuesday lunch would probably revert to what it had been in the past, an Orcas Island soup kitchen, not for the temporarily unemployed but for the hard core homeless, dysfunctional, addicted, and disturbed population of the island that is mostly invisible and can't or simply won't earn a living, existing on the fringes of a society used to abundance.

309: Garter snake - happy or not?

Late in the afternoon after I'd unloaded the wood I cut from logs laid out for me by Pat at his house at the other end of the island and was crossing the studio deck to walk up the three stairs to the house deck, I noticed a smallish garter snake lying in the sun at the point where the first long stair rises from the lower deck, probably, like I was, enjoying the summer warmth. The snake showed some caution but moved little even when I climbed the stairs nearby to get my camera to take a picture or two. Was the little snake happy, content on this beautiful day, having found a slug or two in Yvonne's raised bed vegetable garden nearby? Or was it so slow to move because of the carpenter ant poison that had been sprayed all around the perimeter of the house earlier in the day? Fifteen minutes later as I tested the pH in the hot tub and then added some pH decreaser, chlorine and shock, the little garter snake was gone, probably to the shade under the house deck. I was happy it was about and Yvonne was too but she was even happier she hadn't seen it.

Three-hundred-ten: Fact Finding

"Tell me and I forget, teach me and I may remember, involve me and I learn." — Benjamin Franklin

About 3:00 Yvonne woke me; I'd been snoring apparently and rather than lie useless in bed I got up in the darkness and noticed the carpet glowing between bed and dresser. It must be the moon, I thought, and it was though it took an effort to see it, having risen an hour before probably and now the shape of a fingernail clipping in its lunar cycle. Dew covered the glass panels in the deck railing outside the living room window, the subtly orange predawn sky mirrored in the calm but expectant Salish Sea, and I grabbed my camera from the kitchen counter drawer where I also keep my keys, wallet, my folding reading glasses, spare change, tools, and trays of odds and ends I want handy or can't think where else to put. In less than a minute the sky had lost its peculiar photogenic quality but the fragrances that greeted me when I'd opened the dining room door to go out on the deck wouldn't loose its pungency until the tide covered the exposed seaweed in our cove and the sun dried the moisture from the surface of disintegrating vegetable matter and a faint salt scent would remain. The dawn regulars, a doe with two fawns, grazed on the dry grass below the deck, one fawn turning to look out at the water, ten feet below and stretching to Bell Island and on east for miles, its back legs slightly akimbo and looking fragile and transient.

As usual I was the last to arrive at Howard's though David was still in his Subaru scanning the latest edition of the *Islands' Sounder*, fresh off the presses, that he must have picked up at the marina before coming here. Any news? The most significant was that he had found out that his Eastsound barber, a woman, possessed several advanced degrees, not atypical of Orcas carpenters, mechanics, and other tradespeople. Howard was upset because he'd found one of his cabbage plants he bought and transplanted was infected with clubroot, which could spread to other cabbages, radishes, and turnips in his garden, destroying them, the only cure being to starve the disease for seven years by planting no more of these root crops. When I told Yvonne, master gardener, about Howard's clubroot problem her reply was to say she didn't understand how farmers could grow anything successfully, given everything that stands in the way. She had just uprooted her brussels sprouts after finding them attacked by aphids. The Greybeards covered many of our usual topics — the economy, politics, education, technology, Howard today taking an optimistic view by reporting on a young man who had created a photovoltaic configuration more efficient than a flat row of panels by arranging them around a stem like leaves. That led to Chris and I to wonder how such a structure would cope with wind and snow and why it was better than systems in which the panels moved to follow the sun, acknowledging that nature's optimization of physical properties can have much to teach engineers.

By 11:00 I was at Islanders' Bank in Eastsound talking with Loreen, who'd been at our house on Crane with husband Martin, when Yvonne and I hosted the Library Board and staff two years before. I was exploring bringing Crane Island Association bookkeeping in house, that is me doing it using QuickBooks, something that would save money and provide more control and I was looking for an easy way to issue checks and manage our money. Loreen explained that the bank could make it very easy and inexpensive for the Crane Island Association and me as Treasurer to pay bills and manage our reserves, especially regarding getting a reasonable and safe interest rate.

By 1:00 I was at Bob's Eastsound office, meeting him and his new assistant, Pandora, and we talked through my suggestion for changing the division of labor between his firm and the Crane Island Association, with the association doing the bookkeeping, using Quickbooks, and his firm doing the accounting. They were very pleased at the prospect because he'd never intended to offer bookkeeping services and didn't in his Burlington office but had inherited those obligations for a number of San Juan Islands associations when he'd bought out a firm in Friday Harbor, one that the Crane Association had been using. I found using a remote bookkeeper frustrating and expensive. Bob found providing the services risky from a liability and customer retention perspective. Our joint goal was to make the change the beginning of September.

310: Deer at Raven's Cove

They advised against Quickbooks Online so I'd have to buy and install the software on my Mac, the Mac version, they said, now acceptable though not quite as good as the Windows version.

At our insurance agent's office I presented relevant documents from our Ford Focus purchase and came away with an insurance card for the new vehicle.

Three-hundred-ten: Fact Finding

Even Deer Harbor felt hot and when I got home so did Crane, the outside thermometer registering 76 degrees in the shade. But it was a beautiful summer day.

Three-hundred-eleven: Duck Soup

"Happiness, not in another place but this place... not for another hour, but this hour." — Walt Whitman

    The island was quiet as I walked Circle Road this sunny, warm morning, the community water system water tank at 12 feet and steady, a 10,000 gallon operating reserve over the 20,000 gallon fire reserve starting at the 7 1/2 foot level. I heard chirping from the osprey nest as I passed below, perhaps from the second or third chick the nesting pair was raising.

    Yvonne left for Orcas about 10:00 to fulfill her role as grounds chair (and primary groundskeeper) at the Deer Harbor Post Office (which the Deer Harbor Community Club owns) and the club building itself just north of the Deer Harbor hamlet on Deer Harbor Road, about ten miles south and west of Eastsound, Orcas Island's retail center.

    Now having a reliable process for building EPUB as well as MOBI format ebooks, I began to modify the annotation and book-building software to support a third type of book structure, the first being straightforward annotation, a single layer behind the surface of the book that would contain definitions, explanations of historical, geographic and biographical references, and other helpful hints to the reader, and the second, including the former but in addition essays on specific themes that pulled in relevant annotations into a continuous narrative. The third format, or option would link primary text to specific locations in an essay rather than to an annotation that was then itself included in an essay. Independently of anything I'd suggested, Barbara had conceived of this third way when writing the essay portions of her material for Cather's *My Antonia*. I'd be meeting with her Monday, had the database and word processing files she'd prepared, and wanted to be able to build an EPUB version of her *My Antonia* to discuss when we got together, eager to bring the project to completion, that is publish the eNotated Cather book.

Three-hundred-eleven: Duck Soup

James called to report he'd had a good session with his dissertation committee. They'd approved his proposal. He was now officially a doctoral candidate though at least two more years would be required to finish his research on the genetic basis of impulsivity and addiction in rats. Yvonne was home midday and reported a productive trip to Orcas, the post office and community club grounds looking tidy and attractive. At the post office, Bob had held the dustpan when she picked up the leavings from her sweeping the walk area and around the driveway where she'd been weeding.

Our plan was to leave for Friday Harbor on the early side of 3:00. We'd take a change of clothes and sleeping bags in case we couldn't leave to return before dark. While I sat with my MacBook Pro on my lap doing coding and testing, Yvonne announced that I had to be ready to offer my opinion and she modeled five different summer dresses in succession asking which I liked better. As far as I knew I had never seen these dresses before or the ones she showed me several other times over the last few weeks when she also asked my opinion before needing to look good for some social occasion. I responded to each dress showing, liking some more than others, not seeing any particular relationship between what I said and what she chose, and never had, this a mysterious process for many husbands I think.

Wanting to minimize potential trouble I showed Yvonne what I intended to wear — Levis and a long sleeved knit shirt — and she told me that wouldn't do, we were going out to dinner. I should wear a nice looking short sleeved shirt. I'll be too cold. No you won't. I packed up my computer and other material I'd need for my meeting with Angel and Yvonne preceded me to the *Huginn*, passing Kate and Steve arriving for the weekend, explaining that we had a dinner date on San Juan Island. Then I arrived at the boat, ready to leave when Yvonne pointed out that I wasn't wearing decent slacks. I volunteered to go home and change and did, the phone ringing as I was about to leave, Mick on the other end, telling me something about the handle on the new community club toilet breaking. What? I begged off and walked back to the boat, passing Kate and Steve, holding out my arms and saying nothing. Kate said, smiling, "Women!"

Three-hundred-eleven: Duck Soup

My appointment wasn't until 4:00 at the Griffin Bay Bookstore coffee shop. Yvonne would do some shopping. We had plenty of time. Passing the No Wake Zone buoy a quarter mile west of Pole Pass I took the *Huginn* up on plane and we were soon moving along San Juan Channel south towards Friday Harbor, all instruments in the normal range — and then the oil pressure gauge dropped to zero. Oh oh! I slowed the boat and stopped the engine, Yvonne now in a state, and checked the oil. Normal — as I expected it to be. I concluded that the problem must be with the indicator not the reality, started the engine and cruised the rest of the way to Friday Harbor at a much lower speed — thinking that operating the engine at all with no oil pressure would ruin it in any case. The event did not make a positive contribution to either of our moods.

The county dock area was occupied so I back tracked and went into the marina, finding a small spot at the head of one row packed with big power and sailboats and got permission from the young woman at the nearby marina booth. Yvonne and I agreed to meet at the foot of Spring Street at 5:30. I'd reserve a cab and I walked over to the taxi across from the ferry landing ramp. He'd be there at 5:30. Angel was already in the coffee shop in the bookstore and offered to buy me an ice tea and I consented. For the next hour we talked about her background, then the ideas behind eNotated Classics, showing her a Slocum and a Kafka volume on the iPad I'd brought with, and then talking about Kipling, *The Man Who Would Be King* and showing her the annotation software and talking about the process to create content, edit, and then publish an electronic book. And then I gave her three copies of our standard contract, explaining what each section meant, suggesting she think about whether doing a project with us suited her. She'd get back to me.

I took my backpack to the *Huginn* hiding it in a storage area (we had no lock on the cabin door), and then walked back to Spring Street, saw Yvonne, and we walked together to the cab. We were both in a better mood. Duck Soup Inn is about ten miles north of Friday Harbor, inland, on a little pond, with grape and other vines growing across the arbor that extends from the roof, the building rustic and the parking lot crowded. The summer before we'd done a lot to make Kelly and Tim's wedding weekend work and in gratitude they'd given us a generous gift certificate to this restaurant that we'd tried to use for Yvonne's birthday but couldn't because of conflicts.

311: Evening at Pole Pass

Because the meal would be free we had a different attitude than normal about restaurants and ordered whatever we wanted without reservation. When the bill came the unused balance provided a healthy tip to the staff. Yvonne had two different kinds of wine and then a French 75 cocktail, something she'd had once before with her friend Julie on recommendation of our daughter, Jeni. Yvonne had duck with polenta and green chili sauce and I had chicken with blueberries and potatoes. We'd started with a plate of heritage tomatoes (not as good as we'd had as kids), then a carrot soup, house salad and shared a big piece of cake with blackberry filling covered with whipped cream frosting. The portions were of reasonable size so though full we didn't feel sick or especially uncomfortable. The food was tasty, the service good (the restaurant apparently staffed only with competent women), and the surroundings pleasantly aged and island appropriate. We had talked for quite a while about Eleanor Roosevelt, Yvonne having recently read another book about her and having seen a PBS biography the night before. She was extraordinary, a passionate, persistent, prophet of democracy. And I talked about Steve Jobs, who just announced he was resigning as Apple CEO, having seen him in 1977, I think, at the Computer Faire in San Jose, and having followed his amazing story ever since. Remarkable people who make a difference. The cab driver and his wife had a B&B next door, the Dragonfly Inn, and after a call from the cashier he was back in the parking lot in a few minutes.

The sun was already down when we castoff the *Huginn* but the sky was light. Only a few boats were moving on the water, their navigation lights lit. Because the wind was calm and there were no boats about on San Juan Channel to create wakes, the water was smooth and the *Huginn* skated along the surface like a car on a freeway. The whole western sky was red, San Juan, Speiden and the other islands black silhouettes. We'd left the restaurant at 8:00; we were in the house before 8:40. A few small boats, with red, green, and white lights headed east, having come through Pole Pass and going home, enough sky light reflected on the water to make visual navigation possible, but soon it would be dark and the moon wouldn't rise until early morning. Day was done.

As we hugged on our deck Yvonne said how lucky we were to live in such a beautiful place, to have such a wonderful life, and I agreed. Nothing was forever, even for very long, and that was why sunrises and sunsets were so beautiful. They were transient. So were we and our life on Crane.

Three-hundred-twelve: Earth Light

"We are shaped and fashioned by what we love." — Johann Wolfgang von Goethe

Pink tinted the northeast sky and an almost new moon, a bright sliver, the rest of its face lit by reflected earth light, rose an hour ahead of the sun. Later, the reflection of the morning sun flashed intermittently from the stirring water below the rocks our house rested on, tapping out a watery message in nature's Morse code but I couldn't pick it up. The days had become noticeably shorter, the sky dark by 9:00, an hour earlier than at the solstice two months earlier. Salal, an evergreen bush that adds leaves in the spring our island deer like to browse, now sported bright red leaves here and there in the patch between the high bank and the path to the beach stairs. Why? Dryness?

Not long after noon, with me first checking the oil in the *Huginn*'s engine and at her request, Yvonne was on her way to Orcas to pick up Sheila, Karen, and Lynn in Deer Harbor for a long afternoon with Nancy in West Sound admiring her garden — which was, like Howard's, now infected with clubroot — talking about an Eleanor Roosevelt biography, sharing food, sangria and wine, and planning next month's get together (Gail Collins, *When Everything Changed*). Sheila told an archetypal Orcas story of simplicity and resourcefulness. A few years before the high school sailing team coached by Burke qualified for the nationals competition in San Diego, the young people happy to be going and for a chance to sail in warm water for a change but they didn't have any expectations of doing well against California teams lavishly sponsored by prosperous yacht clubs, so they hadn't brought any nice clothes. But, against all odds, they won and would be feted at the celebration dinner. What to do? Burke took the team to Value Village and treated. They all found something to wear, girls and boys, more likely odd than conventional.

Three-hundred-twelve: Earth Light

312: Kayak fleet heads for Pole Pass

Somewhere thousands of miles to the east and south a huge hurricane would soon make landfall in the Carolinas and then was predicted to migrate up the East Coast to New York City, now under orders from the Mayor to evacuate low lying areas. The president had interrupted his Martha's Vineyard vacation to return to Washington. We expected beautiful, sunny, summer weather for the next week and more, perhaps as warm as 75 at the house and 80 in Deer Harbor. I felt sorry (a little sorry) for the people in New York City; all winter they'd had a new storm every week, then spring storms followed by a very hot summer, and now perhaps a hurricane. Not much fun, I'd say. We hadn't had snow, cold, storms, or heat — though we had had some wind at times, to 40 or 50 mph. Another reason to be grateful. Jens and Susan would be arriving back in Wellesley soon, perhaps just in time for a hurricane.

But we do have trees that fall down sometimes unexpectedly and that's what Dick called me about, one in particular he was worried about, across Circle Road from his rustic inland cabin and near well house #4. He said he'd talked to Pat, the Roads chair and he'd declined the invitation to look as had Doug. The tree was big, two feet in diameter and perhaps 80 or 90 feet high. Had it fallen down? Yes. No. I couldn't tell which. Why don't you put a ribbon on it and I'll look at it when I have a chance. After a spicy chicken soup dinner, Yvonne and I headed up the hill on Eagle Lane and then turned left on Circle Road. The tank level was still at 12 feet. Very good. Near the intersection with Rocky Road I saw a white ribbon hanging on the branch of a small willow by the road, two big dead firs twenty and thirty feet from the road, still standing, but perhaps susceptible of being blown over or just toppling in answer to the earth's pull. I didn't want to deal with it. Farther on we could hear the rapid chirping of what we assumed was an Osprey chick and once positioned at the right place on Circle Road we could see it perched high in the big nest atop a dead, almost branchless Douglas fir. It was hungry. Where were mom and dad, Yvonne wanted to know. Fishing? Or was the big chick ready to fledge, to go out on its own? Yvonne reported that brother Ron and his new main squeeze, probably with her boys, 6 and 11, would be up to the Island from Seattle over Labor Day weekend. We looked forward to the visit.

I'd barely been out of the house all day, ridiculous in a way because the day was so beautiful but I was determined to be able to show Barbara a draft book of her annotated *My Antonia* and besides programming there was data to be massaged. By dinner time I had made good progress and emailed Barbara a note to send me more content if she had any. I hadn't heard back from Angel, consistent with my suspicion that the project didn't fit her.

Three-hundred-thirteen: Tess

"Do what you can, with what you have, where you are." — Theodore Roosevelt

As I lay in bed in the dark about 4:00 doing my normal morning deep breathing — 40 breaths in 30 minutes — I considered — again — how to best architect the annotation services we wanted to provide not only to those adding titles to our library but also to teachers and students as a platform for collaborative reading — active reading in which the student engages both with the book and fellow students to read deeply, critically, and creatively — and a simple solution precipitated slowly out of my out-breathing and in-breathing and I was eager to begin experimenting with it.

But first things first — and that was preparing Hardy's *Tess of the d'Urberville's* for annotation and supplement in a cooperative project by Howard and me leading to an eNotated Tess ebook. That process took all day and even then wasn't quite complete. First I downloaded Tess, in HTML format, from the Gutenberg Library (in the public domain) and then I used Text Wrangler, a free powerful text editing program to clear out excess HTML coding, establish chapter boundaries and rename them for our system, and then convert HTML special character tags to the special characters themselves as well as formatting tags, such as italics with our simple markdown system and then imported the modified text and built a book database. I then created an online book, a local website, I could compare visually to both the Gutenberg original and to a Penguin paper edition, finding formatting and other problems, correcting them and then looking again. By late afternoon I was almost satisfied that Howard and I had a good starting point — except that in two cases at least — the database was showing what should be two or more paragraphs as one. I'd write a utility to read the existing database and create a new one with the right paragraph count — but that would have to wait.

Three-hundred-thirteen: Tess

313: Rain shelter, hers and his sheds at dawn

While Yvonne was making dinner and watching the hurricane news, the DirectTV satellite service began to degrade, the picture disappearing entirely from time to time. Yvonne was frustrated. The other cable, box, and TV in my office seemed to be working — it must be the cable I put a staple through in early summer when remounting it — finally — a year after a buck that had gotten into the front garden pulling the cable down while forcing himself through the deer fence after somehow getting in and not knowing how to get out. I handed Yvonne a walkie-talkie and I took its twin with me, got a ladder, and climbed up to fiddle with the cable from the dish, talking with Yvonne as I did so. The picture would improve, then fail. I carefully put in a new staple when she said the picture looked good but then it didn't again. In the house I looked at the other TV again and it too would degrade at times though not as seriously. Perhaps the problem wasn't in the cable but in the dish or something — tree branches? — had grown in the way of the

Three-hundred-thirteen: Tess

dish — but though branches looked like they might be in the way, why now? They hadn't gotten longer in a few minutes — between the time the signal was strong and when it was weak. After winding my way through a complex automated phone service system I reached technical support — a woman who took me through a few procedures and then scheduled a service call for Friday and I explained that whoever was going to come to the house would need a boat ride over from Orcas and therefore should call me to arrange it. Almost a week with poor service probably. Yvonne, who likes to watch the news would be frustrated. I told the service provider we should get a week's credit against our bill and she said she'd arrange it. Satellite rather than cable service and slow Internet connections are two of the costs associated with living on Crane. Not much, in the scheme of things.

After dinner — leftover spicy chicken soup and a salad: roasted beet, goat gouda, lemon cucumber (all from the Eastsound Farmers' Market where Yvonne was serving in the Master Gardeners' booth and successfully used the iPad to dispense information to customers) and greens from Yvonne's raised bed vegetable garden bordering both sides of the studio deck, and after cleaning up the dinner dishes, I took a short walk, feeling weak, almost sick from being virtually motionless all day long. The community water tank level remained at 12 feet, pumping matching use, Gary having set the timers perfectly, and though he and Wilma would continue to be involved with the Crane community with the water system, over all it would be less because of their recent sale of their landing craft barge and exit from that business. When we moved to Crane most of what we brought from our house on Cayou Valley Road in Deer Harbor came by barge and on those days their service included unloading at our new house as well as transport of the trucks and trailers. When we brought a new refrigerator to Crane they helped get it off the truck and into the kitchen and then helped put the old one on our pickup so I could take it to San Juan Sanitation for recycling.

As I walked I looked closely at four dead trees that had fallen in the last year or two, one close to the Community Center (a silver fir), two near the intersection of Eagle Lane and Circle Road (alder) and one

Three-hundred-thirteen: Tess

to the north along Circle Road between Eagle Lane and Dock Road (silver fir). None would provide the heat Douglas fir does but they were windfalls too and sometime in the next few weeks I'd cut some slices with my chainsaw to see whether the wood was too decayed to bother with. The F150 was in the parking lot at the dock where Margaret had left it when she and Josh took all his tools to her boat for return to Orcas. He had completed the window and door installation project she had hired him to do. Pole Pass and the Crane Island marina were lit by the setting sun, glowing warmly, as was illuminated Bell Island, and Orcas and Shaw to the east, Harney Channel, the foot of West Sound, and the water between Crane and Caldwell point. Our marine neighborhood was now empty of boats — after a busy day of sail and power boats, flotillas of kayaks — one with eight members — dealing with the wakes of some rude boaters, determined to speed in a low wake zone.

I looked more closely at the red salal leaves appearing on many of the plants I passed not sure whether it was normal in late summer and noticed white bumps on many of the leaves, a fungus perhaps — but whether it was the cause or the effect of the dying leaves I couldn't say. Almost finishing my walk and at the community dock a friendly full-sized black poodle I'd never seen before loped toward me and then followed me across the meadow, watching me as I closed the gate when entering Yvonne's front garden, saying goodnight to the poodle who wanted to be my friend.

Three-hundred-fourteen: Wine Tasting

"Wine is sunlight, held together by water." — Galileo Galilei

A pink horizon, one small cloud over Mount Woolard, on Orcas, and lower Blakely Island hidden behind a layer of fog that had come through Thatcher Pass from Rosario Straight. The outgoing tide rushing through Pole Pass spilled across the glassy surface of the Salish Sea without disturbing Bell Island's inverted twin. Suddenly a man standing on the water a hundred yards off shore glided into view, startling me, and then dipped his long paddle and moved quickly south toward Wasp Passage. I realized he was on a paddle board, but that made the image no less striking and I spent the next half hour researching paddle boarding on the Internet, finding that intrepid practitioners were using them to run river rapids in Montana and Colorado. Amazing!

While the sun rose over Mt Woolard, fog continued to pile through Thatcher Pass covering the lower half of Blakely, the reflection from the fog merging with the reflection from the water and so bright it was almost impossible to view, the sun have taken control of water and land, hiding it, not like night behind darkness, nothing, but behind impenetrable glory. A kingfisher hurried south, off our deck, unable to chatter a grumpy complaint because its beak held a small fry. Later in the day, when Yvonne sat in one of the chairs on our point below the house an osprey, presumably a parent to chick we saw in the tree top nest near Dan's driveway a few days before, flew past her not twenty feet away carrying a fish in its talons.

All morning Yvonne cooked, making spinach and walnut empanadas and a marinated tortellini salad for the afternoon's wine tasting fundraiser at the Deer Harbor Community Club, while I tried to complete preparing Hardy's *Tess of the d'Urbervilles* for Howard and I to begin working on the coming Wednesday. I wanted to split each of three paragraphs into two parts and rather than reload the entire book, I'd written a utility to make a new copy of the database, doing the split-

Three-hundred-fourteen: Wine Tasting

ting as it went but by 2:00 when we had to leave for Orcas and the Community Club I hadn't finished what should have been a simple project.

Walking across the meadow toward to the dock I was surprised at how hot the sun felt and again when we walked up the ramp on the Orcas side. Someone had repainted the transient moorage bull rail yellow and loading zone red, covering the faded paint Yvonne had applied three years before and perhaps they had also been responsible for moving Stuart's SeaSport from the transient moorage area, where it had been for more than two weeks, presumably waiting to be picked up by Islands Marine Center in Fishermans Bay on Lopez Island for service and storage. I had been intending to call IMS but hadn't managed to remember at the time a phone was handy. Dick called. Had I cut down the tree he was worried about? No. I hadn't done anything after he'd told me about it and I'd taken a look. And I hadn't wanted to.

By the time we arrived at the Community Club half a dozen cars were parked in the rear lot, behind the building, and the tables inside were already set up, five tables for pouring (one that would also carry desserts), a big table for tapas, and a dozen small tables for seating, those decorated with what appeared to be lit votive candles inside paper lanterns. It looked nice. The kitchen addition I helped build in 2006 was crowded, mostly with women unpacking food they'd made and brought, readying it for the serving table. The wine merchants, sponsors of a tasting room not far from Eastsound, had brought cases of ten Chilean and Argentinean wines — four reds, three whites, a rose, and two dessert wines. Mick and I would have the first shift at the check-in table near the front door where we'd accept tickets ($35 each) and hand back a brochure about the auction items featured and ten tasting tickets — as well as a custom tasting wine glass decorated with the Deer Harbor zip code, 98243, the logo for the successful effort to buy the Post Office building from Wyndam, who intended to close it, and then rent it to the Post Office, thus preserving the local postal service and the building's informal greeting and gossip function.

Three-hundred-fourteen: Wine Tasting

314: Deer Harbor Community Club wine tasting fund raiser a great success

Once I'd been trained on my ticket-taking function, I took a chair and sat on the ramp behind the building in the shade and read some more of *Now You See It*, a book that connects the observation that we see, perceive selectively and the implications for working together and new technology — but I found myself dozing. Clay came by, thanked me for the web link I sent him with strong advice not to varnish teak decks, a response to a conversation he and I had two weeks before and after I'd looked at his boat moored at the Deer Harbor Marina and saw that he varnished the middle deck. He said he decided not to varnish the decks, he'd just let them go gray — except for the middle deck, which he decided to varnish. What?

About 70 people picked up wine glasses; about 100 had bought tickets. The wine cost little, the food came from volunteers; expenses were minimal. About 5:30, Mike started the auction, offering boat cruises, meals, lodging, and other island services volunteered by individuals

Three-hundred-fourteen: Wine Tasting

and businesses, including Howard doing a reading of Dylan Thomas' "A Child's Christmas in Wales" an annual habit of his. The auction grossed more than $4000. The evening was a great success, both in terms of raising money to pay down the principal on the Post Office mortgage and in having a good time. The big room had been very noisy with conversation among diverse economic and social elements in the Deer Harbor area — from one time astronauts to former teachers. I talked with eighteen-year-old Taylor for a while, Pam and Eric's son, about his coming matriculation to the University of Washington, Bothel campus to study electrical engineering or computer science and to, I forget his name, from Oregon, Governor Kitzhaber's assistant in the education area about sensible locally directed reforms they were considering as a response to falling tax revenues and better — and relevant — educational success metrics. He and his wife hoped to move to Deer Harbor soon — one reason being his sense that Deer Harbor was a friendly and effective community, something, because of my experience I knew to be true. The occasion was a success because the group had observed Yvonne's Law: "If you're going to work for a fund raiser you should do something you like to do." This evening it was drinking wine and talking.

Three-hundred-fifteen: Rethinking

> *"It is the life of the crystal, the architect of the flake, the fire of the frost, the soul of the sunbeam."* — John Burroughs (on nature)

As I approached the Crane dock on Orcas Island I saw a powerboat I didn't recognize moored to the outside of the breakwater float, not a good place to tie up because it means being exposed to wakes from passing watercraft. After docking at the west end of the transient moorage area and walking toward the ramp to the pier and parking lot I saw someone vaguely familiar walking toward me, having come from the boat on the outside of the breakwater. It was Keith, of Waterfront Construction, in Seattle, the company that had built and installed the new Crane and Orcas side floats a few years back. He and I had talked three years before when Waterfront was trying to replace two wood with steel pilings inside the float to make possible more dock space. Only one would go in; the other hit rock.

At that time, I was dock steward for the association and he and I toured the Orcas dock as I pointed out problems and asked questions. The dock has a U shaped parallel to the beach and more or less at a right angle to the pier leading from land to the ramp that moves up and down as the floats below, the dock area, rises and falls with the tide. The bottom of the U, the east end float, was attached at either end, on the outside to wooden pilings by heavy chains looped around the pilings that would slide as the float moved up and down with the tide and waves. A third, middle piling, was serving no evident purpose because the U-shaped, sliding device that held the float to the piling was broken, and as Keith explained, the piling wasn't vertical but at an angle that put pressure on the slide as it moved up and down the piling, finally breaking it. But, he assured me, it really wasn't necessary. The pilings at each end were adequate to hold the float. But the broken slide threatened the hulls of any boats parked on the outside of the U, and so the

Three-hundred-fifteen: Rethinking

space couldn't really be used for transient moorage during those rare times the marina was packed. Blair, the current dock steward, had asked Keith to have the broken slide removed while his company did other repair work on the dock.

Basically, the dock can be thought of as consisting of three separate parts, the outer breakwater, a dozen concrete float sections held together by heavy planks running down either side, the bottom of the U, more concrete sections, and the inner float, concrete to the east and newer grating covered floats to the west that allow light to penetrate to the eel grass below. The bottom of the U was attached to both the breakwater at one end and the inner dock at the other by rubber donut shaped hinges that could stretch as the connected sections had slightly different rhythms as the waves hit each one at a slightly different time. From time to time I'd walk the docks looking for problems and in the early spring had noticed that one of the donuts connecting the breakwater to the U bottom was beginning to tear. That would lead to its twin tearing and eventually to the two floats becoming disconnected and that would cause the metal bridge crossing the two sections to bang on the breakwater section, probably damaging the concrete. It needed to be fixed. Blair had made the arrangements with Waterfront but the donuts had to be custom made and had only recently become available. Keith told me they'd be installed in the next few weeks, including the metal brackets, also custom built and waiting to be galvanized. I was glad to hear that the repairs would be made soon.

Another problem threatened the long term viability of the breakwater: half a dozen of the float sections had been installed too close together, without the required quarter-inch gap that would let them flex independently, and the resulting jamming had chipped some of the concrete from the upper portions of the joints. Someone, sometime had applied concrete repair material but it had mostly chipped away. The joints needed to be widened, easiest by sawing. Maybe Pat, who had the equipment to do it could manage it this fall or winter.

Three-hundred-fifteen: Rethinking

315: More than a dozen deer on Crane

I arrived at Enzo's before Barbara and bought a blueberry scone to save me from overwhelming hunger if I couldn't make it home before noon. After she arrived and got her coffee I asked her about her cataract surgery problems; after several days her right eye vision was still clouded. She was frustrated. I showed her the draft *My Antonia* I'd put together and she was pleased to see her work organized into an electronic book. We talked about what was left to do and set a tentative October 1st date for being ready to publish, contingent on her being able to see normally. I had suggested that I would take care of all the semi-technical details, that she wouldn't have to work on the annotation database anymore and that I would make changes to what she'd already given me at her direction and what else she had to do: an introduction to the book, an introduction to her as an annotator, some more theme essays if she wanted to do them, and a short bibliography — and she could do all the writing with a word processing program, such as

Three-hundred-fifteen: Rethinking

Word. She was enormously grateful and that made me consider again what I could expect annotators to be willing or able to do. Rather than make the annotation software more powerful perhaps it needed to be much simpler. Maybe I should do all the book structuring, formatting, and fancy linking and the annotator should be required only to use something more like a word processor and less like a database program. Maybe the elements of the books really didn't need to be stored in a database but could exist as text files that I would manipulate with scripts out of sight of the annotators. And perhaps I now had a way to do this — with Co-ment, an online annotation platform.

About 5:00 I took a quick walk around the island, feeling enervated from being physically inactive most of the day. The tank level had fallen away from 12 feet; I'd have to let Gary know. The tree Dick had called me about had in fact been felled by persons unknown. I'd find out at the first meeting of the new board on Saturday. Margaret came over just after 6:00, Yvonne having made another salad with fixings from her garden and the Orcas Farmers' Market and two kinds of paratha, I think, Indian flat bread, folded over and stuffed with spinach and what else? Margaret reported that she was the person who moved Stu's boat from the transient to the long term moorage area at the Orcas dock, irritated it had been in the way so long. I promised to write Liz to tell her their boat hadn't been picked up. Unlike last winter, Margaret would pull her boat and leave it on its trailer over the winter so it wouldn't be available as emergency backup — and that had turned out to be important to us. But now the *Huginn* had a new (rebuilt) engine and besides it didn't make sense for her to have to pay $60 a month and not use her boat and we didn't want to volunteer to pay the association moorage fee. In the spring, finishing her last year teaching at Ohio State, she'd put her Columbus house up for sale and sort her possessions into what she'd bring to Crane and what she'd sell or dispose off, planning to be on Crane full time by July or August 2012 after attending a number of conferences in Europe and Asia.

Yvonne's peach cobbler with vanilla ice cream was a hit and Margaret and fat cat Moonie left our house in the near darkness to walk the 100 yards home.

Three-hundred-sixteen: The Cable Guy

"Technology is nothing. What's important is that you have a faith in people, that they're basically good and smart, and if you give them tools, they'll do wonderful things with them."
– Steve Jobs

The phone rang about 7:30 and I hurried to answer it before it woke Yvonne. It was Clyde, the DirectTV serviceman, calling from the Anacortes ferry landing. He'd arrive on Orcas about 8:25 and wanted to know where to go for me to pick him up by boat to get to Crane Island. I told him to turn left on Deer Harbor Road about two miles north of the ferry landing and then to drive about five miles, through the Deer Harbor hamlet and marina and then another mile and a half to the Crane Island marina parking lot. He called again when he was driving off the ferry and I walked down to the community dock and took the *Huginn* over to Orcas, moored, and walked up to the road to look for him and he appeared shortly in his official DirectTV truck. He'd come from Anacortes, where he lived, a DirectTV employee for about three years. And he showed me his ID card though I didn't know at the time why he wanted to do that. He carried his tool satchel and I carried a spool of cable that he might need if the problem was related to my having put a staple through one of the cables leading to the dish when re-hanging the cable under the eaves after a buck had somehow gotten inside the deer fence, wanted badly to get out and crashed through the fence at the corner of the house, pulling both the fence and nearby satellite dish cable away from the house.

Three-hundred-sixteen: The Cable Guy

316: Good sailing weather

Two nights before the signal for the cable that fed the kitchen TV had begun to degrade, the picture falling apart and at times disappearing altogether. The other TV in my office showed some symptoms as well but less severe. Clyde checked the signal on the kitchen TV and could see it vary from acceptable to poor. His diagnosis was that the transducer, the device that sends the signal through the cable to the cable box had become defective so he'd replace it and then we'd see whether that fixed the problem. I went next door to pick up one of our extension ladders that Margaret had been using during her window replacement project and set it up on the deck outside the master bedroom, on the east side of the house facing the water, and followed Clyde up the ladder to the roof. While he worked on the dish antenna set just below the peak of the roof on the east side I made an inspection tour of the roof. Parts of sixteen asphalt shingles had disappeared, almost all over the previous winter, leaving only one layer of shingle below. I'd

Three-hundred-sixteen: The Cable Guy

need to do something about that and had a bundle of shingles someplace left over from when the roofing was done more than 20 years ago. I could cut pieces to size and use adhesive to fasten them in place, but I wasn't eager to do that anytime soon.

After my spring moss powder treatment the roof showed almost no sign of that Pacific Northwest scourge. Two years before I'd spent two days on the roof with a pressure washer removing several years accumulation, damaging and shortening the life of the roof in the process. The gutter on the eaves outside the guest room that fed the 450 gallon storage tank wa full of madrona leaves and I'd have to clean them out. For the first time I looked closely at the repairs the roofer had made around the chimney on the studio roof seeing that he had hung a section of sheet metal about halfway up one side and had put new flashing on the roof on the uphill side of the structure, all to cure an intermittent leak that would drip onto the sidewalk leading to the front stairs under a wide roof overhang. His main task was to fix leaks on three skylights, the most important over the guest bathroom and he had. We'd had no more problems.

I walked across the roof to where Clyde was working and asked him if I could watch. Of course. He'd removed the current transducer, about the size of a woman's fist, and was now replacing the connectors on the two coaxial cable ends. It was obvious the four year old transducer had suffered the effects of salt spray blown by winter winds up over the peak of the roof and Clyde confirmed that was a problem for waterfront houses. Once he'd mounted the new transducer and tightened the dish to the roof I asked him whether tree branches might interfere with a clear line of sight to the satellite, invisible to us and thousands of miles away. To me it looked like both madrona and Douglas fir branches might be causing some trouble. He pulled out his cell phone and pointed the back of it at the sky. I knew there were smart phone apps that could show the position of stars and planets, and yes, he said, he could see exactly where the satellite was, and he showed me the screen with a series of red dots, each a different set of signals coming down to the cable box that would untangle them into channels we could watch. Wonderful!

Three-hundred-sixteen: The Cable Guy

We climbed down the ladder and went into the kitchen to check the signal; it was very good and the picture quality was perfect. The transducer had been the problem. He'd been at the house not much longer than half an hour and made the fix. I took him back to Orcas and he headed off to Eastsound for another appointment, probably often busy in the San Juans since virtually everyone that wants cable uses DirectTV or Dish.

Yvonne left for Orcas almost as soon as I got home, carrying a macaroni casserole for the Food Bank luncheon in the Community Church basement, Yvonne in charge of the Unitarian group that served every fifth Tuesday and I spent the rest of the day writing up a Treasurers report on my plans to begin doing the association's bookkeeping for the Crane Board meeting Saturday and then preparing *Tess of the d'Urbervilles* online for Howard, initiating our collaborative annotation project.

After dinner I was happy to go for a walk with Yvonne around the island, uncomfortable at having been sitting most of the day. The tank level was back up to twelve feet; that was good. Gary or more probably Wilma would be taking meter readings Thursday, the first of September and I'd have to begin a new year's worth of reports. We could hear the osprey chick this evening; perhaps it had been recently fed but we could see it, a white head bobbing about the huge nest at the top of a dead fir. Otherwise we saw no one, not even any deer. The sun had come out during the afternoon and now rich and red filtered through the trees almost horizontally. Someone had put gravel in a few potholes close to the community dock but it wouldn't stay, come the first rain and a car driving over it. Yvonne heated up the remains of the peach cobbler she'd made the night before and we settled in a pile in my office watching *"The Conspirator."*

Three-hundred-seventeen: Collaboration

"The ordinary arts we practice every day at home are of more importance to the soul than their simplicity might suggest." – Thomas Moore

    As I crossed to Orcas I noticed that a log boom extended south, just east of Caldwell point, effectively blocking boat traffic between the foot of West Sound and entry to the Pole Pass area. What were they thinking? The *Evergreen State*, interisland ferry, was westbound from Orcas Landing heading toward the log boom. Because, for once, I was early in leaving for Howard's Wednesday morning tea party, I backed off the *Huginn*'s throttle, slowly passing the Crane marina on Orcas, where I was headed, and watched the ferry come closer. What would it do? Then I began to think about the geometry of what I was looking at and realized that though the log boom would interrupt boat traffic trying to come through the pass from Caldwell Point to the north side of Bell Island, it was far enough west that it wouldn't be a problem for traffic turning south to go into Wasp Passage south of Bell Island and then south of Crane Island, just where the Evergreen State was going. Even so, the log boom was right across the Pole Pass marine highway. That didn't seem like a good idea — but that wasn't as exciting as blocking the ferry so I turned the *Huginn* back to the Orcas dock, moored at the west end of the transient area and walked up the ramp to the parking lot.

    I was first to arrive and met Howard at his door, he carrying a tray with pot and cups and we walked over to the garden fence and I opened the gate so he could get through, with his hands full. I followed him up the stone stairs into the garden and we walked between rows of his plantings and I opened the door to the "honeymoon cottage" for him, a shed that served sometimes as an overflow guest room. We knew

Three-hundred-seventeen: Collaboration

that Chris and David were off island and after about 15 minutes, while we were enjoying our tea, Brian hobbled it, supported in part by his cane, and he took his seat on a folding chair, at the head of the two facing couches Howard and I occupied. We talked for some time about how Michael and Kat had gotten themselves into an unnecessary fix with the County government and why. Michael operated a boatyard at the head of Deer Harbor. His neighbors, to the immediate south had, without county approval, converted a shed, only 18" from the lot line, into a guest cottage, and then gotten the county to approve it retroactively even though it violated the ten foot set back rule among others. The county didn't know anything about the violation until it was reported anonymously, probably by Kat, though she denied it to Howard. In any case, the neighbor was granted retroactive approval for the conversion and set back violation. Incensed at the neighbor and County and concerned that having a habitation so close to their work area would result in noise complaints that would then interfere with their boat repair business, Michael and Kat had sued the neighbors and Howard thought had spent $60,000 thus far. The neighbor retaliated by denying Michael access to the small pond that had served as Michael's firefighting water source, something he may have forgotten he depended on the neighbor for. Michael then petitioned the county for permission to build a 30,000 gallon reservoir on his property but was turned down. Then the fire department inspected his property and finding inadequate water for firefighting had the county order him to cease doing business as a boatyard, something that would please many in the Deer Harbor hamlet because the boatyard was an eyesore. Had the County been unusually harsh with Michael and Kat because of their long history of complaining about this, that, and the other thing to the County? Perhaps, but the County had been leaving him alone. It was only when he started to throws stones at his neighbor that his own windows began to break. The three of us agreed that an ongoing affable or at least polite relationship with the neighbor all along might have prevented much of the trouble, for instance by bargaining with the neighbor to get permanent water rights and an understanding about noise in exchange for acceptance of the too close building, which, of course had been there all

Three-hundred-seventeen: Collaboration

along, only having had its purpose change. Of course Michael and Kat wouldn't agree with us but what appeared to them to be a need for justice seemed to us a lazy kind of self-righteousness.

Brian recalled how a business mentor, when listening to Brian's I'm right, they're wrong story had spent half an hour giving him examples of why reality is often shades of gray. I added the observation that focusing on the rules level without seeing the larger purpose behind the rules can cause all kinds of social mischief and grief, and described what I'd seen on Crane at times, with some personalities demanding conformance to rules and ignoring the effect attacking others without taking into account their needs has on the social fabric. Perhaps sometimes war with neighbors is justified but there will always be a cost and tolerance, negotiation, and sometimes acceptance of what you do like, may often be more practical than being right, whatever that is. But since the orientations toward being right versus being practical seem to be so deep and rationalized so thoroughly by those with one orientation or the other, these skirmishes have been and likely will always be part of island life, where we seem to seek insularity and community simultaneously.

Brian was having problems with his tenant, a sixty-one year old woman he provided lodging and some meals to in exchange for some indefinitely specified cleaning, cooking, dinner time companionship, and perhaps occasional chauffeuring services. It had worked for one week and now was failing. She was using the space he provided her but wasn't holding up her end with services. Since Howard and I had heard this story four times before with four other women, the others younger, I asked Brian whether it would be OK for me to offer my suggestions again. Yes. Why don't you rent the cabin for $500 a month and then let the tenant provide you services for which you'd pay as delivered, say $20 for a ride to town and back using your car, $20 to clean the house and so on? Then you can use the balance of the money to hire any number of other Orcas people needing pickup work to fill in when your tenant isn't interested. Brian listened and then said what he was really looking for was companionship. Ah. I was making suggestions for an effective business relationship but what he wanted was love. I had no suggestions. Then Brian asked whether either of us would help him find the cover of his septic tank because he wanted to inspect it. Howard volunteered. I didn't.

At 9:30, Howard adjourned the tea time because the tea had worked its way through his system and was now demanding to get out. Brian left and Howard and I went into his house to look at the on-line site I'd set up for collaborating on annotating *Tess of the d'Urbervilles*. Howard immediately understood the mechanics of the site so we turned our attention to what the annotations should cover. He'd written out a number on a yellow pad and we walked through the first chapter, each with our own book, he pointing to passages he thought should be annotated and what he had to say and me pointing to others that readers might stumble over and could use help with, for instance the "low and plashed hedgerow" — what was plashed? He said he couldn't find a definition anywhere but in other areas he provided fascinating background on 19th century England, the formation of National Schools in 1870 for ages five to thirteen and how his father had an extra year but had left school at age 14. I suggested he cite his own experience where relevant in the annotations, that what he was doing wasn't academic as much as informed by personal experience and that readers would enjoy meeting him from time to time while reading the book, feeling a connection with him to Hardy that wouldn't feel like the typical impersonal, objective approach. He said he wouldn't work on the project until three in the morning the way Chris had on Slocum and Dana and I approved. Work on it as long as it's fun; then do something else and come back to it another day.

I picked up the mail at the Post Office but forgot to get the *Islands' Sounder* and the *Seattle Times* at the marina and so I went back by boat after lunch getting 11 gallons of gas ($50) for the *Huginn* at the marina dock. Before I left to return to the marina, Yvonne commented that she thought I'd been trained to pick up newspapers after Howard's on Wednesday mornings and she didn't know what to do with me when I didn't. Neither did I — since I'd put three quarters in the pocket of my Levi 501s expressly for the purpose of using them in the *Sounder* vending machine on the marina dock; the *Times* I bought in the marina store for $1.

317: Blackberry jam in process

Back home I spent some of the afternoon writing up a status report on eNotated Classics for David, Chris, and Jens and had much that was promising to report. Then I bought and downloaded Quickbooks for Mac and attempted to open the Crane Island bookkeeping database the accountant had sent so I could begin preparing the annual billing and take up the association's bookkeeping but got only an error message and so wrote the accountant who had sent me the file about the problem. For the third evening in a row Yvonne and I walked around Crane right after dinner, something we hadn't done in the four and a half

Three-hundred-seventeen: Collaboration

years we'd lived there in part because my habit had been to do my walks early in the morning but I told Yvonne I like this better, I liked her company while I walked — it was a good time to talk and pay attention to the island — and she agreed pointing out that by winter we'd have to walk before rather than after dinner to do it in daylight.

Three-hundred-eighteen: Turning

"It is not down in any map; true places never are." – Herman Melville

A foggy world greeted me just before 6:00 when I got out of bed, uncharacteristically late, having had a very good sleep even after having taken an afternoon nap the day before when I kept falling asleep typing and encouraged by Yvonne who was already napping on the couch to do likewise on the too short but none the less comfortable love seat. For the first time since June the morning temperature was below 50, a sign of things to come, but slowly here, the changes of seasons deliberate and steady compared with the chaos and volatility we had been used to in Colorado. My habit is to have breakfast at 6:00 and lunch at noon, if I can wait that long, and dinner when Yvonne feeds me, which is almost always exactly at 6:00.

For the last four months my breakfasts didn't require artificial light; now they did, the day shorter by three and a half minutes and in September shortening by close to two hours. Yvonne, who pays attention to the path the sun takes across the sky so she can see what light is available to her garden and what is caught in the still numerous Douglas firs, says she can see the difference day to day, and telling me yesterday that she was now realizing how much sun vegetables required, compared to flowers, for instance, and discouraged about ever having the kind of garden she had on Cayou Valley Road, where the good soil and uninterrupted southern exposure brought explosive growth to squash for instance. And water was a problem here too because it was so dear, unlike our Deer Harbor home where water was essentially free.

Our F150 in the yard reminded me every day that I needed to pick up firewood, five logs waiting at Pat's and four or five more along Circle Road and perhaps two to be felled on the far side of the field next to the community center — but I had too much to do — and with Labor

Day weekend bringing a crowd back to the island I thought it best to wait.

318: Summer at the Community dock

I had complained to Pandora the day before, by email, that my newly installed QuickBooks for Mac couldn't open the Crane Island Association database she'd sent me, probably because it was in PC format. Back came an email that she'd forgotten to tell Linda that I needed Mac format so she had the right format sent via YouSendIt.com, a painless FTP service much better than email attachments for larger files. It loaded without a hitch and I spent most of the day entering the association's new budget, working on formatting our specialized annual

Three-hundred-eighteen: Turning

billing format, and generally understanding how the QuickBook software worked. Bob and Pandora had assured me the Mac version, though inferior to the PC version, was still very good, but I was prepared to be disappointed because of all the negative reviews it elicited on Amazon, where I bought and downloaded it from. Actually I was very pleased, more, I was impressed with how well the system was put together, for my limited purposes, anyway.

For the previous ten years perhaps, the accounting firm had also done the bookkeeping, using QuickBooks, and that detail was available in the database, so I'd be able to do year over year reports and look for trend lines — all easily and all relevant to the Board's upcoming long term planning project — especially with regard to reserves, expected expenses, and the revenue needed to make it work. I wanted to do budgeting month by month, that is when I could anticipate more or less similar billings each month, like the community center phone bill, but those amounts in or when I knew we'd have to make a large specific payment, D&O insurance for instance, I wanted to put that into the month it belonged, reasoning that the more exact I could be with the budget the more meaningful the monthly actual to budget reports would be — and though the bookkeeper hadn't done this I found it easy to do. Setting up the invoices proved more complicated since I had to experiment a good deal with the custom format process to get what I wanted — something that would show the dues, water meter fee, and water usage fees, amounts I knew the values for by member — but allow the member to report on their moorage, parking, and other fees, add it all up and send it back to me with a check.

Grace's Rock the Rock choir had been idle for the summer but had it's first practice, Yvonne leaving the house about 4:00, confident she'd be back before dark, the sun setting about 8:00, and she was — with a load of groceries I helped her bring in from the small folding dock cart she'd bought at Joyce's yard sale. I'd cooked myself poached eggs with toast covered with the blackberry jam Yvonne had made the day before from blackberries she'd picked on Orcas, the jam delicious and more sugar than berries, but because I was so focused on Quickbooks I hadn't gotten up to make myself dinner until after 7:00, leading me to conjec-

Three-hundred-eighteen: Turning

ture that without Yvonne's creating a regular dinner schedule and putting it on the table I'd go off on a tangent, not eating regularly and probably poorly, compared with the dinner the night before consisting entirely of cheese and fresh vegetables from the Farmers' Market, Howard's garden, and her own, along with fresh homemade bread.

She was happy to be back singing, especially this session since the focus was on "Unforgettable" (Nat King Cole) and "California Dreaming" (The Mamas and the Papas) where the altos would carry the melody and she sang a verse for me. I told her about how pleased I was with QuickBooks and how I had set up the Crane Association detail budget and sent it to the Board for review before the coming Saturday meeting and that lead her to describe again her frustration with the Food Bank board and its failure to create and manage their finances with a budget.

Three-hundred-nineteen: Veterans

"Success is the sum of small efforts, repeated day in and day out." – Robert Collier

Just before 6:00 when I went into the kitchen to fix myself oatmeal for breakfast the under-cabinet heat came on briefly, the first time I'd noticed it since June, telling me that the temperature in the room had fallen to 65 and that meant that the temperature of the mass of the house was falling a bit, the daytime sun now at an increasingly lower angle in the sky and thus not warming the house as effectively as it had done earlier in the summer. There are two under-counter heaters in the house, one in the kitchen and one in the master bathroom, both electric resistance heaters with blowers and they can heat a small area more quickly than the electric baseboard heaters we have all through the house but they're noisy. This morning, because the kitchen heater hadn't run in several months I could smell the dust on the coil being burned and that reminded me of a story Howard had told about one of these heaters having started a fire. When we had remodeled the kitchen in December I'd taken the heater out thinking to discard it, thought better of it and instead cleaned it thoroughly of all the dust bunnies and what all that had made their way inside. I should do the same for the bathroom heater although perhaps because it's used every day the accumulation of dust may be less of a problem.

Yvonne spent much of the day bustling about the house preparing for the company that would arrive the following day, brother Ron, his new girlfriend, and her two sons. I asked what I needed to do to help and it wasn't much but I did move my Crane Island Association bookkeeping/QuickBooks operation from the living room coffee table and my favorite wicker chair next to the wood stove (that would again be in use in a few weeks) to my office at the other side of the house, away from the water, the place where we watch Netflix DVDs and sometimes television, where I have a desk and more than a thousand books. Finding that it was more comfortable using my MacBook Pro in my lap leaning back in the wicker chair than on my desk in a hard wooden chair leaning forward, I had favored that arrangement for working for the past two years or so though it did have the effect of sometimes cluttering the living room and thus causing Yvonne some mild mental anguish but it prevented the tightening in chest and throat I'd develop when sitting leaning forward. I spent much of the day perfecting the invoices I'd soon be sending the Crane Island Association members, both in their layout and in their data content until finally they looked pretty good and the invoicing run totals matched the revenue budget for dues, water meter fees, and water usage — except that the water usage total, about $9000 was $27 and some cents lower than the total on the annual water use report I'd distributed to the members, though I had triple checked the water usage totals for each member in the invoices and they matched the water report — but the totals didn't jibe. I'd have to figure that out.

 Midafternoon Yvonne asked me to go out with her to pull up Margaret's crab pot and retrieve any keepers and drop her own pot in West Sound east and south of Double Island in about 100 feet of water (now at high tide and determined by running the depth sounder in the *Huginn*). A purple/pink starfish sitting astride the bait wrapped in hardware cloth and five Dungeness crabs huddling in the corners came out of the water dripping as I pulled Margaret's cage into the cockpit. Two crabs were keepers and Yvonne picked each up by a back leg and tossed them into a five gallon bucket she'd half-filled with sea water, then lifted the trap, tipping the open end toward the water and the smaller crabs clattered (if I could have heard it) back into the water though the starfish remained draped over the bait so Yvonne pulled it free and tossed it into the water as well. Since her crab trap line was shorter than Margaret's by about ten feet she directed me to shallower water closer to Double while I watched the depth sounder and told her the current readings. It was a glorious day, especially on the water, a high pressure north wind rippling the surface of an intensely blue sea under a dark blue sky; a sense of freshness and energy everywhere, the *Huginn* bobbing on the wakes of boats that had passed on their way toward Pole Pass and now out of sight.

Early in the day Jim had helped Margaret pull her boat out of the water and park it in her driveway where it would remain, covered, until she returned from Ohio, retiring from teaching in Columbus to live full time on the island. Because it hadn't been out of the water in two years and because she wanted to put on a new coat of antifouling paint, she had spent the afternoon scrubbing the hull, at some points crawling under the trailer and covering herself with a layer of ooze and the need to clean up before beginning cooking for the dinner she'd invited us to along with John and Liv meant that it would be late. I suggested an island walk to Yvonne and once she had fortified herself with a little chardonnay she consented and we took a stroll, talking about her call wth Jeni who reported she was to have out-patient surgery on her right wrist soon to repair torn ligaments caused by the repetitive movements she made handing surgeons instruments in the OR for more than a decade and she'd be laid up for a month or so, not being able to work. Yvonne offered to come to Seattle to pick her up after the surgery, take her home and spend a few days with her and Jeni gratefully accepted.

We arrived at Margaret's not long after 6:00. Her house was a mess because of all the construction that had been going on inside during the summer with the installation of new double paned wood windows. I talked with her about her boat cleaning, remembering that I had a pressure washer I should have offered to her to use though she said she thought hand scrubbing was better and Yvonne went back home to get some cheese and crackers to snack on while Margaret worked on the salmon she'd caught off the west coast of Vancouver island on a fishing expedition earlier in the summer. About 7:00, the dinner nearly ready, John and Liv appeared at the door, having driven from the other end of the island in their 1968 soft top VW van and all of us sat and talked in the living room while the salmon cooked briefly. They'd been to Paris and France generally on an Elder Hostel trip focused on Impressionist paintings and painters (wouldn't that be fun!) and we talked about travel, Crane history, and then retirement, their practice, somewhat different than ours perhaps because they're older, of extended leisure, ours being, apparently extended work.

319: John, Liv, Yvonne, and Margaret

About 9:30 when the party was breaking up, Liv felt something on her cheek and in swatting it discovered that it was a yellow jacket, the hornet that is so irritating when it appears in August, and it stung her on the hand. Margaret mixed up a poultice of baking soda to apply and Yvonne and I volunteered to go home to get some antihistamine and then, without a flashlight, found the outdoors very dark, with nearly invisible trees everywhere, as we made our way home, determined not to fall or crash into anything. While Yvonne found the medicine, I found my headlamp and we walked back much more confidently than we'd come. Liv took the pill, we returned home and they drove off in their ancient van, and then while Yvonne got the crabs cooking (she'd dismembered them earlier on the "killing rock" on the point above the water outside the house, screaming as she did it), I got into the hot water as well and Yvonne soon joined me, crabs in their pot and us in ours.

Three-hundred-twenty: Arrival

> *"Community is much more than belonging to something; it's about doing something together that makes belonging matter."* – Brian Solis

My Treasurer's report and the new fiscal year's budget (from QuickBooks) had already been mailed to Board members and there wouldn't be much to say about the water system since there were no real problems or need to do improvements immediately, so I didn't have anything much to do this morning besides walking up to the community hall/fire station setting up the conference speaker phone for the first Board meeting of the new fiscal year. Martha had already arrived and I was happy to see her, having heard that she might not be able to attend because her father was ill. She was secretary and did a good job in the role, taking careful minutes, and was also a check signer and I had three (two I'd prepared with QuickBooks) that needed a second signature. Dan, the Board fire and safety chair walked in next and then Dave, long term planning and Mike, who I didn't much know and who was new to the Board, Kate and Pat called in but then Pat, on his cell phone, was gone.

The first order of business was to establish officers for this new Board term and Dan, who had promised Jan he wouldn't do another term as president but finally agreed when Mike was nominated for VP with the understanding that he was an understudy to Dan and would succeed him next summer. Martha would continue as Secretary and I would as Treasurer. Next came appointments to the various committees. Then I had a chance to discuss my suggestion that we move banks, from Friday Harbor, which had been convenient for the bookkeeper there but not the Crane association. All were in favor and I had Dan and Martha fill out account applications so they could, with me, be signers on the new account and have access to the online banking module. After the meeting, Dave, who with Caroline would soon be heading to

Three-hundred-twenty: Arrival

Nepal to hike for four weeks, showed me the well production, usage, and loss chart he'd put together as part of his package to request the state to raise the number of potential water taps from the current 55 (we used 47) to 69, the actual number of lots. It was interesting to see the patterns for the last five years — except for most of the 2007-2008 fiscal year which Gary had yet to supply from his archive. Though we'd had some leaks, totaling more than 20,000 gallons, the background leak rate was under a gallon per minute throughout the miles of piping.

When I got home after the meeting Yvonne had already gone to Eastsound to the Farmers' Market and I walked right past the crab bucket on the back deck without looking inside. As I found out later it contained five crabs, keepers of the fifteen Yvonne had found in the trap when she took Margaret out to retrieve her trap as well. Because there had been some wind and with all of the boat traffic, the mouth of West Sound was bumpy and Yvonne didn't like that one bit. Then after Yvonne, while driving, had told Margaret she would be taking her trap out again soon, Margaret took out her bait and threw it in the water, annoying polite Yvonne because she would have just taken it home and frozen it for reuse.

The two of us started off in the *Huginn* to the ferry landing before 1:00, Ron, with friend Aileen and her sons Icarus (11) and Isa (6) expected about 1:30. Big wakes at the dock caused by the Labor Day weekend traffic tormented the small boats tied to the dock, like us, waiting to pick up friends and relatives — and then the ferry was in and we walked up to the road to watch for them in the wave of walk-on passengers. The landing was crowded with high school kids, some dressed in green football and cheerleader uniforms and their parents waiting to return to the mainland, the game with the Orcas High School Vikings apparently having been early in the day. And then Ron and party appeared, Aileen warm and friendly, immediately engaging us, Icarus (Icky for short) appeared and turned out to be a confident, friendly studious type and his little brother friendly but anxious and on the ride back to Crane Isa begged me not to go fast, so I slowed down and offered to let him steer and later Icarus greatly enjoyed it.

Three-hundred-twenty: Arrival

320.1: Aileen murders her first crab

Back home on the deck we got to know each other a bit, Aileen having grown up in western Washington, now lived in downtown Seattle and liked the hustle and bustle. Oscar, a sweet black and brown Dachshund-Chihuahua mix, who had been carried in a crate, explored the yard while the rest of us took tea and fresh-baked cookies in the dinning room.

At 6:30 the six of us walked up our driveway carrying a sack of flashlights and another with cooked beet greens, turned left on Eagle Lane rising steeply between dense salal and small struggling firs, willows, and ocean spray, the tall trees along the road shutting out almost all direct sunlight, and found the shortcut path farther up hill to Rupert and Rachel's lodge, in the middle of forest with an obstructed view of the water over the top of Mike's property. Rupert confirmed that Mike had approved his plan to cut down several firs that would open up a window to the water. Icarus, Isa, Sophie (16), and Lucy (10) hit it off immediately though Sophie spent more of her time with the adults. Though Margaret hadn't yet arrived (she was late) Rupert served salmon and Rachel pasta, with Yvonne's beet greens providing salad. Rachel had just started her directorial efforts with a western to be shot in Calgary and had already chosen the location, had access to a warehouse of costumes that had recently been used in a western series, and was in negotiation with some "names" for the cast. Rupert's production efforts were focused on a sensational Vancouver documentary with the script in process. And Rachel described more of her ideas for film direction software that would take advantage of Apple's iPad.

320.2: Looking for and finding bioluminescence

Halfway through the evening, Icarus said he needed his charger for his Nintendo 3D so he, Lucy, and I walked back to our house in the dark, Lucy with our big flashlight, and she and Icarus were soon so far ahead of me that I had to move vary carefully along the rock and root strewn path through the salal we'd used earlier. Before we headed back I found another flashlight I could carry so I could see as I moved much more slowly and carefully through the night than the kids had to.

About 10:00, after finishing most of the blackberry (from the Crane parking lot on Orcas) and apple crumble, Rupert told us about the bioluminescence we could see at the end of the community dock if we stirred up the water and all of us, except Margaret who had left earlier, walked through the dark, half a dozen flashlights and head lamps lighting the way and onto the dock. And Rupert had been right. As the kids and the adults leaned over and stirred the water it glowed and then faded. Up above the Milky Way was visible and I told the kids how to find Polaris, the North Star, by projecting seven lengths from the outer side of the Big Dipper — and there it was, with the Little Dipper there but much harder to make out. Rupert then told us that Mercury was just above the horizon, in the east, that Mars was somewhere in the Milky Way because it always was this time of year and that the moon was about to rise, pointing directly south. I didn't argue with him but it was all wrong. And then I understood the difference between producers and directors: the former are sales people and the latter technicians, both of course with an obsession for film and an artistic bent.

Three-hundred-twenty-one: Kayaking

"It is not what we have, but what we enjoy, that constitutes our abundance." – Epicurus

The day dawned cloudless and calm and I took a series of pictures of the changing light and color in the sky in between putting away dishes and cleaning up what was left from the night before, the most challenging a pot Yvonne had used to cook five crabs, the sides being coated with something that required fifteen minutes of scrubbing to remove. I had my usual oatmeal but Yvonne served raised waffles to the group about 9:00, the group not having shown up in the kitchen until about 8:30. I was hungry again so I had two and could have eaten more but because I didn't need them didn't — but the temptation was strong because they tasted so good with the new blackberry jam Yvonne had made.

Lucy came over about 10:00 with a jacket Icarus had left at her house the evening before, so we asked her if she'd like to go sightseeing on Orcas; she would, so Yvonne called Rachel who consulted with Rupert and after seemingly interminable delays, for what purpose neither Yvonne nor I could determine, Lucy, Ron, Aileen, Icarus, and Isa were finally in the *Huginn* and Ron cast us off for our short trip to Orcas, the water of Pole Pass sparkling in the sun. I parked the *Huginn* near the west end of the transient moorage area and the group headed up the ramp, me carrying a car seat for Isa. They were on their way. Back on the dock I saw Steve painting the bull rail along the Northfield section of the dock (for nearby Orcas residents) and walked over to kid him about feeling embarrassed because its chipped paint now looked so bad in comparison to the recently painted yellow and red transient and loading zones at the other end of the float and he acknowledged that was exactly right. Returning to Crane I could see that Rupert had backed his C-Dory up to the beach and he was doing something with the propeller on the Yamaha outboard while Rachel watched, Sophie

Three-hundred-twenty-one: Kayaking

back at the house perhaps reading one of the two Camus books she showed me the evening before.

Then it was lunch time, after which we planned to kayak following a short nap for each of us — but it was interrupted by Margaret's call asking me to come over and help her hang the mostly glass door on what would be her office once she lived full time on Crane beginning late next summer. With Josh's help, I assume, she'd put the door on two saw horses and put on a new coat of varnish. She'd taken the whole hinge with the door off the house so I suggested separating the frame sides from the door sides and screwing the former back in place and then to remount the door, sliding the two hinge halves together and inserting joining pins to hold them. Her approach was to keep the hinges together and slide the frame side of the hinges into their slots in the wood and then screw the hinges to the frame. My suggestion prevailed in this little kerfuffle; perhaps hers was the better approach but in all the door hanging I'd done over the years I'd always slid the two halves of the hinges together rather than rely on a few screws to hold the door while the the rest were being screwed in. But the door was back in place and she could close the room to the outside world and the wind and rain to come in the winter.

I retrieved two paddles and two life jackets from the tool shed while Yvonne swept off the two single kayaks and then I carried them down the stairs and along the path lowering them down to the beach one by one with Yvonne waiting to catch and carry the downhill end. The tide was high and the beach in our little cove next to the house covered with rock weed debris that had been carried in and left by the last advancing tide. I helped Yvonne push off in her orange and red kayak and then I did in my light and dark blue model, only to realize that I hadn't adjusted the pedals and they were too far toward the front of the little boat so I returned to the beach, pulled the kayak out and made the adjustments, Yvonne by now out of sight around the rocky corner of the cove.

I caught up quickly while Yvonne dawdled off the beach at the foot of the meadow next to our property and we were soon crossing a watery field of bull kelp on our way to the east side of Pole Pass, our intent

Three-hundred-twenty-one: Kayaking

to cross to the red warning light device on the Orcas side of the pass, and we did it during a lull in traffic. Though we could see the intermittently flashing light from the Pass through our bedroom window, I had never looked at it closely. Years ago a kerosene lantern had sufficed, tended by Cal's grandfather. This light — number 2 on the navigation charts — was powered by a photovoltaic array that fed a battery in a white case below it, and I assumed that because the flashes were so brief and so far apart that the system was self-sustaining, though perhaps an OPALCO cable ran from Deer Harbor road through an easement across Howard W's yard.

We hugged the Orcas shore, looking closely at the water side of houses we'd passed on Deer Harbor Road and wondered why we had never done this before, our Crane kayaking over the past five summers confined to circumnavigation of our island. We passed under every dock, Warren's having a special significance because two years before when I was backing up the *Huginn* to park at the Orcas dock in a heavy wind the engine stopped and because the throttle interlock chose this time to fail I wasn't able to restart the engine. The wind carried me and the *Huginn* directly toward Howard W's dock, 100 feet to the west and I imagined how the resulting crash would damage the SeaSport's cabin roof when it collided with the edge of the ramp above. Margaret, who happened to be on the Crane dock, ran up the Crane ramp, went through the parking lot gate into Warren's yard, tripped, hurting her leg, and continued to his dock hoping somehow to help. During that minute or so the *Huginn* had already been blown to the dock and I could see that it would probably pass under the ramp and between the two sets of pilings that held it up. I briefly grabbed the pier as I passed under, thought better of it and let the *Huginn* continue its wind-driven trip west toward Pole Pass. With the immediate danger of a collision with Warren's dock averted I banged my fist repeatedly on the part of the throttle that contained the misbehaving safety mechanism that had put the boat and me in danger and suddenly the engine started and I was able to recover and get back to the dock. Not long after I had the mechanism intended to prevent starting the boat in gear replaced but occasionally it continued to prevent starting — until corporeal punishment was applied.

Warren's dock also held traumatic memories for me from late January 2007 when we had recently moved to Crane and I was returning from Eastsound late in the evening after dinner with a friend. Yvonne was in Seattle with daughter Jeni. The wind was blowing that night too and the tide was very low, with little water under the Crane dock on Orcas. I didn't know that rocks lurked under the water just west of the end of the dock where I'd parked, now only a few inches below the surface and the boat was soon caught on them and the engine stopped after the prop caught on the rock and the engine stalled. I reasoned that I could throw the anchor out into deeper water and pull the boat free and I did but I hadn't noticed that in climbing back and forth to the bow I'd knocked the starboard dock line into the water so when I started the engine and began to move south to go around Warren's dock, the line was caught by the prop, wound around it and the engine again stalled. I was at the wind's mercy and it blew the *Huginn* against Warren's dock and I jumped out and secured it, standing there thinking what to do next. Then a voice behind me asked if I needed help and I turned to see that the Coast Guard had come in silently in the darkness perhaps suspicious or perhaps concerned for my safety. They offered encouragement while I raised the outdrive but it wasn't possible to remove the line now jammed between the prop and the fitting it spun on. The lead officer, understanding I needed to get back to Crane, offered to inspect the *Huginn* while tied to their boat on route to Crane and I readily agreed. I used the officer's cell phone to leave a message on Yvonne's and was finally home by about midnight and I let our pooch Samantha out to relieve herself.

After passing under the Crane pier, Yvonne and I continued paddling east, and I pointed out where I'd seen a dog chase a buck into the water last year, the deer swimming toward Bell Island with the dog 100 yards behind. The buck continued around the little island toward Wasp Passage and Shaw Island, the dog prudently giving up and paddling back to Orcas. Eventually the buck was too far away to see so I couldn't track his fate but watching him swim all that way, half a mile that I could see, in 50 degree water, I now believed what others told me of the willingness and ability of deer to swim among the San Juan Islands.

321: Rachel, Lucy, Yvonne, Margaret, Rupert

Around the corner of Caldwell point we found a rock formation that waves had drilled a three foot hole through into a small cove walled with grey layered rock, sedimentary rock, in an area of mostly igneous basalt. Then we turned around and paddled south toward Bell Island across the No Wake lane where we'd seen so much boat traffic today, some of it big or rude fast boats leaving large wakes. At the north end of Bell a white sign with black letters affixed to the rocky bank announced that the area was a bottom fish preserve. At the southwest corner of Bell we turned west and headed back to the central part of the east side of Crane island, passing the southernmost No Wake Zone buoy for the Pole Pass area, and then saw Nancy on her dock and paddled up to visit. Jim was working with a small dozer, earthmoving around the site of the addition to their house he was building. Back in our cove, I laid the two kayaks upside down on drift wood logs at the upper part of the beach that wouldn't be disturbed again until the winter storms. The Livingston still sat inverted, the aft end on a log I'd wired to two steel posts I'd pounded into the sand, the bow end on logs.

Moving the F150 out of the driveway to the area closer to the rain shelter and the two sheds I found two nylon straps on the passenger front seat left there by Margaret so I took them to her house and called out for her, had no answer — but then heard noise from under her back deck so I ducked down to look. I could dimly see Margaret through the two by three foot entrance to the crawl space doing something — probably in preparation for leaving her house for almost a year. Did she need any help? No, Jim was going to help. She went on to say something about a manual and I realized she was talking about the outboard on her boat now on its trailer in her driveway, the cover off the Yamaha, looking as if some maintenance operation had been interrupted. Now I knew why.

At 4:00 Ron called from Eastsound announcing that they were leaving and I picked them up about 4:30 at the Orcas dock. He'd enjoyed driving our new car to the 2400' summit of Mt. Constitution which had been warm and windless with a hundred mile view. They'd dawdled at Cascade Falls and then swum in Cascade Lake, toured Eastsound and then stopped at the Anthony Howe wind-driven sculpture studio to admire his amazing stainless steel windmills.

Home, the kids piled into the hot tub, and when they'd had their fill, Yvonne prepared snacks and we assembled on the deck in the afternoon sun to drink wine and hear about the day. Rupert and Rachel appeared to fetch Lucy and stayed to eat and talk and then Margaret came over in her paint stained clothes, setting, as Yvonne described it, a new standard for Crane Island cocktail party attire. Rupert, Rachel, and Lucy went home and then Margaret and Ron helped Yvonne grill chicken on skewers for dinner — with a peanut butter hot sauce and cabbage. Noah called; I would call him later. After dinner, with Ron, Aileen, and Yvonne looking at a family photo album, I called Noah and learned that pooch Sugar's recent near messy death experience had cost $900 at an Olympia emergency pet service, that a half-hour of child care for the two kids before school would cost $400 per month, that Natasha would have a second interview for a UPS sales rep job in Tumwater and that they would put their Harstine Island house, where they'd lived for ten years, on the market, hoping to move to Steamboat, close to Olympia, where the kids could have friends nearby and the trip to school and work would be much shorter. In the past the kids fretted at the possibility of moving; now they seemed to favor it.

While I talked with Noah, everyone else walked to the community dock in the darkness, Rupert and family coming along, the object for Icarus and Lucy being jumping into the water at the end of the dock, something Icarus had been talking about wanting to do for more than 24 hours. As it turned out Aileen decided to jump in and went first, opening her eyes underwater long enough to see the water luminesce from her disturbing it. Then Icarus made his jump, after a long series of "1-2-3"s and paddled quickly to get back to the dock to be pulled out. Rupert and Rachel decided Lucy should not go in, concerned that later she wouldn't be able to get to sleep, that being a problem because they would leave early in the morning. Yvonne and I retired to our bedroom by 9:30 and I fell asleep before 10:00.

Three-hundred-twenty-two: Departure

> *"Even if I knew that tomorrow the world would go to pieces, I would still plant my apple tree."* – Martin Luther

Even though I had had a nap the day before and been asleep before 10:00, I slept, with only a few short interruptions until past 5:30 and didn't appear in the living room until 6:45, after having done my morning deep breathing. The morning was very different from the last, fog enveloping the house that receded and thinned all morning, the wind picking up out of the northeast, and the sky clearing by noon. Though the temperature wasn't lower, at 63 degrees, the wind made the air feel much colder outside. It was close to 9:00 before the others made an appearance.

Though I'd already had my oatmeal breakfast I was happy enough to have another breakfast, this time a poached egg on a day old waffle and we all sat around the dining room table with little motivation to do anything outside because of the cold-feeling north wind and foggy atmosphere. Ron and Aileen explained that once the two boys were asleep in the studio loft, they sat in the hot tub sipping raspberry wine and then took a walk around the island with the help of flashlights, uncovering our local raccoon foraging at the compost pile and scaring up deer here and there that would stare at the lights and not know quite what to make of them, Aileen concerned the deer might bolt and run them over. Living in Seattle they were surprised at the night darkness on Circle Road, the moon having set not long after the sun and the trees blocking starlight. At the intersection of Old Road and the continuation of Circle Road they mistakenly chose the former, climbing the step hill toward Brook's which would have taken them across the airstrip but realized they'd make a mistake and turned around retracing their steps. Walking at night in Seattle my sense was that neither had much anxiety about it but they did on Crane because they could see no further nor wider than a flashlight beam.

Three-hundred-twenty-two: Departure

322.1: Icarus powers back from Bell

They had met through Ron's practice as an acupuncturist but once they felt a sense of attraction, Ron said he could no longer treat her so they changed their relationship and followed their feelings. She lived not far from the Public Market, right above a McDonald's and I found out from the boys that the building had a center courtyard, an air shaft, where they could walk Oscar without having to go out on the street. The prior fall, Ron had broken up a fight at that very McDonald's and as it turned out Aileen and the boys had been in the restaurant at the time, making up for pizza that had burned in their apartment upstairs. Aileen had hustled the three of them out of McDonald's as soon as she could, not meeting Ron but recognized him when she sought acupuncture treatment months later. Fate?

Icarus was willing so Aileen wanted to take him kayaking and since he'd told me he'd had experience with mini-kayaks at Camp Orki-

Three-hundred-twenty-two: Departure

la on Orcas this summer, I recommended they go out in the two singles that were still sitting on logs on the beach in our cove. Though Aileen hadn't kayaked she had paddle-boarded on Eliott Bay in Seattle so I was confident she would be comfortable on the water, even if sitting rather than standing. I gave them both a few minutes of instruction, helped Icarus adjust the pedals in his kayak (Aileen's were fine) and launched them, first Icarus and then Aileen into the calm water of our sheltered cove, while Ron watched. I had recommended that they stay away from Pole Pass, suggesting that they follow the shore around the cove, knowing they wouldn't be out for long, and I was surprised when Aileen took them straight across to Bell Island, Yvonne and I not having had the confidence to do that until the day before even after having spent five summers on Crane. First Ron held Isa outside on the deck and they watched the two paddle away and then Isa and I watched them come back with the binoculars we keep on a windowsill in the living room. I could see that Icarus was tired because he stopped frequently to rest. Back on the beach in the cove, both reported having enjoyed the trip and Aileen commented that perhaps she'd switch from paddle boarding to kayaking since that might work better for the boys.

Ron had packed and once Aileen made some peanut butter and jelly sandwiches, all of us, including Oscar, made our way to the community dock where Ron put Oscar in his crate. Yvonne hugged them all and waved as I backed the *Huginn* in a half circle and then motored forward, falling in line behind a big powerboat with a small powerboat and then a sailboat lined up behind. The marina, behind the breakwater, had been relatively calm but the water was choppy on the east side of Pole Pass. Isa peeked out of the V-berth where he felt safe and reminded me not to go fast so we made our way slowly the two miles to the ferry landing, the *Hyak* pulling into the ferry slip just before we made it to the county dock, already populated with five other small boats that were being tossed about by waves and wakes.

Three-hundred-twenty-two: Departure

322.2: Brother Isa watches

Ron tied us up and I helped carry their luggage up to the picnic table on the pier on the level below the street near the whale boat office and gift shop. The boys handed me their life jackets, I hugged them and told them how much we enjoyed their visit and invited them to come again, hugged Ron and then Aileen and we confirmed that we'd see each other at a happy hour Friday in Seattle. Leaving the ferry landing I finally had a chance to go fast and it was exhilarating to flying across and sometimes up and over the waves in Harney Channel and then the mouth of West Sound. A green hulled sailboat, perhaps the *Eileen*, with Howard and Sheila aboard, made way across West Sound at high speed, heeled over from the fresh northeast wind.

Yvonne had grilled me a sandwich and we sat at the counter talking about the weekend, having had a thoroughly good time, Yvonne enjoying yesterday's *Sunday Seattle Times* and soon we were each back at work, Yvonne with the Food Bank donor database and me with the Crane Island member billing, printing, folding, and inserting the invoices into envelopes. I had two mailing labels left over and realized that I'd put two bills into one envelope and quickly found it. After a little research I realized that I hadn't billed one homeowner, someone with a vacant lot who never comes to the island, and that I hadn't billed him the year before either so I created an invoice showing two years of dues ($1400 payable) and was embarrassed to have skipped him last year but pleased that we'd have revenue that wasn't anticipated by the budget. The recycle containers were full so I carried the contents out to the former privy where we keep four big plastic cans, two for trash and two for recycle. All were full, so I pulled the big empty plastic bags from between the two trash cans sitting on the shelf with the toilet seat, watching a big black spider intently and put recycle into it. I'd need to go to the transfer station soon.

Three-hundred-twenty-three: Cutting Up

"The sky is the daily bread of the eyes." – Ralph Waldo Emerson

At dawn the sky was clear but fog lay in front of Blakely Island, having come through Thatcher Pass from Rosario Straight, the eastern connecting channel between the Straight of Juan de Fuca in the south and the Straight of Georgia and Canada in the north. About ten years before when flying back to Orcas from Seattle after returning from the East Coast, in the midst of "Harry Potter and the Philosopher's Stone" we passed over the Straight of Juan de Fuca, entirely blanketed with fog, perhaps 100 feet deep, only the superstructure of a container ship bound for Admiralty Inlet and Seattle visible. Some years later when returning to Orcas from Sidney by the Sea on Vancouver Island in our pocket trawler, *Gumption*, Yvonne and I foolishly opted to proceed through the morning fog over Haro Straight, the western shipping channel between the Straight of Juan de Fuca and the Straight of Georgia in the west, passing other boats patiently waiting for the fog to lift. Our radar would presumably show us any freighter or tanker bearing down on us from either direction as we crossed this busy shipping channel and the GPS would point us toward Speiden Channel close to Orcas — but would we have shown up on the radar of an approaching ship (not all pleasure boats showed up on our radar) and even if we did, would the helmsman be able to change course? Not likely. And so we strained our eyes looking through the fog and watching the radar and came out of the fog near the entrance to Roche Harbor, having apparently learned nothing, since more recently we tempted fate again by making our way from Orcas to Crane at night and in a dense fog, apparently enjoying the intense anxiety it produced. By 8:00, this morning, the fog surrounded the house, intensely white in the morning light. By

Three-hundred-twenty-three: Cutting Up

10:00, when I took Yvonne to Orcas the fog had receded to Blakely, five miles away and looking back toward San Juan Island while in Pole Pass I could see fog over San Juan Channel, that finger having come in from the Straight of Juan de Fuca through Cattle Pass.

Margaret wouldn't need a ride to Orcas until at least noon so I took our pickup, with my chain saw on a tarp on the back seat and gas and chain oil in cans on the floor of the front seat and drove the mile or so along the south section of Circle Road to the place Yvonne and I had seen the newly fallen tree the evening before, just outside the pasture that had once been home to Rachel and Marilyn's milk cow. The 60 foot silver fir had fallen from a stump about eight feet off the ground and across the road, breaking into four pieces, and someone had somehow moved the piece that blocked traffic to the side. The year before on Labor Day weekend another Silver fir had fallen, like this one, without apparent provocation across Circle Road near the boundary of what had been Bob and Nancy's farm and Dick's cabin property. Jeni and two of her friends were visiting and later in the day I'd sail them around Crane in the *Discovery* but I spent about 90 minutes slicing up and bringing home that tree. Last year's windfall didn't produce much heat when burned, compared with Douglas fir, but it was convenient and it did need to be cleared from the roadway area, so I began by cutting the upper end of the tree, on the far side of the road from where it had fallen, and then the section lying across the near side and then one of the two sections still pointing at the stump. The salal and new and old fallen branches for the most part held the sections of the tree off the ground so I could do some of the cutting without having to raise the sections. The upper part of the tree I cut into four foot lengths (that would become three sixteen inches sections at home) but the lower part I cut every sixteen inches since triple or even double that length would be too heavy to heave into the bed of the pickup. The cut up tree filled the bed of the truck and once home I emptied it into a pile I'd started near our sailboat's trailer with three logs I'd cut at Pat's and hadn't yet moved to the firewood area outside the deer fence and Yvonne's garden at the front of the house.

Three-hundred-twenty-three: Cutting Up

323: Contrail at dawn

Margaret said she'd be ready to leave at 2:00 so I backed our F150 pickup into her driveway and filled the cab back seat with what she had ready. Just before 3:00 we'd loaded into the *Huginn* what she would take back to Ohio where she was returning to finish her last year teaching before retiring and as I backed past the *Kelper*, Cabot called out that he'd found one of the *Huginn*'s mooring lines untied this morning. Uh Oh! That didn't make sense until I remembered that I'd replaced the line on one of the forward fenders and had untied the forward mooring line during the process and then not retied it, distracted by John and Liv who were leaving the island in the *Argos*, their now ancient Ed Monk designed boat, to return it to the Cayou Quay Marina, on their way back to Seattle. On the dock John had told me again how he had been thinking about my telling him a few days before at Margaret's for dinner, that the prevailing winter winds were from the southeast, not the north as he'd believed, his house facing north, ours east. Most Crainians are on the island a week or two a year, at most, and then in the summer, and have no idea what the island is really like. Perhaps John and Liv would now more likely come to and enjoy Crane in the off-season.

Yvonne was already on the Orcas dock waiting with a cart to use to move Margaret's travel trove up to the parking lot and we accomplished that quickly, hugging her, and wishing her a safe trip, not expecting to see her again until late in the next summer. At dinner, the second night of chicken with chili peanut sauce, this time on vermicelli, with a beet and goat cheese on spinach salad, the beets especially tasty because Yvonne served them with pickling juice left over from her Sunday beet pickling session, we were already missing Margaret, the island now populated only by Lou, Tom, Jim and Nancy, Cabot, who we saw and talked to on our evening walk around the island (the tank at 13' 6" — I'd have to email Gary so he could dial down the pump timers) who reported that two of his sons would be visiting this week. We had re-entered the quiet time of year. There'd be a few busy weekends in September and October but the summer season was over even though the weather was better than ever — though the days were shortening quickly and the change in light, especially obvious as we climbed the grade below the north end of the airstrip and saw the setting sun on the Douglas firs, so rich and soft, and then again at the community dock before we went through the break in the split rail fence to walk across the meadow and home, the little community marina protected on the east by the rocky breakwater and to the south and west by Crane Island, glowing like the far side of Pole Pass, in a warm, loving solar light so beautiful that it almost made me cry.

Three-hundred-twenty-four: More Wood, More Wood

"All truly great thoughts are conceived by walking." – Friedrich Nietzsche

Below 50° again before dawn, a doe browsing near Yvonne's little pond, one fawn exploring the most recent contribution to the compost bin, and its twin on the far side of Margaret's driveway. A pinkish orange line, straight but not quite parallel to the horizon and darker than its background crossed the sky above Blakely Island, the contrail of a military jet flying south (or north) in the dark some time before. By mid afternoon the temperature at the house was in the high 70's, the warmest day yet this summer. Under a cloudless sky. Less than an inch of rain had fallen in the last two months, July and August typically the driest months in a year that sees rainfall in inverse proportion to temperature, November, December, and January by far the rainiest.

Late afternoon the day before I'd thoroughly washed the pickup, parked in what had been the driveway, outside the studio deer fence, scrubbing the roof and hood especially with a soft brush to removed a year's tree droppings, black spots on a otherwise dirty dark brick-red surface. This morning, from the kitchen, the 1999 truck looked new, the places I'd missed when washing it not visible at this distance nor the paint spots and scratches that had accumulated from heavy use hauling appliances, trash, potted plants, furniture, construction debris, top soil, gravel, and lumber and towing trailers (from as far as Colorado) and boats back and forth to Seattle. The truck looked so good and had performed so reliably I was motivated to make two minor repairs, both the result of the truck having been broken into in Seattle years before: a slipping AC/heat control knob where the dash had been removed to get at the stereo and a passenger side door with an ineffective lock and handle that had been pried off for entry, operating now only from the inside, the repair having lasted a few years and then failing. And the cab was dirty, with gray mold here and there especially on the vinyl door pull, encouraged in the winter because of the dampness inside that I finally started to treat with a chemical dehumidifier.

324: Great dry wood at Pat's

About 10:00 I drove the truck to the other end of the island, to Pat's property, where six of the nine logs he'd left for me lay next to a gravel pile near the unfinished house, the gray metal roof in place but the walls bare oriented strand board with gaping holes for windows, his construction schedule interrupted along with his Seattle excavating business when the Seattle construction market collapsed in the spring of 2008. I began by cutting the two logs that were stacked on others, one so

Three-hundred-twenty-four: More Wood, More Wood

big that it was hard for me to lift sixteen inch sections I'd cut into the bed of the pickup. Two more, smaller logs I was able to wrestle on top of other logs and cut them in that position. The last two I cut halfway through, then rolled to the other side to finish the cut. The results of the cutting process filled the pickup bed more than two feet above the sides in places. A bright green tree frog showed itself on the ground when I was ready to back the truck up to receive the wood so I shoed it to the nearest tree so I wouldn't run over it. Off and on during the cutting, yellow jackets (hornets) would hover above the whirring chain of the saw, not caring about the noise I had to protect myself from with earmuffs, attracted perhaps to the chain oil or an aroma released from the Douglas fir. It was 1:00 before I got home and Yvonne met me on the back porch ready to leave for Orcas and a little worried that I had been gone so long. After she left for Oras and I had lunch, I unloaded the wood to a growing pile that I'd have to move to the front yard.

I spent the afternoon bringing Slocum's *Voyage of the Destroyer* and *Voyage of the Liberdade* forward to our latest ebook format in preparation for updating the Amazon Kindle inventory and listing them as well in the Barnes and Nobel Nook catalog. After a dinner of salmon, boiled potatoes and a beet salad, Yvonne and I took a walk around the island, for the first time bringing with the binoculars we keep in the living room for viewing the watery world to the east. I could now see the level gauge on the wall of the community water system tank, 200 feet away on its hill from my observation spot on Circle Road; 13' 10' — the tank was at capacity and water being pumped in would overflow to the ground, wasting it and adding to the volume of unaccounted for water that indicated a leak — and because of the spillage misleading. I hadn't had a reply from Gary to my morning email about the high water level — with the implied need to adjust the pump timers for wells 5 and 6. Along the road a downy woodpecker let us get close and then flew 20 feet along the road, perched on a fir, let us get close and moved farther on. We used the binoculars to look at the osprey nest we'd been monitoring: no sounds and no sign of the chick we'd seen a few days ago, at the time suspecting that it was a fledgeling and would soon be on its own. The cliff swallows, so evident at the community dock and over the meadow nearby all summer, were gone now and we weren't seeing hummingbirds at the feeder above our front deck.

As we climbed the hill at the north end of the airstrip, the more than half-full moon came into view down the 1500 foot grassy field with dense forest on either side. Flying back and forth about 100 feet above the airstrip, a bat fluttered back and forth catching insects, some of them flying red ants (harvester ants?) we'd seen all along our walk, sometimes flying across the face of the moon. Perhaps that same bat would fly a foot above our heads as we sat in the hot tub later in the darkness with the starry sky above.

Three-hundred-twenty-five: Cleaning Up

> *"We are what we repeatedly do. Excellence, then, is not an act, but a habit." – Will Durant*

Yvonne had picked up the number 9 envelopes she'd ordered at the Office Cupboard in Eastsound, none otherwise available on Orcas, that she'd include in her Food Bank fund raising mailings to return with generous donations. I needed number 9's as well to stuff inside the number 10's I was using for the Crane Island Association annual billings — also to encourage responses — with completed forms and a check. I'd left the uncompleted mailings on the dining room table and now added stamps (that Yvonne had picked up at the Post Office) to the outer envelope and Association address labels to the smaller envelopes and put them inside the larger, 49 in all.

One envelope would go to Rupert in Vancouver so I checked the USPS Web site for postage to Canada (I'd use two 44 cent stamps). I asked Yvonne whether we had a scale to check that the mailings were under an ounce and she produced one she used for cooking. I put a blue rubber band around the sealed envelopes and left them on the bench in the entry hall for Yvonne to take with when she went to Orcas after lunch. I'd completed the first step in generating revenue to support the Association's budget for the new fiscal year.

Jens had forwarded to me the names and email addresses of his eight Wellesley students enrolled in his fall Kafka class that they used for their Amazon accounts and then through Amazon I "gifted" them copies of *The eNotated Metamorphosis* ebook that he would then use as a text for his course, followed later by *The eNotated In the Penal Colony*.

Thus far we'd published six Amazon Kindle ebooks between January and August and one, *The eNotated Sailing Alone Around the World* also in the Barnes and Noble Nook catalog. The plan was to make the

Three-hundred-twenty-five: Cleaning Up

other five also available for the Nook. I could convert our Kindle ebooks to Nook format easily using the Calibre app but first I needed to make corrections to four of the ebooks and make all structurally and cosmetically alike — because the format had evolved over eight months — and then republish them on Amazon before publishing them on Barnes and Noble.

325: Afternoon treat

What seemed straightforward turned out to be complicated because I'd changed the software and the database somewhat with each book over the eight months, and most recently to accommodate *My Antonia* and I hadn't paid enough attention to whether the changes would work with the earlier books. They wouldn't. I'd broken the system and even the book I'd already published for Nook would no longer process.

I spent the rest of the day making repairs to the software and corrections to the book databases and by supper time all but *The eNotated In the Penal Colony* seemed to be in order, though I'd have to proof each

Three-hundred-twenty-five: Cleaning Up

before republishing for Kindle, publishing for Nook, and gifting Jens' students the *Penal Colony*. I didn't want to have to go through this process again and hoped I wouldn't or that it would be easy because all the books were now consistent with one another and would work with the book generating software in its current state correctly.

Yvonne came home briefly after having her hair cut and tuned it up with some tools I don't understand and then returned to Orcas for Rock on the Rock choir practice in the Madrona Room at the Orcas Center just north of Eastsound next door to the Orcas Medical Center. She walked in the door about 8:00 as the dusk was rising and the moon had turned the whole sky silver. I was on the couch reading a new book, *Now You See It*, that connected neuroscience findings, emerging technology, and education and I was surprised at how much I was enjoying the author's insights and their application to my publishing and organizational experiences, later telling Yvonne when she got home a bit about it as we tried to stay awake for a few minutes.

Three-hundred-twenty-six: Earthquake

"No man is an island, entire of itself; every man is a piece of the continent, a part of the main." – John Donne

We were already in Seattle by the time the earthquake struck the north end of Vancouver Island, perhaps 300 miles from Crane Island. James called later in the day to check on us and then we had an inquiring email from Tim and Kelly in Paris. Checking *Bullwings* and the *Islands' Sounder* websites I found no reports of the quake being felt in the San Juans.

We left the house at 7;15, a little earlier than usual to make the 8:50 ferry to Anacortes, because we had a cartload to carry up to the car on the Orcas side. We had been storing an old Sony computer and three keyboards, an old HP printer, and my old MacBook Pro because they couldn't/shouldn't be discarded with the trash at the county transfer station — but recycled — and RE-PC in Seattle would take them. This was the first time we'd had to put much in our new little Ford Focus and though it all fit the lack of capaciousness compared with that van we'd given up was sobering. The Friday ferry to America wasn't even half full but when we got to Anacortes the Orcas waiting line was full all the way to the back of the lot. The tourists were still coming — after Labor Day — the weather a motivation because it was absolutely perfect. We were going to Seattle to cat-sit Lola in Jeni's apartment near the Pike Place Public Market, and looked forward to being in the big city for the weekend.

Since the Friday afternoon plan was for Yvonne to shop, starting with H&M, at my instigation we talked almost the whole way to Seattle about women's clothing styles and shopping techniques, something we'd never done much of before, but I was curious to understand better this mysterious process, prompted in part by a recent New Yorker article in which the woman author took a series of men clothes shopping and was baffled by their near universal desire to avoid or minimize the activity, an attitude I shared. I knew that Yvonne and most women wanted to look nice and that many men didn't care. In the San Juans most women wore jeans or slacks; Yvonne was an exception, often wearing a dress when out and about. She liked close fitting, younger looking, non-traditional clothes — no collars or layers that made her too hot. We talked about the styles her Orcas friends affected, each different, each appropriate to rural, island living. She liked J.Jill and H&M, which she'd first seen in Edinburgh, Scotland, five years before.

326: Childhood home

After dropping Yvonne at the H&M store at Pike and Sixth, I drove south and found the RE-PC store close to the Seattle Mariners' stadium

Three-hundred-twenty-six: Earthquake

and they were happy to take the equipment and would delete all data from the old MacBook Pro's hard drive, a service I paid them $5 for. But I was disappointed not to find any used Mac notebook computers for sale — while hundreds of Windows-based machines sat in counters or in bins. RE-PC had few desktop Macs, the newest probably seven or eight years old. Interesting.

I'd hoped to waste a good amount of time at RE-PC but it made no sense to stay there and since Yvonne and I had planned to meet at the Tulley's near Jeni's apartment building at 4:30, I had to find something else to do for several hours, so I drove north to Alaska Way and the waterfront and parked under the viaduct, walking across to Starbucks and spent an hour nursing an iced tea doing email and research at a metal table outside on the sidewalk, watching tourists meander and locals hustle. But then I couldn't stand sitting and walked uphill to Barnes and Nobel to look at new fiction and non-fiction — and computer and web technical books — but got bored there as well and walked back to Tulley's, sitting outside at a table waiting for Yvonne, who soon appeared with the key to Jeni's apartment she'd retrieved from the concierge.

We hadn't heard anything from Ron about having Friday happy hour so Yvonne used the iPad to find candidates nearby and we walked south on First Avenue a few blocks to two prospect locations but both were noisy pubs so Yvonne suggested we go uphill to the Hotel Monaco restaurant where we'd been once before and sat at a table outside on the sidewalk enjoying and commenting on the passing scene. From there we walked to where we expected the Regal Theaters to be (north of the Pacific Place theaters), couldn't find them and asked a young woman with a smart phone to help. She did and we found the theaters close to the Convention Center and a block from H&M, where Yvonne had shopped earlier. Since we'd been to those theaters many times before it was disconcerting to not be able to find them again. Later, walking back to Jeni's apartment we found the evening still warm and the streets crowded with people.

Three-hundred-twenty-seven: Exploring

"The city is not a concrete jungle, it is a human zoo." –
Desmond Morris

At Jeni's apartment at Harbor Steps, and after sharing oatmeal I'd made, Yvonne and I took our car out of the garage under the building and drove south to the Georgetown neighborhood, an area of warehouses, factories, train yards and truck depots with small houses and little retail, at the north end of the Duwamish Waterway, an estuary of the Green River that flows into Eliott Bay and Puget Sound where the container ships come to be unloaded by huge orange cranes. Our destination was the Georgetown Farmers market and we found it on Airport Way north of Boeing Field just off Interstate 5, having appeared for the day on a new blacktop parking area next to the skeletal remains of the red brick Seattle Brewing Company, with a bakery, a pizza joint, and an indoor beach for playing volleyball.

Fewer than twenty booths covered an area that could have accommodated three or four times that number. Yvonne wanted to buy vegetables — to cook for dinner and to take home — as well as just look. I had no agenda but soon found a booth with what looked like Northwest Indian art — in copper pressings and a black, stone type material I didn't recognize — with a very complex design that seemed to me superior to the imitations we saw so much of in Washington. The proprietor, tall, gray haired and in his early seventies appeared and I began to ask questions and he answered and explained. The black material was a combination of ground slate and binders, the 12 x 16 dark gray panels, castings from moulds he had spent a great deal of time carving and was struggling to find an efficient way to retail his creations, which also included copper medallions in silver and gold frames, miniatures of native carved wool spinning devices. He began to talk about form line, Bill Reid, and Bill Cole, and I was drawn into his story since it related to what we'd seen in Vancouver and the reading I had done afterwards. He had met Reid and admired him, especially his inclusivity about Northwest Art, with a focus on the art itself not on the ancestry of the artist. Cole, he said had just the opposite point of view. Yvonne and I both liked the panels and bought one for $100. I walked to the car and put it in the trunk and then rejoined Yvonne who picked out vegetables from three different booths.

327: From Georgetown Farmers Market

Next stop was Columbia City, a place where Yvonne had spent some time in her youth, east of I-5 and a bit south, a few blocks of restaurants, a bakery, bookstore, music venue, beauty shop, barber shop, and generally looking like a redecorated scene out of the 1950's, lots of trees lining the street, a place serving locals, a mixture of colors and ages, clearly an area young families could afford more readily than Wallingford, Greenlake and other neighborhoods north of Lake Union. Yvonne found a consignment store to explore while I spent half an hour in the mostly used bookstore, tidy and well-stocked, the owner working the whole time preparing and shelving books. I found an illustrated Kipling biography and joined Yvonne at the bakery across the street where she bought a baguette and italian lemon soda.

Driving north and then east we found our way to Lake Washington just north of Seward Park, left the car in a lot and walked to a bench in the grass along the shore looking out at Mercer Island to the east. As she had on Friday, Yvonne made us chicken salad sandwiches served with San Juan corn chips and we shared the lemon soda while watching a few speed boats tow tubes, perhaps with children aboard, over the surface of the lake corrugated by a fresh northeast wind. Soon two sailboats motored from a marina to the north and soon raised their sails and were scooting across the lake on different courses. A couple in their thirties got up and walked away from a nearby bench facing north and we moved to have a view towards the floating bridge that carries I-90 across the Lake Washington to Mercer Island.

As a teenager Yvonne had spent many hours, mostly with girlfriends, sometimes with boys, in Seward Park, a peninsula that juts into Lake Washington not far from the neighborhood she grew up in so we went there next, driving the perimeter of the park, big, spread out, with several big picnics in progress, one a birthday party, another a company picnic, with beaches on the south and playgrounds. A nature walk would begin soon but we chose to move on, first to Pritchard Beach, another place Yvonne visited often, and then drove by Rainier Beach High School, almost new when she attended there in the mid 1960's, and then to her childhood home, a craftsman style, up the hill from Rainier Avenue that Opal, her mother had sold and retired from in the early 1980's. We'd passed by a few years before and the house had looked a little neglected; now it looked almost abandoned and Yvonne felt very sad. Opal's successors, first Yvonne's friend Julie who had painted the house and improved the property, but now, more than 25 years later and with no apparent maintenance, the area around the house and yard had become a jungle, the paint peeling and the front stairs failing apart. Opal's house had become a neighborhood eyesore. Why?

Neither of us had been to Mercer Island, a Seattle bedroom community surrounded by Lake Washington and fairly close to the southern end of this big lake so we drove north again and used the iPad and Google Maps to get directions to the closest eastbound entrance to I-90 and were soon on the floating bridge we'd watched while eating lunch. Mercer Island is heavily forested and subdivided so as to have few through roads. It isn't possible to see much of the island without great difficulty. Many beautiful houses, some right on the water, with docks outfitted with ski boats on lifts and the occasional float plane, like the San Juans but completely different. Some Orcas and Crane Islanders had their own docks, boats, and even a float plane, but the boats were heavy duty, either enclosed, like our SeaSport or self-bailing Boston Whalers, intended for sometimes rough conditions, our part of the world, on salt water, actually rugged and remote just as the ads say.

Back at Jeni's Yvonne made an early vegetable and pasta dinner and we were soon on our way on foot to the same theaters to see a different film, tonight Woody Allen's *Midnight in Paris* — which both of us savored. A walk in the rare warm evening air and we were in the Public Market area and then down on the waterfront watching one ferry come in from Winslow and another from Bremerton, the container ship dock farther south at the entrance to the Duwamish Waterway, the Sea Hawks and Mariner's stadiums just to the east of the docks and a full moon rising to add silver to the white, orange, and yellow man-made light. Three Argosy Cruises boats, one pretty big, rocked in their slip on Elliott Bay, rising and falling on the wakes of the ferries now unloading walk-ons and drive-ons. A magic evening in Seattle. Lola, the cat, needed company, so we walked back to Jeni's apartment and gave her some attention and then sat on the balcony absorbing life in the big city.

Three-hundred-twenty-eight: East Shore UUs

> *"Life is a journey to be experienced, not a problem to be solved." – Winnie the Pooh (A. A. Milne)*

The garage downstairs had a special 5:00 to 8:00 overnight rate so I was at the pay station at 7:58 and handed what I thought was the parking ticket to the attendant and he asked me whether I was inviting him to a movie and then said it didn't matter, to go on, and opened the gate for me to exit. As on the day before I'd unintentionally handed over the receipt for the movie we'd seen the night before rather than the parking ticket, not to the same attendant. Perhaps he thought I was an addle-brained old person. In any case, the parking was free. I parked on the street now, taking advantage of Sunday's free parking: we didn't need to leave for the east side of Lake Washington until 9:30 to be in time for the 10:00 service at the East Shore Unitarian Universalist Church just off I-90 and south of Bellevue.

Saying goodbye to Lola and assuring her that Jeni would be home later, we carried our luggage and food purchases to the elevator, then across the street to where I'd left the car, Yvonne observing that apartment living was just as inconvenient as our dealing with a boat transfer except that we had the use of dock carts and they weren't approved for elevator use. The iPad helped us find the church, a busy place this in-gathering Sunday, the end of the summer holiday and the time when the congregation reconstituted itself. Tables were set up outside of the sanctuary for the annual salmon bake potluck following the service on this gorgeous late summer morning. We were greeted and welcomed, filled out name tags and then found seats on the right hand section and were immediately struck by the scene that filled the windows that made up the entire wall behind the choir and pulpit, not much different from Crane Island, bushes and trees, and no sign of human presence. It was a

Three-hundred-twenty-eight: East Shore UUs

huge window into the natural world, the world Emerson and Thoreau, patron saints of Unitarians, made sacred for generations of Americans. In the fall, the turning leaves would lend color and in the winter occasional snow would lend contrast. The sermon turned on the interaction of Priam and Achilles, enemies in Homer's *Iliad*, the scene in the midst of the Trojan war in which they recognize and honor one another as fellow, feeling human beings, Priam having snuck into the Greek camp to retrieve his son Hector's body, Achilles having sought Hector out and killing him for his killing of Achilles' friend Patroclus. The meeting didn't stop the war, the minister pointed out, but the compassion it released was an occasion for hope and an end to hate and revenge, what these Sunday morning services kept reminding us about, a coming back to our better selves amid the temptations of tribalism and xenophobia, a fitting comment ten years after the beginning of a war that seemed to have no end. When the offering was taken up, this Sunday in support of a water protection organization, the minister encouraged the congregation to talk to one another and they did. We met the couple to our right and then a joyful octogenarian with her grandson who explained that she knew Rachel and Marilyn and had been to Crane Island in years past. The big choir and the congregation sang loudly and well, one piece being Bill Withers' "Lean on Me." Yvonne was surprised at the extreme casualness of the group, describing it as suburban compared to the University district UU church we'd visited last year, more formal, less friendly, with fewer children.

We didn't stay for the potluck and Yvonne made sandwiches we ate in the car as we drove north toward Anacortes and the ferry. I dropped Yvonne at Costco, filled the Focus' tank, pleased at the relatively small charge, and crossed I-5 to pick up license plates at the Ford dealer. A young salesman put them on and I asked for instructions on how to reset the trip odometer (when it's showing on the readout, hold down the OK button, until it's reset to zero) and then how to pipe music from the iPad through the car's sound system and he took me through the Sync System's voice menu until Van Morrison could be heard. I'd need to study the system more but at least now I knew how to make music and audio books available from the iPad.

Three-hundred-twenty-eight: East Shore UUs

328: Harbor Steps world

The line at the Anacortes ferry landing was shorter than we'd expected and we left on time, Yvonne staying in the car for a nap and me going up to the galley level to write. We'd seen Wilma walking her dog and Gary's some distance away at the ferry landing and here they were upstairs at a table at one end, me in the middle so as to have access to a 110 volt outlet to keep my MacBook Pro charged. Gary took a nap and Wilma left for a time and once I'd finished, just past Thatcher Pass I approached them and asked Gary if he could stand talking about the Crane water system. He could, so we reviewed the unfinished two hydrant installations, Larry's need for a meter where he intended to build, next steps for the Cross Connect Policy implementation, Dave's project to get the State to approve more potential water connections, the County's order to improve water sampling, and the project to add a tank switch to the system, all items that we'd talked about for some time.

Gary said he would be working on all of them this month and next. And then I asked Wilma about Ruby, freshly graduated from Orcas High School and still very eager to spread her wings and leave the island as her older sister Edie had done by spending eighteen months in Vietnam but now back on Orcas and not quite as anxious to leave.

CeAnn was on the Crane dock, on her way back to Orcas, and told us a carpenter would soon be on Crane, repairing their deck. The air was warm, about 75°, and we were very happy to be back in our quiet beautiful home, the almost full moon turning the Salish Sea silver as we luxuriated in our hot tub before bed, only a few lights visible from Orcas and Shaw Island, giving us a sense of neighbors but not crowding, unlike places like Gig Harbor, as Yvonne pointed out, where houses were close together and people lived cheek by jowl. Yes.

Three-hundred-twenty-nine: Frustration

"The struggle itself toward the heights is enough to fill a man's heart. One must imagine Sisyphus happy." – Albert Camus, The Myth of Sisyphus

Rose in a smudged pink sky but by 8:00 a.m. low clouds were racing north from the Straight of Juan de Fuca and by 9:00 the sky was completely overcast, not clearing until mid afternoon, the wind shifting to the northeast and freshening. But it wasn't cold so the house was comfortable

Jens students at Wellesley had picked up their copies of *The eNotated Metamorphosis* I'd gifted them through Amazon and they'd be using the ebooks immediately in Jens' Kafka class but they'd need *The eNotated In the Penal Colony* to study and *The eNotated Hunter Gracchus* to annotate. I spent an hour or so experimenting with putting *Gracchus* online with Co-ment, setting up a separate copy of the story for each student and then creating a simple help file that explained how to format italics, bold, and create new paragraphs and then I sent Jens an email telling him the site was ready, to take a look, and then let me know when email invitations should be sent out.

The version of *The eNotated In the Penal Colony* listed in Amazon's Kindle catalog had two small errors Jens had written me about and I wanted to fix them before gifting the ebook to the students but while doing a new edition I wanted to bring the other five books forward so that they would be consistent in formatting and structure and ready for conversion to EPUB from MOBI and upload to the Barnes and Noble Nook catalog. I'd begun the process days before and continued to struggle with it, in part because of a bug in my software that hadn't shown up before for some reason. It was nearly 6:00 when I felt comfortable about all six books and especially about *Penal Colony* since I'd found that the upload I'd done early in the day had introduced worse errors than the ones I'd fixed. What would seem on the surface to be a mechanical process wasn't, in part because the software and procedures were more ad hoc than finished. We hoped to be able to scale the book building and publishing process, that is have hundreds of books in process with as many eNotators but that wouldn't happen until it was automated or at least well documented — with check lists.

329: Glory before the grey

The summer light was clearly disappearing quickly, more than three minutes per day; in September we'd lose close to four hours of daylight and the familiar fall feeling of loss, even some anxiety, waxed and waned during the day. I was eager to complete all I needed to do before mid October when the rains and wind would come in earnest and there didn't seem to be enough time. I associated fall with James

Whitcom Riley's poem "Little Orphan Annie," something I heard more than once in grammar school and each time it gave me the creeps. And I had a strong memory of John T. McCutcheon's "Indian Summer" page, created in 1912 and that appeared every autumn in the *Chicago Tribune*, the top of two pictures showing at old man sitting, smoking a pipe, holding a rake and a young boy standing, both watching smoke curl up from a pile of burning leaves and the bottom picture, with the light mostly gone, showing corn shocks morphed into teepees and the smoke into dancing Indians.

Yvonne had sent out a short news bulletin to the Borg (family) units, especially to describe Jeni's wrist surgery, now only a few days away and that Noah and Natasha were listing their house as part of a process to move closer to Olympia schools and work. Within minutes Corrina had responded from Philadelphia and had news of her own including being hired as a TA through her art graduate program and having secured acceptable housing nearby. Great news since she finally seemed to be on a path that could bring her the kind of employment and life she'd finally come to understand she wanted.

Yvonne continued to work on her Food Bank fund drive mailing, now with a substantial list of potential donors (more than 500), perfecting the solicitation text, but still frustrated because she couldn't get the financial and usage information from the Treasurer and President she needed to make the pitch concrete and specific. I was frustrated because I'd thought I'd begin to have plenty of time to spend outdoors on projects and instead I was spending whole days staring at a computer screen.

A big envelope had appeared in our PO Box, a mailing from the York/Willowbrook High School 50th Reunion committee containing a group photo of 47 of my classmates and a bound booklet with directories and lists. I'd signed us up for the event but we hadn't attended, one reason being that day was the Crane Island Association annual meeting and I'd be doing two presentations but more significantly perhaps, was the cost of the travel, a couple thousand dollars, and the likelihood no one would be there that I wanted to see. My sisters, having attended the same high school, advised me to go saying I might be disappointed in

Three-hundred-twenty-nine: Frustration

going but surely would in not going; but we hadn't and I wondered a little whether I'd made a mistake. I took a magnifying glass out of the dictionary stand Yvonne had Bill make for me 25 years before when I fantasized about being a writer and studied the photo, recognizing almost no one at all in the group of, for the most part, 47 gray and paunchy old people. There were some exceptions, women who had taken care of themselves and still looked good, but no sign of any of my friends, the smart boys that made fun of everyone else. Where were Larry, Doug, Mike, Bob, Vince? They didn't even show up in the directory listing. Of the 422 in my graduating class, 31 were known dead and another 145 were whereabouts unknown. I knew the whereabouts of a few, I'd found them or they had found me on Facebook, but beyond an initial contact, they hadn't responded to my notes. If we were friends then, why 50 years later wasn't there even a modicum of politeness or slight interest? Was the view of high school now so completely different from what it had been at the time? For the most part, the directory listing in the booklet had few facts beyond address, spouse, children and grandchildren, but in a few cases notes told stories of achievement or lack of it that I never would have predicted and retired life that was a conventional mixture of travel and family. Over the past 50 years I'd thought from time to time about the reunion and looked forward to it as a time to reflect on our lives, our struggles, what we'd learned, what made us happy, but when the reality of the reunion materialized my interest in the past was minuscule compared to my interest in the present and future, and the flesh and blood friends of today much more important and superior to the friends of half a century ago. For some time I'd thought of high school as being a kind of golden time. I no longer did. This was the golden time. I'd have to think about this some more.

Three-hundred-thirty: Bzzzz, Bzzzz

"Do not dwell in the past, do not dream of the future, concentrate the mind on the present moment." – Buddha

Waking about 1:30 a.m. and not being able to go back to sleep, thinking about software changes I wanted to try, by 2:30 I was sitting in my favorite wicker chair, a view of the outside darkness to the left, behind me, the wood stove, cold since May, to my right and behind me, my MacBook Pro warming my lap. Two weeks before I had loaded *Tess of the d'Urbervilles* into Co-ment as 59 separate chapter files. I now thought that was too complicated and that the book should be one file with a table of contents at the beginning linking to each chapter and each chapter heading linking back to the table of contents, so I created a new kind of output format from the *Tess* database — one continuous book file (without any annotations) — a very different from the MOBI creating a folder of files, one per chapter. By late morning I had imported *Tess* as one file to Co-ment. The next step would be to create annotations, export the file from Co-ment and then read the file, extract the annotations and insert them into the *Tess* database.

But that was enough programming for the day. I took a quick walk around the island, walking by the water tank without stopping to note the water level, seeing virtually nothing on my walk, so preoccupied with system and business design ideas. Yvonne was on her way to Friday Harbor for a county Master Gardeners Foundation meeting and once I ate leftovers from the prior evening's dinner and an open-faced peanut butter and jelly sandwich, I went outside, retrieved extension and step ladders from behind Yvonne's shed and set up the tallest step ladder next to the south side of the rain shelter roof, got the push broom from my shop, climbed up on the ladder and began to sweep the roof. The rain shelter is an open-sided 12' x 12' light brown (treated), post and beam structure with a translucent, corrugated polycarbonate roof — just a skeleton with a glowing roof, an attractive structure, the design copied from a picture in *Sunset* magazine, though the translucent roof, giving a sense of lightness in two different ways (internal illumination and not heavy) was my idea and polycarbonate, which I'd gotten to know something about years before when contracting with a CD manufacturer to press monthly copies of an insurance reference library my company would send to subscribers, was a terrific material, surprisingly tough rather that brittle and which would stand up well to the elements, better than fiberglass panels, for instance.

I wanted to do the roof sweeping now, while it was so dry because moisture in the debris that collected in the corrugation valleys was less likely to clump together and stick to the surface of the roof. Two years before I'd taken a hose up on the roof with the intention of using water pressure to remove the debris. It was a messy process and an extravagant use of precious water. I wanted to approach the problem in a different way. It worked and I was happier with the result. The rain shelter looked cared for, its original lightness mostly recaptured. The ground around the shelter was now covered with fir and cedar droppings but it didn't matter; the area was rustic and grazed by the doe and twins that came through the yard every morning. And then I saw the huge mushroom, next to the big green tent Yvonne had raised under the shelter for overflow summer guest housing, somehow not noticed and eaten by the deer that grazed through the yard every morning. The stem was four inches across and the head more than six, the whole mushroom about eight inches high. Later I took a picture of Yvonne holding it. She fixed half for dinner and would take the rest to Seattle to share with Jeni.

Yvonne's shed roof was next and I set up an extension ladder in front to get access to the roof. Three and a half years before, in the spring, I had the lumber yard bring over all the wood and materials I'd need for the rain shelter and two sheds. I built the rain shelter first, assembling the two gable ends on the concrete driveway (before I covered it with a wood deck), disassembled it, and then reassembled them, one on the front two poles of what would be the rain shelter and the other on the back two and then turned my attention to creating pads over which I could build the hers and his 16' x 12' sheds. Since a hill rose behind the sheds I had to excavate the rear area for each shed, cut out roots from the immediately adjacent big cedars and firs and in one case remove the stump of a small fir. The roof extended two feet past the walls, front and back and two sides, and since the sheds were up off the ground allowing space for storage underneath and to protect from wood rot, the front of the roof was at least twelve feet off the ground, high enough to want to be careful.

330: Prince mushroom

During construction of my shed, begun after mostly completing Yvonne's, the ladder slipped sideways along the flashing at the front of the roof and fell over, me with it, though without injuring me in any way. In the past, the roof fronts had seemed high; today they didn't and

Three-hundred-thirty: Bzzzz, Bzzzz

I was completely comfortable, though very careful, and the sweeping down the corrugated panels, not quite half way, as far as I could reach with the push broom from the ladder, the debris piling up in a line across the roof. There was enough moisture left in some clumps that they didn't sweep away easily but had to be jiggled to loosen. Moving the ladder three more times along the edge of the roof, I finished the front side, walked around the back, on the hillside and put up one section of a shorter extension ladder which made it possible to climb up on the roof.

Because the hill rose around the sheds to the rear and because the roof was about two feet lower in the rear, the roof was only about seven feet off the ground. Once on the roof on my knees I was careful to put my weight only where there was skip siding, that is, cross supports, under the polycarbonate panels, though generally speaking it probably isn't a good idea to climb on a polycarbonate roof and I was concerned about cracking the material around the holes through which hold-down screws with silicon washers passed. I'd attached the panels in an unconventional way. The right way was to put wood supports cut in the same pattern as the corrugation under the panels and put the screws through the peaks, not valleys. I'd done it the other way, since no appropriate precut supports were available and I didn't want to create my own, a laborious and time-consuming process. But it worked; after adjusting some of the screws there were no leaks in either shed. The roof looked much better and there was more light inside. The roof on my shed didn't have near as much tree droppings and it swept much more easily. I was pleased to complete the roof cleaning process; they wouldn't need attention again for two years probably. One surprise: the right end of the beam that held up the front, high end, of the roof extended two feet beyond the wall and on top of it, under the polycarbonate panel, birds had built a handsome nest, lined with moss taken from a nearby tree. What kind of bird I couldn't tell but it wasn't small. When working on the other end of my shed roof I noticed that wasps, I assume, had built a paper nest, hanging it from the skip siding that extended beyond the edge of the roof, but I didn't see any.

Three-hundred-thirty: Bzzzz, Bzzzz

Close by I'd created a pile of sixteen-inch trunk sections I'd cut and carried back from the eight fir trunks Pat had pulled out of his pile for me. They needed to be split and they needed to be moved to the front yard with all of the other fire wood. Thinking I might split them before moving them, I fetched my two splitting mauls, sledge hammer, and two metal wedges, one steel and one aluminum, and began to work on the pile, taking a whack with the maul and then if the stroke didn't split the wood, pulling the maul out and substituting a wedge in the cut, using the sledge hammer and wedge to complete the split (and when that didn't work, turning the trunk section over and repeating the process from the other end). After about 45 minutes of this sweaty work, Yvonne showed up with the new maul I'd bought a Lowe's in Seattle Saturday and left in the car because we had too much to carry when coming back to the house on Sunday. I hadn't paid attention but this maul's fiberglass handle was six inches longer than the one I'd been using (and ruined by whacking the back of the head like a wedge with my sledge hammer) and maybe too long but the longer radius of my swings brought more energy to the head of the ax and the wood split more often on the first whack. I'd noticed that yellow jackets (hornets) congregated around cut would, perhaps preying on small insects that feed on or in the wood. After about an hour of splitting, perhaps 100 yellow jackets buzzed around the growing pile of split wood and increasingly around me so I used that as an excuse to quit for the day, came inside and talked to Yvonne sitting on the couch reading catalogs and asked her about her day with the Master Gardeners in Friday Harbor. Most interesting for her was getting to know better a new Master Gardener who had recently moved to Orcas from Palo Alto and who with her husband had started a micro brewery but would probably abandon it because of licensing problems with the county.

Three-hundred-thirty-one: Chores

"Work is love made visible." – Khalil Gibran

A little past 6:00, the sky dark gray except for a north south stripe to the east that let a little light through from the sun still below the horizon, a dividing line between America and the Islands perhaps, duplicated in the glassy surface of the Salish Sea, Bell island bracketed by matching above and below lines, interesting enough for me to take my camera out on the deck twice to record the scene.

331: Doe and twins browse beneath bedroom window

Three-hundred-thirty-one: Chores

While I sat at the kitchen counter eating oatmeal and reading the *NY Times* online, Yvonne, getting dressed, beckoned me into the bedroom — something to see outside. The doe and its twins were browsing right below the bedroom window, between the house and the trees on the rocky bank not ten feet away. One of the fawns was stripping the leaves from a prickly wild rose, further evidence favoring my hypothesis that these deer were unpaid grounds keepers for us.

Yvonne was on her way to Seattle and would go directly to Swedish Hospital to be with Jeni for her outpatient wrist surgery, then take her back to her apartment and look after her for a couple days. Howard had again demurred from his normal Wednesday morning Greybeards hosting so when I took Yvonne to the Orcas dock and helped carry her luggage, store returns, a plant for Jeni, and what not to the car, I went back home in anticipation of a day outside working.

In early July Yvonne had raised our big green two-room Coleman tent in the rain shelter, outfitting it with a comfortable inflatable bed covered with a layer of memory foam and even a light and table/dresser. I took it down and found the waterproof floor wet on the underside near the middle of the rain shelter; the wood chips making the floor of the rain shelter were also wet and had been for almost twelve weeks, during a time of little rain. The roof must leak, I figured, and over the winter and spring had soaked the chips and ground underneath, the floor of the tent drawing it out. Next rain I'd look to see where the leak was coming from. Then I dragged a tarp loaded with wood chips into the shelter and dumped them in the center. As we needed them sometime in the future I could shovel them into a cart and move them.

The 450 gallon water tank at the northwest corner of the house, intended to catch rainwater to irrigate Yvonne's front garden, had tilted and was leaning against the house. It was too heavy to budge. The remaining water was lower than the level of the hose bib so I removed the bib and reducers, opening the inch and a half port close to the bottom of the tank and slid in a hose to siphon out the remaining water. I could now wrestle the tank, four feet across and six feet high away from the corner of the house and lay it on its side to let any remaining water out. I'd dug out an area to place the tank on and smoothed it with sand, not

Three-hundred-thirty-one: Chores

a good foundation for anything but it did protect the tank bottom from rocks below and it would work if it didn't move. Assuming the problem was that I disturbed the sand when I slid the tank into position initially, I decided to try smoothing and leveling the sand again, covering it with plywood and then sliding the tank onto the plywood. Since the three reducer fittings between the tank and the hose bib had leaked a little I took them apart, applied plumbers putty and reinstalled the assembly. Time would tell whether the sand approach would work this time. The gutter that fed the tank was filled with madrona leaves and bark so I cleaned it into the five gallon bucket Yvonne had used for crabbing.

Before bringing the two single kayaks up from the beach to join the two doubles, I put down two planks for all four to rest on up off the ground. They were made of indestructible polypropylene but sitting directly on the ground mud adhered to the contact point. Better to be higher.

Since it might not be long before we'd want a morning fire, I swept the front porch and moved the bench to the house side, leaving an 8' by 3' area against the railing facing the garden to store firewood for the heating season. Two years before I'd found sections of a cedar trunk near Circle Road someone had abandoned years ago and brought them home in our dock cart as a source for kindling. I used my short-handled splitting maul to make enough kindling to fill three orange crate boxes that might last the winter. I had enough cedar for at least another winter I could use next year. Then I brought the remaining split firewood, three cart loads, to the porch and stacked it and then brought three cartloads of split wood from the other side of the house, the yellow jackets still in abundance around the split wood and the big stack of trunk slices. I'd move the rest of the wood to the firewood area the next day. The front porch looked very satisfying, wood stacked four feet high in places, probably enough for three weeks beginning in October.

I used the big tarp I'd covered the split firewood with to now cover the wood from the six trees John had felled for us, potentially a pile of split wood about sixteen feet long, eight feet wide, and four feet high, perhaps two cords, but I didn't expect to use that wood this season. Nearby was the wood Tim had cut in January, the three logs I had cut and brought back from the community beach in March, and the three trees Yvonne and I had felled in May. And then there was most of the pile from the eight logs Pat had let me cut and take and the windfall on Circle Road — and all of this I could use this season and all of it would have to be split — a little at a time all fall, winter, and spring. I hadn't yet figured out whether I had enough for the heating season — but while the pickup was on the island it made sense to pick up more.

After a spaghetti dinner using the sauce Yvonne had left out for me, I called her in Seattle for a report on Jeni's surgery, talking first to Jeni and then Yvonne. Jeni had worked in the O. R. with this surgeon on precisely the same procedure so she knew exactly what was happening and the doctor let her watch it all through a camera focused on her wrist. She was nonplused; I would have fainted. The ligaments were abraded, not torn, from rubbing on the joint because her ulna was slightly too long, not uncommon and generally not a problem except with repetitive motion, what she did for doctors in the O. R. The surgeon shortened the ulna by 25 millimeters, about a tenth of an inch, which would take the pressure off the ligaments. She'd need four to six weeks of recuperation but she was optimistic that she'd have the use of her right hand back and wouldn't have further problems with it. Given that Jeni would have to feed herself and wouldn't be able to get out much during the recovery period, Yvonne proposed to Jeni that she come and stay with us at least part of the time. Jeni thought she would. That would be nice for all of us.

Three-hundred-thirty-two: Bang!

"If you're going through hell, keep going." — Winston Churchill

By midmorning the rain predicted materialized but only for a few minutes though the sky was mostly cloudy all day. Mike had written me the day before asking for help with his crab catch reporting. Like everyone else with a 2011 license he was required to report how many crabs he caught on which day — by October 1st — or he would have difficulty getting a license next year. The state uses the information to help it set dates for the coming season in ways I don't fully understand. Yvonne would be reporting soon, which she could do through the internet. Mike had left his crab license and catch information in his house two doors south of us assuming he would be back before October 1st but as it turned out his boat had developed a serious outdrive failure and because of the unavailability of parts wouldn't be in the water again until winter. His front door key was in a lock box next to the back door and he provided the combination. I'd helped in the past from time to time, checking the heat, for instance and it wasn't much of a problem. The license and catch records for Mike, Bethany, and Kevin were in small plastic envelopes hanging from a lanyard in a bowl with keys to his Explorer parked in the driveway. I took the lanyard home, examined the catch records and sent him an email with the details. Mike had been the first to return his 2011 Crane Association annual bill — filling in details about car and boat usage and what he owed, adding that to the dues, meter fee, and water usage fees that I'd included in the bill I sent him, and then sending a check for the total. Because I'd listed the Orcas side trailer parking fee as $100 when it was actually $50, I'd have to refund that amount to him eventually.

Three-hundred-thirty-two: Bang!

332: Waiting wood for drying then splitting

Now I had a check to deposit in the bank account the Board agreed I should open for the Association at Islanders' Bank in Eastsound and I had applications filled out for the three of us who would be on the account as well as a Board resolution for the account — but the bank wanted meeting minutes that reported on the resolution and they wouldn't be approved until the next meeting, October 15th, and though we could conceivably approve the minutes by an email vote, the Board Secretary hadn't responded to that suggestion from the Board President — so it was likely we'd continue to use Keybank for annual bill deposits and write checks out of, but then we'd have to go through an application and signature card process with them because Dan at least, I assumed, wasn't a signer on the account though I thought both Martha and I were. And then the phone rang and it was Debbie at the Eastsound Keybank branch. She had been reviewing accounts and had

Three-hundred-thirty-two: Bang!

found that the Association's was out of date and as we talked she realized was seriously inaccurate. She couldn't find a record of last year's applications and changes of Board members on the account though somehow she had my name and phone number. For the last year they'd been honoring checks they technically shouldn't have. We finally came to an understanding after I'd provided her with the information she needed for Dan and Martha — which I got from the Islander Bank application forms: she would send all of us signature cards to sign and return and she would change the mailing address for the association so I'd start getting the monthly statements rather than the accounting firm that had done the bookkeeping in the past. I asked about savings account and CD interest rates and as I suspected they were terrible, much worse than Islanders' Bank. Debbie apologized and said she understood that I would want to move our savings someplace else. I sent emails off to Dan and Martha alerting them to look for a note from Debbie.

Our son, Eric, and others had told us they weren't able to leave us voice mail messages though when we tried it we had no problems. Yvonne, using her cell phone and calling from Jeni's now found she couldn't leave a voice mail for me and we realized that the problem was for calls coming from outside the local area. I called CenturyLink service and after being on hold for some time finally talked with someone who recommended resetting our system. What? She said I should disconnect all the phones for at least 30 seconds and that would cause their system to do some kind of reset and that she'd call me back in five minutes. She never called back but when Yvonne called later while I was outside she said she got the proper voice mail system response and was gratified that problem seemed fixed.

Late afternoon I took a walk around the Island on Circle Road. The tank level indicator showed a bit over 13'. Good. I took a close look at the big Silver fir someone had felled a few weeks before, at Dick's request, to see whether it would make good firewood but the trunk was spongy and Dick was right that it might have fallen over in the wrong direction, with or without a wind. Then I walked back off the road to well house #4 to check the tree, another Silver fir, that had fallen behind it, missing the little building by about four feet. I was doubtful it would make good firewood either. I noticed that Gary hadn't filled in the trench where he'd run a new line from the chlorine mixing chamber to the main line on the road. The line was exposed and would freeze sometime over the winter unless it was covered up again. I'd have to write Gary.

Three big contractor trucks occupied Ilze's house where Josh had been working on a remodel off and on over the past year and seeing him and a worker near the road, I said hello and inquired about his progress. The current project was to install wall insulation. Normally that would be easy but Ilze, an architect did want to use fiberglass bats so Josh had hunted down scrap denim and then had it ground up and made into bats — at great expense. The five workers were installing the denim bats and anxious to be finished by the time the barge came at 6:30 to transfer the trucks to Orcas. He reported seeing a big boat fire in Deer Harbor over Labor Day weekend but we hadn't noticed it so later I checked the *Islands' Sounder* website and sure enough a fire had destroyed a 35' Bayliner the owner had for only three months.

Home again I picked up where I'd left off the day before moving wood from the back to front yard, again confronted with an army of hornets buzzing over or crawling the log sections I needed to split. Picking up a four foot section I'd need to cut into three pieces something dislodged and fell on my left big toe. Ouch. I did another load and then could barely walk, so came in and wrapped some ice around it. The skin wasn't broken and it would heal but every so often I'd feel a shot of pain, like a needle going into it. Oh well. Yvonne called while I was fixing some spaghetti and in Seattle she was cooking for Jeni — who was getting along. Yvonne had seen her niece, Samantha, and her boyfriend during the afternoon and Samantha was happy to see her — but talked the whole time about how broke she was, her job plus her monthly check from Boeing following her father's death two and a half years ago just wasn't enough to put food on the table. But it was good to see her, Yvonne said, and she learned that Samantha rarely saw her sister, Sarah, who had withdrawn from her and everyone else, the loss first of her mother and then her father pushing her into a difficult place.

Three-hundred-thirty-two: Bang!

Yvonne would try to make the 12:30 ferry tomorrow and I would be happy to have her home. I took two ibuprofen and crawled into bed.

Three-hundred-thirty-three: Wings

"The world is a fine place and worth fighting for and I hate very much to leave it." — Ernest Hemingway

OPALCO, our local power utility, had scheduled a power outage for the San Juan islands overnight from 11:00 to 6:00 that was mandated by the North American Electric Reliability Corporation, a group focused on the reliability of the North American bulk power system so I wasn't surprised when I woke up in the darkness and saw no glowing clock readout on the dresser, so I went into kitchen and pulled my watch and headlamp out of the drawer where I keep them — 3:30 a.m. After an hour I resigned myself to being awake and since I'd been thinking about JavaScript, a web page programming language, I fetched one of my books on it and read by LED light, not the best for reading. At 5:30 the power came on, so I could begin my day and after 30 minutes of slow and deep breathing and thinking, I got up to fix myself breakfast. I looked at my right toe, the one I dropped a log on the day before and was pleased to see that it looked normal — but strangely all the toes on my left foot ached — so I looked there. Ah! Red and purple and dented.

Jens and I had scheduled a phone call for 8:00 to prepare invitations for his Kafka class students so each would have access to their individual online copies of *The Hunter Gracchus* so they could work on the annotation assignment he'd given them. Because we both had access to the same web pages I could walk him through the process of inviting a student and then setting up permissions so the student could see only her own *Gracchus* and the shared help file I'd prepared and none of the other 69 files that now populated the eNotated Classics site. After doing two it was clear this wasn't something he really wanted to do so I offered to do the rest and he readily consented. One of the students must have been checking her email because she almost immediately signed on and her pending status disappeared.

Three-hundred-thirty-three: Wings

333: Whose wings?

Almost right after we hung up, Chris called. Wasn't our monthly business meeting scheduled for right now, 9:00 a.m. on the third Friday at David's? Was he there. Yes? Could he pick me up at the Cayou Quay marina? Yes. Then I told him I hadn't yet taken a shower and he said he hadn't either. He'd pick me up in fifteen minutes. Because we hadn't discussed or confirmed this date both David and I assumed we wouldn't be having a meeting but Chris was right, I realized, we should catch up. After flattening my hair, I hobbled to the community dock and in five minutes was backing into the slip next to Chris' Catalina sailboat and as he grabbed the lines he told me the slip belonged to Mike, a nemesis to each of us, he because he had to deal with Mike when trying to upgrade the Cayou Valley neighborhood water system and me because Mike had been a sometime summer neighbor on Cayou Valley

Road and had been infuriatingly difficult, one reason we were happy to sell and move to Crane more than four years before.

Besides our little meeting, which convened in David's office downstairs, Maxine was hosting a yoga session in the living room, whose members I didn't recognize. First we talked bookkeeping with QuickBooks; I'd take over as soon as David had set up the "inventory" and "billing" systems that would help us track sales and pay royalties. We all agreed that Islanders' was a more responsive bank than KeyBank. I reported on Barbara and *My Antonia* — going well though because of her aversion to computers I was doing more work than would make sense in the scaled up business we imagined. Tom had finished his *Death in Venice* translation but I had been after him. Angel had said she wanted to go ahead with *The Man Who Would Be King* but I wasn't sure that would happen and Chris added that she had gotten "flakely" now that her mother had come to live with her from Texas. Though *Tess of the d'Urberville's* was ready for annotation on Co-ment, Howard was missing in action. That was disappointing because with his background in historic rural England he had much to offer. Then we talked about Jens' experiment, teaching Kafka from his ebooks, projecting *The eNotated Penal Colony* from his iPad to the class, who also had the text on their notebook computers, iPhones, of whatever, and the imminent *The Hunter Gracchus* annotation assignment he'd given them that they'd use Co-ment for as I had set it up and to which they were now invited. Finally we talked about Co-ment and how we could use it in lieu of the annotation software I'd written, the advantages being that it was online and intended for collaboration and would eliminate or greatly simplify the software I needed to create and maintain, and that the Co-ment software was available for free should we want to set up our own server. With Co-ment we were closer to our vision of a multi-layered annotated classics service — online for libraries and ebooks for consumers and a do-it-yourself annotation platform for teachers and their students and for us and our annotators.

Yvonne called from the Anacortes ferry landing to report that she didn't make the cut on the 12:30 ferry and was second in line for the 4:00. After a mid-afternoon nap I hobbled along, pushing the dock cart

Three-hundred-thirty-three: Wings

to what was left of the wood pile behind the F150 and while trying to avoid the hornets that had become so numerous around it, moved successive loads to the front wood pile, some hornets coming along for the ride. I thought I could see where they had their nest, under a piece of wood and I let that be. When I got to the bottom of the pile I saw what looked like hundreds of winged insects crawling around but as I looked closer I saw only gray wings stirred by the breeze into motion that looked like flapping — hundreds and hundreds of wings. At 7/8's inches long they looked bigger than what the yellow jackets wore. Where did the wings come from? What left them and went on without them? There was no sign of insect bodies. Could it have been the orange ants I had seen a few weeks back? Or carpenter ants as Yvonne later suggested? But why would they crawl under this new (and temporary) wood pile, drop their wings and then go — where?

    I walked up to the Orcas parking lot about 5:30 and helped Yvonne carry bags down to the boat. She was happy to be home and so was I. We talked for a long time about her Seattle visit with Samantha, her niece, who continued to struggle financially and emotionally since the death of both her parents. Jeni was doing OK, the percocet helping her manage her post-wrist-surgery pain, but once she felt better but before she could go back to work in perhaps a month, she'd become bored so she was open to the idea of coming to Crane for a while but the date was left open. After dinner Yvonne needed to use her iMac in the studio but it wouldn't turn on and the site was disheveled. What had happened? I'd forgotten to return everything to its upright and locked position after taking it apart to disconnect the telephone from the printer and handset so the phone system would reboot and fix the phone mail system problem. That was the mess. But why didn't the eight year old computer boot up? Did it have something to do with the power outage overnight (we generally leave our computers turned on and let them go into sleep mode when not in use)? The iMac wouldn't boot with the keyboard plugged into the USB port on the back but would plugged into a USB port in the keyboard. Yvonne was back in business but I didn't try to figure out exactly what was going on. She would be busy and off Crane every day for the next six, until we left for Harstine Island and I'd be a little lonesome — but had plenty to do.

Three-hundred-thirty-four: Island Farmers

> "The human capacity for burden is like bamboo — far more flexible than you'd ever believe at first glance." — Jodi Picoult

Though the decks were wet from a little early rain, it didn't continue and by afternoon some sun peaked through the clouds, more sun in Eastsound from what Yvonne described, and it wasn't cold, starting at 52, the thermometer rose into the low 60's by afternoon.

I was determined to bring all six of our eNotated Classics books up to date for Amazon's Kindle catalog and make them available in Barnes and Noble's Nook catalog and by late morning everything was uploaded and would be processed overnight and perhaps ready some time Sunday. I reported on the development to David, Chris, and Jens and all found it an encouraging step.

Because Yvonne had been so busy and I considered myself off the eNotated Classics critical path for a day or at least a few hours, I asked for and got an assignment and spent about an hour sweeping, vacuuming, and cleaning the guest bathroom and then checked the pH level in the hot tub and added chlorine and shock.

I'd gotten a heavy duty angle bracket a week before to fix the leaning and wobbly post at the head of the stairs from deck to ground outside the dining room door that made it difficult to open and close the gate that was supposed to keep deer out so I found some lag screws in my shop and brought them back to the deck with a corded drill, positioned the bracket, fastened it to the flooring and then to the post, making it plumb, which in turn fixed the gate problem.

The pickup was still reasonably clean on the outside from when I'd washed it a little over a week before but I hadn't cleaned the inside in more than a year and it wasn't a very pleasant place to be. I'd expected to move it closer to the house, right outside the garden gate at the south end of the studio deck but Yvonne had taken my keys so she could get into the Crane Island Association Post Office box and bring me the completed annual bills and payment checks I was certain were now finding their way into it but I realized the yard power post was only ten feet away from the truck and I could plug in the portable vacuum there. Though only scraps of bark remained from the pile of wood I moved to the front yard for splitting, the hornets were still active though perhaps not in the numbers I'd seen the day before but they buzzed around my head and legs, curious about everything in the vicinity. I shooed them away and they took the rebuff graciously.

334: Early fog will burn off

I took everything out and put it on the ground for the hornets to examine, then swept and dusted the interior. The the vinyl-covered part

Three-hundred-thirty-four: Island Farmers

of the two front door pulls/armrests had suffered an attack of mold — dark gray spots — that may have come off hands grasping the pulls and then encouraged by the over-winter dampness in the truck — something I finally addressed with a chemical air drying system in the spring. The mold wouldn't wash off, even with bathroom cleaners Yvonne used, so I applied Comet from under the guest bathroom sink, something Yvonne warned me not to get on the floor or rug and that worked pretty well. I took the floor mats to the house to scrub and spray off and then hang over the south railing to dry. I'd been storing my chain saw, two-stroke gas and chain oil in the back seat of the pickup, the saw in its black plastic box on a tarp on the bench seat and the gas and oil cans on the floor. In cleaning the truck cab I'd been reminded that the two sections of the back seats would lift up from under the seat backs and rotate seat down, exposing metal backing. I decided that's how I should carry my chain saw kit, folded the seats over, put down the tarp and put the gas and oil in separate boxes so they wouldn't fall over and emptied a rectangular deck screw pail I had in my shop into a jar and then put the chemical drying water receptacle/pellet holder ball device in the pail and then on the backseat platform. The 1999 red F150 was now good to go — on more wood foraging missions on Crane and then once barged back to Orcas be socially acceptable transportation.

Yvonne came home from Orcas about 4:30 having spent the day until 2:00 at the Farmers' Market helping staff the Master Gardener "Answer" booth and then with Joyce outside Island Market soliciting donations as part of the day's Food Drive. She'd prepared "shopping list" handouts showing what the Food Bank needed — to be handed to responding citizens as they entered the store but by 2:00 few had been given out and only a dozen shopping bags were next to the table. The Food Bank volunteers had probably been doing too much gabbing with friends and neighbors shopping at the Market and not enough solicitation. In the two hours Joyce and Yvonne sat at the table they doubled the Food Drive take.

Yvonne had bought fresh chard from the Farmers' Market and used it to bake a gratin that she served with a fresh beet and goat cheese salad. Delicious. The Farmers' Market was finally coming into its own, she said, the Orcas farmers really producing, especially the Black Dog and Maple Rock Farms. We'd had wonderful produce this summer from Yvonne's raised beds on either side of the studio deck (that we felled trees to bring more sun to) from Howard's garden and from Orcas farmers. What a treat! Yvonne's back was acting up so she was happy to get into the hot tub. Another busy day.

Three-hundred-thirty-five: Preparing for Winter

"Autumn is a second spring when every leaf is a flower." — Albert Camus

The light rain that became visible as the morning darkness gave way to a gray light had stopped by the time Yvonne appeared about 8:30 a.m. Both Yvonne and her garden badly wanted rain. Summer drought is our normal weather pattern but June to date we'd had half the average rain, not a problem at first because the spring was so wet, but now it was and some of her plantings were dying and she was pulling them out. Normally we'd have had more than two and a half inches from June 1st.; this year we'd had less than an inch and a half and most of that in June and July. The fall rains won't begin for a few weeks, usually mid October. Until then green things will continue to suffer. Because our autumn is wet and we're unlikely to have frost and because most of the trees are evergreen in this eponymous state, we don't have the beautiful fall colors of much of the country, the big leaf maples an exception but their color usually muted by the almost continuous dampness of late October and November.

My need for a haircut could no longer be ignored, so after Yvonne had finished breakfast and was reading the *Sunday Seattle Times* she'd bought the day before when she was in Eastsound at the Island Market, I brought out the clipper kit and extension cord, folded over the corner of the dinning room rug to keep the falling hair off, put on the black plastic sheet and sat myself down in my kitchen counter chair, dropping the seat to its lowest position. Trim on the sides, not too short on top,

Yvonne was determined to finish preparing materials for the Food Bank fund raising mailing so once she finished editing her 600-address mailing list in Excel, I helped her create labels using the Word mail

Three-hundred-thirty-five: Preparing for Winter

merge process and as usual it was frustrating to get through it to the right result and since her HP printer didn't seem to register correctly on the Avery 5160 labels, I volunteered to complete the process on my computer and printer, turning to Mac Pages and then to Address Book once I understood Pages wasn't intended to be the all-purpose program Word is. Importing to Address Book and then printing labels took only a few minutes once I understood how to do it.

All afternoon Yvonne worked on preparing her garden for winter, putting away or moving and covering what ought not to get wet. I helped carry the teak deck table and chairs from the deck off the dining room down three steps to the more sheltered area against the studio deck and Yvonne would put a tarp over it and tie it down. While she worked outside I used QuickBooks to complete the six annual billing invoices Crane Island Association Members had returned with their checks, finding that I'd made not one but two errors on the form, the first inadvertently raising the fee for storing a trailer in the upper lot on Orcas and lowering the fee for bringing a heavy truck to Crane. Of the six invoices, two had unwittingly overpaid and I'd have to create and send them refund checks. The six checks had brought in nearly $10,000 of our $84,000 revenue budget. I'd been sitting on two bills to be paid, having thought that I'd be able to use a new account at Islanders' Bank and their electronic banking system for the process but with their need to see Board meeting minutes and those minutes not available until October 15th that wouldn't be possible. On the other hand, Debbie, and KeyBank, had told me a few days before that we really didn't have any signers on our account because they didn't have the correct paper work and though she'd promised to send out whatever Martha, Dan, and I needed to sign, it hadn't appeared in the PO box by Saturday and Debbie was leaving for the East Coast for a month to resolve matters after the death of a parent. Since it was obvious that KeyBank didn't compare check signatures to cards on file, I decided I might just as well write the two checks on the KeyBank account, sign them, not go to the trouble of a second signature, and get them in the mail.

Three-hundred-thirty-five: Preparing for Winter

335: Cocktail time

Since I'd seen her about two weeks ago, Barbara had sent me additional material for *My Antonia*, an introduction and a short bio, as well as about twenty annotations she wanted added, happy not to have to use my annotation software to do it herself. She'd listed the Penguin paperback page number with the passage and its annotation and it was easy to find and add the notes to the database but I didn't want to have to do much more of this, too labor intensive to scale for a real business and so was determined to see Co-ment used for all new books.

Howard called in the midst of my working on *My Antonia* saying that he'd been adding annotations to the latest version of *Tess of the d'Urbervilles* I'd put up on Co-ment, one file with a chapter table of contents versus having had a file for each chapter previously. He wanted me to look and offer my opinion as to whether he was on the right track. Later, I did and was pleased with the notes he'd done so far, both for what he chose to annotate and what he wrote to provide the reader background on Nineteenth Century life in rural southwest England. I wrote him a note of encouragement. I was well into the Hardy biography I'd been reading, now in the late 1890s when he published *Jude the Obscure* to sometimes vicious reviews that didn't make sense after *Tess* was so well received, tipping the scales in favor of giving up novels in favor of his greater love, poetry.

Yvonne had harvested her Romano beans, steaming them for dinner and serving them with fried beet greens, with a white sauce over cauliflower on pasta. The beans literally melted in my mouth. Why didn't everyone eat these wonderful Italian beans. Yvonne didn't know but the long, flat beans weren't readily available, even from the Farmers' Market. She'd grown them before and had gotten the seeds at the Seattle Garden and Flower show in January. The beet greens were especially tasty as well, a byproduct of the beets she'd roasted in the late afternoon, cooked in olive oil with garlic salt. Years ago I wouldn't have eaten or if I had wouldn't have enjoyed the dark green plop on my plate. Yvonne wrote emails, one to a high school friend she'd just reconnected with through Facebook while I read more about Hardy and tried to stay awake. I hadn't walked around the island in several days and hadn't today because I'd wanted to do it with Yvonne and as it turned out she didn't have time but as we sat it the luxurious warm water of the hot tub I could feel the lack of exercise and I didn't like it. Tomorrow.

Three-hundred-thirty-six: Discovery

"The only way to discover the limits of the possible is to go beyond them into the impossible." — Arthur C. Clarke

As sometimes happens I woke up about 2:30 and couldn't go back to sleep but was enjoying myself thinking through problems and solutions especially relating to the (illusion of?) what eNotated Classics could or better, should be, all elements of the book and reading environment collecting themselves into a mental table with business/needs areas across the top and market, technology and other details down the left side. The overall metaphor that described what we were trying to do, it seemed to me, was to focus on reading as an active, sometimes social process rather than on books as fixed objects transferred to customers. Yvonne was also awake as she often is in the middle of the night and she put her arms around me for a while, sharing and enjoying our sleeplessness.

The dawn sky was completely clear, the day very promising for hauling out the *Discovery*, the one big fall task yet to accomplish, and practical because the tide would be in at six feet from noon on, with no second low tide until night. There would be plenty of water at the beach next to the Crane Community Dock so I wouldn't have to back the pickup and trailer into the mud exposed at low water but could stay on the sand. Yvonne would be going to Eastsound for the afternoon to have Food Bank fund drive letters duplicated at Rainbow Services and then attend a Master Gardeners meeting — and besides she didn't feel strong enough or confident enough with her unpredictable arthritic hands to help. Though I wasn't eager to ask others on Crane for help since it created an obligation, I called Jim and when I got no answer drove to his house, a quarter mile by almost impassable beach path and a mile by road.

I hadn't seen his new garage/shop yet this summer and I was impressed at how nice it looked, the exterior finished and stained. Nancy

Three-hundred-thirty-six: Discovery

nowhere in sight, I found Jim inside their cabin, or what had been their cabin, now with a new framed addition that wrapped around the back and the original house gutted, the glass roof replaced with a conventional beam supported wood roof covered with plywood and that with a huge blue tarp. Jim showed me around explaining that once he began the remodel in the existing structure he found the walls and especially the corners compromised with rot where the roof, without flashing and with no overhang had leaked rain water for years, Jim's continuing efforts to repair the leaks unavailing. The house had been built by an architect with an interesting idea — open the house to the sky — but the practical reality was that it didn't work. We talked about the tarp and certain problems with the winter winds it would confront when he and Nancy were in Mexico — for sunshine and warmth — and the need to cover the plywood with roofing felt at least but he wasn't certain that what he'd bought was heavy enough, especially in comparison with what he'd used for his garage/shop but he wasn't able to find a supplier now for the heavier grade. The new thinner felt seemed adequate to me, plenty tough — but what did I know — still — my opinion was that he ought to make the roof water tight and not depend on the tarp, apparently the same advice his next door neighbor, Doug, had given him. Jim was having fun with his project, liking nothing better than working, but like me wearing out. I offered to help him put the roofing felt down on some nice day soon. Basically Jim was expanding and rebuilding his house, a huge job that would take years but he and Nancy had made the decision to do that rather than look for property someplace else, enjoying their lot with a low bank facing east and a serviceable dock. Yes, he'd be happy to help me step the mast on the *Discovery* at 3:00 that afternoon. As he walked me back up his driveway to my F150 we stopped at the big trailer hitched to his green John Deere tractor, now covered with a tarp, to look at the dual glazed roof panels he'd removed and now didn't know how to dispose of, each an 8' by 2' panel weighing about 150 pounds. I could think of several people who might be interested. I'd contact each. Later, Howard replied to my email about the glass saying he wasn't interested but suggested Don and Terri.

Three-hundred-thirty-six: Discovery

336: Discovery wrapped for winter

Yvonne ate lunch sitting in the sunshine in one of the chairs we keep on our knoll on the edge of the ten foot rocky bank above the water and just below the east deck of the house and I joined her once I finished the eggs and cheese on toast I'd started eating earlier. Several sailboats were in sight riding on an adequate wind, with large and small power boats heading east and west and a few smaller zippy craft going south to Wasp Passage. An intensely blue sky peeked through the shiny green madrona leaves above our heads. An otter appeared intermittently about 100 feet off shore. Two Kingfishers squabbled (why don't they just relax for a change?), broke off and then separated, one flying over our heads into the firs on Margaret's property across our cove to the south. Yvonne observed that this beautiful view she saw every morning as she slowly woke up would be forever etched in her memory.

Three-hundred-thirty-six: Discovery

    I spent more than an hour getting the boat trailer ready, towing it to the beach and backing it to the edge of the water and then on the *Discovery* at the adjoining dock taking the mainsail off and folding it, removing and stowing the boom, and then removing the rudder and two fenders, taking them home by dock cart and hosing them off. Two ravens, perched in tall firs on the west side of our little harbor called to one an other, likely not about the two-legged on the dock but something more important, perhaps flirting. I moved the *Discovery* to the dock loading zone, about 100 feet from the beach. I was ready for Jim but still had a few minutes and had hatched an idea about a simple way to get the sailboat onto the trailer from its temporary position at the dock. The prior two years we'd used the motor and paddles but that was clumsy. Why not run a line from the bow of the *Discovery* to the trailer and hand pull the sailboat to where it needed to be? I retrieved two 100 foot polypropylene lines from my shop, tied the smaller diameter line to the trailer at the crank and walked with the line along the dock and down the aluminum ramp. The line was twenty feet short so I brought the *Discovery*'s bow mooring line up the ramp and joined the two lines. I was in business. Jim drove up in his little Suzuki, the most popular car on Crane, though tractors and Gators are the more popular vehicles, and I explained the plan. It made sense to him. He'd stand in the bed of the pickup, trailer and rear wheels of the pickup in the water, and he'd pull on the line, drawing the sailboat onto the trailer. I'd be on the bow of the sailboat to do whatever was necessary.

    But the sailboat resisted coming aboard the trailer, drifting first to the left and then when I paddled it back out aways, drifting to the right of the trailer. When the third try didn't work, with the sailboat just to the right of the trailer, I got off, standing on the trailer, the water coming halfway up my legs and filling the boots I was wearing and I pushed and pulled the sailboat into place and then tied the crank line to the tow loop in the bow and drew the bow to the trailer rollers. I was wet but the water didn't feel very cold and after emptying my boots and with Jim in the truck bed I started the engine, checked that the transmission was in four wheel drive and towed the *Discovery* out of the water, up the short beach and then onto the gravel at the end of Dock Road. Jim climbed up on the bow and I got into the cockpit, unfastened the back stay while Jim held the mast and the two of us let it fall forward slowly until it was resting on the bow pulpit. Then we pulled the foot of the mast out of its bracket and I carried the foot to the stern while Jim supported and slid it aft, then laid the head on the pulpit. The black mast, about 25 feet long, and aluminum, was lighter than it looked. I thanked Jim and he could go back home to continue work on his house, the pulling out and mast stepping process having taken less than 30 minutes.

I used bungee cords to secure the mast to the pulpit and aft rail and sail ties to bundle the six wire stays and shrouds and three halyards to keep them from falling out of the boat and then used a mooring line, running it from the starboard winch under the keel and aft trailer support to the port winch. I was ready to tow the *Discovery* home.

I parked the truck and trailer on level ground before Eagle Lane heads steeply down hill to the cul de sac that feeds Mike's driveway to the right and the upper driveway we share with Margaret to the left. I wanted to get out of my wet clothes and then reconnoiter our driveways to decide whether to bring the truck and trailer in forward or backward. The year before I'd backed the truck down the steep, curvy driveway and it seemed to me it would be easier to pull in, turn right at Margaret's driveway and then back straight into our property and leave the sailboat under the willow. It was easy enough coming down the driveway but as I turned the truck right into Margaret's driveway I could see that it would be impossible to pull the trailer in behind me. The Douglas firs on either side, perhaps ten feet apart wouldn't let the boat clear. I backed the trailer a little ways up the driveway and then pulled straight forward into our driveway stopping just outside the deer fence and bamboo gate just south of the studio deck. Now what?

I considered backing up and swinging the trailer to the right into our yard, threading the Douglas firs on either side of my destination but I could see I'd have the same problems I had trying to get into Margaret's driveway. The truck and trailer, almost 50 feet long, didn't have enough clearance. I'd need to back the rig up the driveway, take it out to Circle Road, turn it around, bring it back down Eagle Lane, pull into

Mike's driveway on the right and then back down the upper driveway we shared with Margaret. It had been an ordeal backing down the driveway last year with Margaret my eyes behind the trailer. Backing uphill? With no help? It couldn't be helped. I'd deliberately put myself in a pickle and I needed to get myself out of it.

    I put the F150 in low four wheel drive to get the most power and twenty minutes later was backed into Mike's driveway 50 yards up hill ready to pull out on Eagle Lane. I hadn't driven the truck off the narrow driveway on to the wooded hillside that fell away to the east or gotten stuck in the rocks as the hill rose to the west of the driveway. Backing down the driveway was easier on the truck and somewhat less stressful for me and after many backing then coming forward sessions, the *Discovery* was berthed under the willow, its leaves beginning to yellow. It was 5:00. I'd spent an hour and a half moving the boat, perhaps an hour of that time the result of my trying to take a shortcut. It wouldn't be the last time. I was relieved because I'd accomplished what I considered the most challenging element of our fall preparations to be but I didn't feel it. I just felt worn out. And I was glad no one had watched my towing.

Three-hundred-thirty-seven: Break In

"A garden is always a series of losses set against a few triumphs, like life itself." — May Sarton

Our neighborhood doe and twin fawns browsed outside the south deer fence, stopping often to look and listen, perhaps to the small noise I made in the kitchen fixing my breakfast, their ears independently twisting this way and that, sound scoops to a world I'd never know. As I'd seen before and had marveled at, they seemed intent on keeping our yard trimmed, munching encroaching salal as well as the little amount of grass we have in our yard. The Salish Sea was completely calm this morning, Bell, Shaw, Orcas, and Blakely resting on and reflected in a huge mirror. The base of Blakely was invisible, smudged with a light gray that had made its way through Thatcher Pass.

Yvonne would be leaving for Eastsound for a Food Bank Board meeting intended to confirm an addition to the Board who would focus on publicity, an area that had received too little attention. Then Yvonne, Joyce, and others would finish the fund drive mailing. Joyce had asked Yvonne whether I could provide her some of the pictures I'd taken at the Food Bank open house in July. Not having any idea which pictures of the 80 I'd taken that day would be relevant I made a CD and gave it to Yvonne to take with to town.

The *Discovery* was parked under the willow in front of the storage tent and next to the light green privy-cum-trash and recycle shed and the forest green yard tool and flammable liquids shed but the job I started the day before wasn't done. I removed the tools aboard, anything that might grow mold, and the four horsepower two stroke motor hanging from the movable bracket on the stern as well as the gas tank under the aft cockpit seat, then dragged my power washer out of my shop nearby, unreeled the 100 foot hose hanging on the skirt of the hot tub, added another reel parked near the boat, joined the hoses and the power washer, plugged it into the yard power pole, turned on the water at the hose bib back at the foot of the hot tub and cleaned the green scum off the *Discovery*'s hull and salt from the trailer and running gear. Halfway through I noticed a small doe grazing in the salal along the studio deck deer fence. The gate was open. The doe might enter the garden. That would be bad. I walked quickly to the gate, walked in, closed it, and concerned that the doe might have already spent some time in the yard looked for damage but seeing none was ready to return to the *Discovery* when I noticed that the doe had moved around to the sunrise gate and had stuck its nose through the fence netting and was chewing one of Yvonne's plantings. I yelled and charged the doe and it ran off but it would be back.

I pulled five brown tarps out of the storage tent, stretching them out on the ground, still folded lengthwise, to find the longest, twenty feet long and dark brown. I found another matching tarp but eight by twelve and spread both, the larger from the stern forward and the smaller from the bow aft overlapping the former, both draped across the mast now sitting on the bow pulpit and the stern rail, overhanging two or three feet at each end, and adjusted the tarps so that they dangled the same length down the hull on each side. I found the scraps of rope I'd used previously, threading it through some of the tarp grommets and tying it to the trailer. Since the winter rains blew from the east and the bow pointed that direction I folded the tarp around the extended mast and tied it in place. Rain wouldn't blow in and wind wouldn't carry away the tarp.

After coming in from my work in the yard I picked up a voice mail from Margot telling me Susan's new Orcas UU uebsite contained a factual error in stating that the group had formed in 2003 and would I confirm that and let Susan know. In fact the fellowship formed in 2000, founded by Nanette and Jack and Nan. Only Nanette was among the living, now in Bellingham where many Orcans retire after they retire. In 2009 I had prepared a document that listed talk topics for all UU services from the founding so made a PDF copy and sent it on to Susan with a note — to which she quickly responded with a thank you.

Three-hundred-thirty-seven: Break In

337: Crystal clear Salish Sea

The temperature control in the F150 didn't work because the nylon shaft for the knob was stripped, that is too small, so that when I turned the knob the shaft didn't follow suit. I'd read online that wrapping the shaft with teflon tape and then forcing on the knob would do the trick but there was no clearance to wrap the tape — but putting a piece of toothpick in the knob receiving hole might work. I found some fancy toothpicks in the kitchen, fancy because they were in a variety of shapes, thicknesses, and colors and took them in their plastic bag out to the pickup. I found a fairly thin pick, broke it off the right length, stuck it into the knob hole and pressed the knob onto the shaft. When I turned the knob and encountered some resistance, it felt like the temperature setting shaft was turning. I'd know whether the toothpick fix worked once I ran the truck long enough to try out the heater but that wasn't now.

Three-hundred-thirty-seven: Break In

Jens had written that he'd wanted to have his own copy of *The Hunter Gracchus* on co-ment.com so he could experiment and also that a colleague had agreed to write an Amazon review for *The eNotated Metamorphosis*. Good news. I set up the *Gracchus* file, from time to time pausing to watch two cormorants sharing Mike's big white spherical mooring buoy in front of Margaret's house, and wrote Jens a return email.

When Yvonne returned from Orcas she toured her garden to see what needed watering and discovered a deer had gotten in and browsed through the strawberries. I told her about the doe near the open gate as a more hopeful hypothesis than a break in. Her thought was that a fawn had crawled through the fairly large openings in the west gate so she stacked some patio chairs against it as well as against the south deck gate. We hadn't had much trouble in the four years since we, mostly Yvonne, put up the deer fence, but once they find an opening they'll exploit it repeatedly and destroy the garden. She looked in the morning to see whether her temporary measures would hold.

Yvonne told me again that Larry couldn't access the Food Bank website from his PC in the office. She saw it. He got only a blank page though he'd been able to pull up the home page in the past. The new publicist got a blank page as well. While Yvonne worked on dinner, turkey burger chili, I tried the page and also had a null result. It was broken. On August 26th Yvonne and I had made a change to the page and I had tested it, at least to the extent that I could call up the home page — but I hadn't looked at it closely. Apparently I had actually looked at a copy of the page in the Safari browser's local cache; I hadn't forced the browser to reload the page from the internet. Looking at the HTML page source online I could see that it was a mess. No wonder browsers looking at it couldn't render it. I'd saved the old source online and confirmed that it worked then made a copy and made the textual changes right into the source HTML, tested it and then uploaded the revised page to the Food Bank site, made it the index.html page, confirmed that it worked and told Yvonne she could let Larry know the site was back in business. I was embarrassed. I hadn't checked my work properly in the first place.

Three-hundred-thirty-eight: Another Break In

> *"In three words I can sum up everything I've learned about life: it goes on."* — Robert Frost

I was dimly aware of a movement in the Douglas fir, determinedly growing out of the rocky bank on the eastern, open end of our cove, hard to see at half past five, lit only by a rosy glow seeping through a crack in the clouds over Orcas that I had gone out on the deck to photograph. Another movement — our small local raccoon had spent the night in the fir apparently and was now awake looking for breakfast. First stop, our compost bins. The little raccoon kept his eyes on me as it moved along the ground but didn't seem particularly worried. My photos, taken in the darkness and with flash, showed only two small bright spots on a dark background.

Howard had reconvened the Greybeards after a two-week hiatus so I was due there at 8:00 but Yvonne wanted to leave Crane for Eastsound at 9:00 for the monthly Garden Club meeting (today Dry Shade and Wet Shade) and we had only one vehicle on Orcas. Either I'd need to leave Howard's early or have someone give me a lift back and forth the two miles to Howard's from the Crane parking lot — or — I had an idea — what if I rode a bicycle to Howard's? We had two in the storage tent. Yvonne thought it made no sense since one of my friends would be happy to help. But what if I wanted to try it? To be self-reliant? All this thinking had happened the day before in the late afternoon before Yvonne returned from Orcas when I'd taken the red Scott mountain bike out of the storage tent, topped up the tires from the canister I keep filled from my air compressor, rode the bike across the meadow to the dock and turned left on Dock Road. Normally I walk Crane clockwise and that means climbing the steep hill at the foot of the north end of the airstrip, not a problem on foot but certainly one on a bike.

Three-hundred-thirty-eight: Another Break In

I hadn't ridden at all in several years and only twice on Crane before and a few times on Orcas and not having the balance I once had and riding on a narrow gravel road I wasn't very confident or very comfortable, especially on the hard, narrow saddle that hurt my rear end. The bike had sixteen gear ratios in two sets of eight and I couldn't remember how to shift and besides was too focused on just remaining upright so I stayed with the low gear Morgan had left it in when he used it at Borgfest in July. I rode slowly, was very careful coming down the airstrip hill, and only once came close to going off the road into the ditch. At the short but steep hill at the south end of the airstrip I had to get off and walk the bike. And my legs got tired. But I managed the two mile ride and I had decided I would bike to Howard's.

Now it was Wednesday and I woke Yvonne at 7:30. She got dressed quickly and she and I and the red Scott mountain bike walked to the community dock where I set the bike in the cockpit. Yvonne dropped me at the Orcas dock to go home and get back in bed and I walked the bike up the the ramp to the lot and then through the two levels of the lot to Deer Harbor road, narrow at the point close to its terminus but paved. I wouldn't be wearing a helmet. Maybe that was stupid but when I was a kid no one did. And then I was off. Shifting turned out to be very easy and smooth though I found myself using the very lowest gear going up some of the steeper hills on the two mile ride to Howard's, past the Arkady farm and its open meadow fenced with split rail cedar and lined with poplar and aspen at the north end, pond well to the west of the road and Carousel Buffalo Ranch with its cattle guard drive, high, strong plank fences, Douglas firs and pastures and pond often frequented by local Canada geese. I let the bike accelerate now going downhill to the Four Winds Camp road, struggled up hill past Chase and Mary's and then swooped past Gene and Judy's, Terry and Carol's and Bob and Sue's to the bottom of the hill, the Post Office, the resort and the marina, then up hill again past the old dance hall and then left on Channel Road, past Michael's Boatworks, across the wooden bridge and around the corner to Howard's driveway. The two mile trip had taken eighteen minutes. Walking the bike up Howard's steep driveway I parked it near his outdoor bread and pizza oven and below

Three-hundred-thirty-eight: Another Break In

his fenced garden just as he came out his front door with tray and tea bound for the honeymoon cottage in the garden. He was surprised to see me with my bike. He rode his regularly to the post office to pick up mail. Chris drove up shortly and did a double take at the bicycle. I felt contentedly self-satisfied.

338: Varmints below the deck

After tea and discussion on recurring topics — education, politics, finance, history — Chris excused himself to pick up up Lynn for their Wednesday morning Library volunteer session and Howard and I moved to his living room to talk about Brian who now found it very difficult to walk and attend these gatherings and Bob, who Howard had seen the previous week at the nursing home in Friday Harbor, doing well and enjoying the close proximity to many people who responded to his infectious enthusiasm and appreciation for books and ideas. Howard was having no problems with Co-ment, having created annotations for the first four chapters of *Tess of the d'Ubervilles* and I talked about how we could use the platform to collaborate, me commenting on some of his annotations and suggesting more perhaps, and he commenting on the essays I had in mind writing, all accomplished on-line through a browser using Co-ment. We tentatively set year end as a target for publishing our book.

On the way back to the Crane parking lot on Orcas, I stopped to pick up the Crane Island Association mail and saw that more annual bill responses had come in as well as invoices forwarded from the Crane accountant and now former bookkeeping service in Friday Harbor. Yvonne, now in Eastsound, had left the *Huginn* at the dock. I'd pick her up when she called following Garden Club adjournment and clean up. Cabot and Cynthia's *Kelper* was still at the Crane dock. They'd been on Crane for three weeks now though we had seen little of them. Later while cleaning up for lunch I saw three small mink each about a foot long, with dark ginger coats frolicking together on the patch of luxurious green grass adjacent to Yvonne's pond, at one point all jumping into the water and splashing about. I tried to take pictures from in the house but they moved too fast and after perhaps two minutes they bounced away to the west, perhaps on their way to the community dock cove.

Yvonne called not long after 1:00. Would I like to pick blackberries with her in the Orcas parking lot? Could I bring two buckets I would find in her shop? Yes, indeed. An old Bayliner, perhaps 25 feet long came through Pole Pass but otherwise no boats were visible. The boating season was nearly over. I saw myself as the helmsman in the Bayliner in route to the Gulf Islands from Anacortes perhaps, wondering who the white haired guy was untying his SeaSport from the private dock on Crane Island and wondered what it would be like to live in the San Juans or especially what it would be like to live on a small private island not served by the Washington State Ferry System. Many years ago when Yvonne, the kids and I would take the Winslow or Bremerton

Three-hundred-thirty-eight: Another Break In

ferry from downtown Seattle on a sunny summer afternoon I coveted the sailboats on Elliott Bay and the waterfront houses on Bainbridge Island and the Peninsula the ferry passed and then later when we'd cruised through the more remote and wild-seeming San Juans. Now I had that house, was on that dock, and I knew it was both work and wonderful. Passing through Pole Pass the world felt calm and right and perfect and then as I walked up the Orcas dock ramp I knew why: rain drops created dark stains on the sun and salt grayed wood walkway. I had been feeling the deep calm before a Northwest female rain.

Yvonne, in her red raincoat, was already picking blackberries in the parking lot and I passed her a rectangular two gallon bucket keeping for myself the cutoff bleach bottle I'd lined with a white paper fruit bag. The sprinkles didn't turn into rain; that would happen later, and the bushes were thick with ripe blackberries that would fall off their stems if disturbed even though they'd been picked through several times earlier in September and even in late August. In half an hour, less actually, we had more than a gallon of berries, our hands purple and red (for me perhaps because I'd stuck myself so many times on the prickly shoots). Home again, Yvonne made a big batch of blackberry jam and filled 20 jars and then after dinner a blackberry cobbler we ate half of for dinner dessert. We'd eat the jam over the next year and Yvonne would give some away as gifts, very happy to have had this second chance to make blackberry jam this summer.

In the morning before she went to Orcas, Yvonne had made another inspection of her garden and though we had protected the gates she thought a small deer might have wriggled through the two days before since more damage was evident. Half of her favorite Japanese maple had been stripped of its leaves. She was very discouraged. After dinner she checked the fence line that passed through heavy salal west of the house and discovered where the deer had been entering. The nylon net fencing had been chewed through here and there the spots merging and then opening a big enough hole for a deer to crawl through. We both thought the chewing of the fence hadn't been deliberate — with the goal of creating a gaping hole — but a byproduct of chewing the salal that lined and sometimes penetrated the fence. Yvonne tied a layer of

Three-hundred-thirty-eight: Another Break In

plastic bird netting she she'd stored back by the old privy sealing the accidental opening. I volunteered to remove the steel fencing from around the storage tent — that had not kept the mink out — to protect the nylon garden fence from the outside where it passed through the salal. That would fix them. To keep the mink out of the storage shed we had changed tactics from obstruction to openness. Since we'd left the door tied up and open we'd had no problems, the mink apparently seeking privacy. Then the rain came more seriously and all of us on Crane, green and brown and white were happy, content in the good rain.

Three-hundred-thirty-nine: Heightened Security

"Life isn't about waiting for the storm to pass, it's about learning how to dance in the rain." – Vivian Greene

As the day brightened I could see the decks were wet, rain dripping off the eaves. The first ferry was docked at the landing two miles to the east, mist, hanging clouds, scraps caught here and there in the big Douglas firs that cover these islands, no wind, tide out and rock weed exposed in our cove, the Salish Sea outside the windows puckered in a million places except where unseen boats had passed smoothing the water, leaving their own kind of contrail that slowly changed shape as the currents pushed and pulled it, like a trowel passed across wet stucco.

Our neighborhood doe and two fawns made their way around the yard, the doe checking first at Yvonne's compost bins, finding something tasty that hung down from its mouth until her tongue could bring it all inside. One of the fawns grabbed for the overage and the doe drew her head away. You find your own. They browsed salal here and there but showed no sign of heading toward the section of the deer fence that passed through eight foot high salal just west of the house, twice the scene of break-ins. Yvonne had patched the sections of the soft nylon netting with plastic bird webbing. I wanted to add another layer of protection, metal fencing. I now understood what had happened. One or more deer had browsed on the salal that came through the netting from the inside of the fence, inadvertently chewing holes in the netting and pushing on it to reach the tasty looking salal on the other side. At some point they'd chewed enough that that they created a large hole and with their pushing they found themselves inside the fence. From my observations deer aren't clever but they do remember and they'd be back again and again unless prevented.

Three-hundred-thirty-nine: Heightened Security

Two years before mink had invaded our 10 by 20 foot storage tent at the back of our lot, using it as their privy. James and I put a green metal net fencing around the tent and then plastic bird netting between the fence and the tent. For eighteen months the mink stayed out and then found an entry point we couldn't find and kept coming back, Yvonne cleaning up a few times until she decided we'd do better leaving the tent open so we rolled up the door creating a ten feet wide by eight feet high opening to the outside world. Mink like privacy; they hadn't returned so far. I had some ideas about how to keep the door open and the blowing winter rains out, and I'd work on that in the future, but today I'd remove some of the perimeter fencing and move it to protect the 40 feet of deer fencing that passed through the salal that deer had come through. It was no longer needed at the storage tent.

James and I had fastened the five feet high green metal fencing to the ground — so the mink couldn't crawl under it — by pounding stakes into the ground and using fence tie twists to hold the fencing to the stakes. The fencing is clumsy to handle and each end of the first section I worked on tried to grab everything nearby and hold on as I tried to pull it away from the tent. Then when I drew it through the salal it tried to grab the nylon web the deer had been munching. I found my supply of ductile bare wire I'd bought for our house on Cayou Valley Road five or six years before to tie up insulation that was falling from its position between the floor joists in the crawl space. Today I cut pieces to tie the green metal fencing to the white topped green poles I'd put in four years before to hold up the nylon deer fencing and to tie the bottom of the metal fencing to logs that held down the netting. A second section of green metal fencing, about fifteen feet long, from the north side of the storage tent was just the right length to cover the balance of the nylon fencing that passed through the salal. The mesh size of the nylon fencing was about four by four inches and encouraged deer to push their muzzles through, The mesh size of the green metal fencing was two inches by three inches, stiff, and thus much less accommodating. Because the metal fencing was in the salal it wouldn't create visible ugliness, one reason Yvonne had chosen the nylon fencing in the first place. It was almost invisible.

Three-hundred-thirty-nine: Heightened Security

339: Pink, grey, and Bell

In the afternoon I had taken Yvonne over to Orcas for her Rock and Roll Choir practice and had an early dinner of left over turkey chili and then took a walk around Crane. I saw that the door was half open at well house #1 and approaching it that it was locked open. I didn't know the combination to the lock, so I closed the door and propped a rock against it. I'd let Gary know. The tank was at 13 feet — good. A flicker flew past me into the trees. The girdled branches on the huge big leaf maple at Skip's had turned dark brown, the rest of the leaves, especially at the end of lower branches were yellowing with the loss of light. That was normal. The upper part of the tree had been badly damaged, big swaths now dead. I still had no idea what had stripped the bark on this tree and a number of others along Circle Road but where the branches were stripped completely around the branches were now visibly dead. Farther east I saw dead vertical branches as opposed to the mostly horizontal branches I'd been noticing and I thought a little bit about the physics of something having to hold on to the branch and have enough leverage to strip bark. A mystery. When climbing the hill at the north end of the air strip I looked up at Matt's huge tree house that encircled a big Douglas fir, looking for ideas for building one as a Borgfest project next summer, linking it to the existing two level fort with a suspension bridge. A big pileated woodpecker watched me and then flew deftly through the dog's hair that grew up when this section of the island was clearcut in the 50's. It was getting dark. I'd wait for Yvonne to call from Eastsound before she drove back to Deer Harbor and take the *Huginn* over to Orcas to bring her home.

Three-hundred-forty: Harstine Island Rumpus

"Do not go where the path may lead, go instead where there is no path and leave a trail." – Ralph Waldo Emerson

Yvonne was ready early so I walked up the hill to our water meter, opened the metal door in the concrete cover, reached in behind the meter and turned the valve counter clockwise until I hit the stop. Whatever might happen in the next four days at least we wouldn't be responsible for loss of water to the community system. Coming back in the south gate I bungeed the bottom and looped the top to the bamboo frame and then walked to the studio door, locked it from the outside, and then walked up three stairs to the house deck, went in and locked the kitchen door from the inside. I'd already locked the dining room door from the inside. I picked up my small pack with my MacBook Pro, a small, green soft-sided suit case (Yvonne had its twin) we'd gotten on our trip to Africa in 2000, a book bag with card decks and games for our upcoming trip to Ocean Shores with grandchildren Morgan and Opal, and a soft-sided cold storage bag with food for today's drive. Yvonne had her suitcase, purse, and a pack of food. We wouldn't need the dock cart. The *Huginn*'s windows were frosted with dew — in fact the boat was wet everywhere — almost always true of anything sitting above the water overnight on the Salish Sea.

We were about the 20th car in the ferry landing line — there wouldn't be much traffic to America today — and while Yvonne took the path through the open gate in the fence on her way to the Orcas Hotel coffee shop, I walked down to the Market to buy the *Seattle Times*, noticed the new sliding door and complimented Ron on it as he took my dollar for the paper. He commented that he should have put an automatic sliding door in long ago referring to the fact that the pair of manual swinging doors had been hard to open and tried to close before one could get through them. I climbed the stairs and noticed all the rabbits in the vicinity, one hopping past me, nose quivering, and then walked through the fence toward the hotel — past the yard where I officiated Kelly and Tim's marriage ceremony a year ago July, the couple now proud parents of baby Noah — and I noticed a big, white fluffy cat looking at me and eating something on the grass — a headless and earless rabbit. The barista behind the counter acknowledged the carnage outside saying that it had been going on since at least 5:00 a.m. when she came to work. It was all right she said. Not a problem. I wanted to say what about the guests but didn't.

I handed Yvonne the newspaper and she reminded me that though both of us had been on Orcas Wednesday neither had gotten a copy of the latest *Islands' Sounder* so she expected me to have brought one back from the Market with the *Times*. Back down the hill, this time via the Hotel's front stairs. The Tazo Awake tea was just the right temperature when I sat down with Yvonne in the coffee shop.

On the *Yakima* we walked up to the galley level, the second floor of passenger seating, and picked a table on what would be the south side of the boat as it cruised to Anacortes by way of Shaw Island across Harney Channel. Then Ruthie on her way to a doctor's appointment joined us and then Howard on his way to pick up his sister coming from England at SeaTac, both welcome and both unexpected. Ruthie began recruiting me for a collaborative literature class on Orcas to begin in January. She was considering teaching Aeschylus' *Oresteia*, three dark plays connected with the Trojan War as one session. What did I want to teach? Her mention of the *Oresteia* reminded me of the Dreyfus-Kelly book *All Things Shining* and I suggested to Ruthie that it might be a way to focus the class and used the iPad to find its catalog listing on Amazon, pointing to the subtitle "Reading the Western Classics to Find Meaning in a Secular Age" and we went on to look at the Table of Contents and to talk about Homer, Aeschylus, Augustine, Kant, Melville, and David Foster Wallace, me pointing out that the book had defects but was suggestive and a way to provide a theme for the class. We agreed to meet before Thanksgiving with others who might want to do a class session on one of these authors or another that fit into the overall *All Things*

Shining theme. Howard and Yvonne talked first about Gail Collins' *When Everything Changed*, and then about women's situation generally and the difficulty men had understanding it from the inside.

340: Noah, Yvonne, Morgan. Natasha, Opal

From Anacortes to Edmonds I talked with Yvonne about what I now saw as the opportunities and near term tasks for eNotated Classics — the way Co-ment filled a crucial need, about the January MLA convention where we'd have a booth, about my thoughts of offering a classics library, an eNotated subset, an on-reserve service, and a teacher-student annotation and ebook creation teaching tool — all connected and all feeding off one another, individual books for sale but everything else a subscription service sold especially to academic libraries. She liked the concept but pointed out that in the past when I built a business around a set of ideas — at the intersection of unrealized need with emerging technology — I had an infrastructure I could immediately make use of. I couldn't do this all myself. Of course. I'd need help and money but until the last few weeks I thought the project was too vague to justify seeking help beyond what David, Chris, and Jens were providing. Now, it seemed to me, I could put a prototype of the business together for the MLA show, offering the service as a beta test, for free for the next year, and look at bringing in early, angel funding once we'd proven ourselves at the MLA. She pointed out we'd need a professional looking booth, materials, computers for demonstrations, and so on, what I hadn't thought much about. David, Chris, Jens (via Skype) and I would meet October 14th to go over an outline for the MLA convention that I'd prepare. That would get the process started.

Having taken the Edmonds-Kingston ferry to the Olympic Peninsula, our normal route to Harstine Island, home of our son Noah and family, we planned to stop first at a small housing development just south of historic Silverdale and then do a little shopping just north of it in a big commercial area. The development consisted of seven cottages, all about 1500 square feet, four on one side, three on the other, the rows facing one another except that the houses were sited at an angle so each had some view of the water. Beach access, a small community building, seven attached garages and parking close to the street, and extensive landscaping completed the development. Someday we expected to move from Crane, maybe to Eastsound, maybe someplace else closer to our family and we wanted to understand what the alternatives looked like. This cottage development, one of a series done by the developer over many years was very attractive and physically at least a place we'd be happy to live. After some Costco and Target business we continued on our way and arrived on Harstine Island about 5:30.

The day had been surprisingly warm for late September or any time in this part of the world so we all sat outside on the deck enjoying the improved view of Pickering Passage because Noah and Natasha had employed some arborists to trim a few Douglass firs and cedars on the bank above the water that obstructed their view. They had just listed their house with Windermere and had had one showing so far and hoped for but didn't expect a quick sale given the current real estate market. They'd looked at houses to buy in Steamboat, much closer to Olympia, Noah's work and the kids' school, and presumably to where Natasha would be working. Natasha had interviewed several places and had been the semi-finalist out of 108 in one case but she expected this process to take some time as well. Morgan, 10, and Opal, 6, were all energy, noise, and enthusiasm, excited about our taking them to the ocean the next day. We ate dinner on the deck outside as well, homemade lasagna, talking until it grew too dark. Noah showed me the major repairs he'd made to the deck and then when we were inside brought us a fat white three ring binder with his finished novel in it. Would we be willing to read it? Of course. He'd been struggling to find an agent and had had good response from several who enjoyed the book but thought its prospects not sufficiently commercial. We talked too about our good tenants on Grant Street who had given notice and intended to move out because he had lost his job. Natasha would find out whether our providing a free month or reduced rent would help them adequately with their financial bind.

Three-hundred-forty-one: Ocean Shores

"The sea is as near as we come to another world." – Anne Stevenson

Natasha went off to work early in the morning, Noah served Opal some frosted flakes and me oatmeal for breakfast and then he and I talked about his book — from the point of view of self-publishing it in electronic and paper (print on demand) format. Frustrated with the conventional publishing path, he was interested, and happy to provide me the Word file that contained the book. I showed him Co-ment and explained how I'd put his book up on that service and create annotations that he could then look at and make changes, if he chose, to either the Co-ment or his Word original, and that I'd then create MOBI, EPUB, and PDF (for printing) versions.

Before 10:00 we were packed and ready to go, the kids in the backseat of our new Focus — which they liked a lot — their boogie boards in the trunk with their wetsuits and clothes, Opal's doll Carisa less than a arm's length away. We took a shortcut to 101 from Route 3 going through McCleary, a mill town like all the others in western Washington that had seen better days. We were south of the Olympics, the landscape flat with some rolling hills, dense with fir, cedar, alder, and some maple growing in luxurious profusion, the area receiving twice the rain we enjoyed on Crane Island. Some swaths had been clear cut, stumps and a few seed trees remaining, others ten or twenty years into regeneration. The trees here, opposed to the San Juans, looked picture perfect, not having had to struggle with rocky ground, wind, and drought.

Aberdeen, at the upper end of Gray's Harbor, and Hoquiam immediately adjacent had been trying for years to stay alive, the disappearance of the mills and the near demise of fishing having clobbered these once thriving towns, Aberdeen claiming the late Kurt Cobain, of Nirvana, the father of Seattle Grunge music and John Elway, always exciting, now retired Denver Bronco quarterback, as its native sons.

Three-hundred-forty-one: Ocean Shores

341.1: Ocean Shores attraction

We'd been to Ocean Shores with Morgan and Opal in October five years before when Opal had begun to walk and talk, but just for the day. Now we'd be staying overnight and would meet Noah and Natasha at the new Hoquiam YMCA with its outstanding water park the next day. Today we had the kids to ourselves. Arriving just before noon and all hungry we picked Our Place as our lunch destination, the same place we'd had lunch the last trip, an authentic Washington, breakfast all day long spot, the kids sharing a cheese burger and Yvonne and me a Denver omelette with a large pancake on the side. We were all looking forward to a round of miniature golf and were pleased with the 36 hole course that Ocean Shores offered. Though a little windy, the day wasn't cold and though we wore jackets most of the other putt-putt golfers wore t-shirts and shorts. Morgan had played before and had an aptitude for the game, scoring well when he took his time. Yvonne did as well, acing the 16th hole, a complicated one with a big rock in the center of the fairway in front of the cup. Opal struggled to understand how to hold the club and where to put her feet but like the rest of us had a very good time.

We'd seen a few families riding bicycle surreys and stopped there next. Morgan and I pedaled, Morgan steered, Yvonne sat in the center, and Opal in a basket in front of us. Going first two blocks west to the beach we found it easy to go down hill on the packed sand over which countless cars had driven (on this beach at least, autos were welcome and common) but once we were on the beach proper pedaling was a great deal of work if even possible so we left the beach and pedaled a bit around the bike and moped rent shop and within twenty minutes of starting our cycling we were happy to turn it in. Since I had done a little riding the previous week I managed to hold my own but Morgan not much more than half my weight was the spark plug.

After checking in at the Shiloh Inn right on the beach, our third floor room providing a good view of the dunes, beach, surf, and endless ocean, the kids put on their wetsuits, we retrieved their boogie boards from the car, and we walked on a path through the dunes' vegetation to the beach. The wind was out of the south and blowing hard, big colorful kites taunt on their tethers and the first six inches above the beach was a blizzard of blowing sand. These Washington beaches are almost flat, the space between the water and the farthest travel of a wave 50 yards or more. That meant that Morgan, in order to catch a wave, would have to wade out a good distance from where Yvonne and I stood, higher than the highest wave, though the water came only halfway up his legs. Opal didn't venture into the waves but waited in the alternately wet and dry area to flop her boogie board down. Not comfortable with Morgan so far away, I took off my shoes, rolled up my pant legs, and waded into the shallow surf between Morgan and Opal keeping an eye on both, Yvonne watching all three of us and taking pictures. The water was cold but not painful though my pant legs were soon soaked. Opal managed some short rides on the surf up the beach but Morgan, watching for the biggest waves had some 100 foot rides, delighting himself and us and Yvonne reported later many people on

Three-hundred-forty-one: Ocean Shores

the beach who were watching him, themselves unwilling to enter the water. Yvonne and I were impressed with Opal and Morgan, who hadn't wanted to go to the beach but finally acquiesced at Opal's insistence. Intrepid.

341.2: Morgan seeks the surf

341.3: Morgan and Opal warm up in the jacuzzi

Back at the hotel we all went downstairs to the pool and spent half an hour warming up in the Jacuzzi, the kids in the pool most of the time. We'd seen a pizza restaurant nearby and went there for dinner, sharing a twelve inch, half just cheese, which the kids devoured, and half their Sicilian recipe that Yvonne and I consumed. Back in the hotel room we played Crazy Eights, Black Jack, with fruit treats and chips, and then Go Fish. The hotel TV/Movie system was offering a Wimpy Kid movie so we got ready for bed and watched it though I fell asleep halfway through. What fun we had!

Three-hundred-forty-two: Running on Empty?

"What good is the warmth of summer, without the cold of winter to give it sweetness?" – John Steinbeck

Yvonne, Morgan, and Opal slept until after 8:00 — with two interruptions I was almost oblivious to: first Opal got teary about missing her mother and when Morgan's efforts failed to comfort her he came to me and tapped me on the shoulder but it was Yvonne who got up to sooth Opal. Later, I understand, Opal needed a drink of water and Yvonne fetched it, these experiences reminding Yvonne of the challenges of raising children and her thankfulness that she'd already done that. Then there was the question of breakfast. Opal was in a very grumpy mood, not unusual for her first thing in the morning. Rather than get everyone ready, it made more sense to Yvonne that I go out and bring food back — but what did the little darlings want — Morgan an Egg McMuffin and milk, Opal a cinnamon roll, Cocoa Puffs and juice and Yvonne egg, cheese, and bacon on a bagel and a latte. The wind, at gale force outside, blew intermittent rain. First the bakery, then McDonald's, then Tulley's and then the IGA market for a ten pack of little Kellogg cereal boxes. That worked and within minutes everyone was in a good mood having a good time. Yvonne called Natasha. We'd meet at the YMCA in Hoquiam at 11:30. They'd take the kids and spend a few hours at the water park in the new Y. Yvonne and I would drive north, our destination Port Angeles. As it turned out Noah and Natasha were about 30 minutes late but that gave Yvonne and me a chance to pick up lunch at Subway in Hoquiam. We'd had such fun with Morgan and Opal we were sorry to have to give them back to their parents but Natasha told Yvonne they were available for pickup any time.

Three-hundred-forty-two: Running on Empty?

342: Huge, ancient cedar - host for other big trees

We drove north out of Hoquiam on Route 101 in the rain noticing how high the Hoquiam river was, one of two, the other the Chehalis, that fed Grays Harbor, the big bay interrupting the Washington coast with Ocean Shores on the north and West Port, the fishing town, on the south. Thirty-five miles north we turned off the highway to look at the lodge on Lake Quinault on the edge of the rain forest, a place Yvonne and I had visited about 30 years earlier and with Jen, Noah, and Eric a few years after that to walk with them among the huge trees, eight and ten feet across and 300 feet high, firs and cedars a thousand years old irrigated by about 150 inches of rain a year. Farther north, after entering the Olympic National Forest we turned off the highway again to view a huge cedar at least fifteen feet across that though still alive was the nurse tree to a big fir that had taken root in the cedar about thirty feet off the ground, and bushes, and a variety of other vegetation. Not much

Three-hundred-forty-two: Running on Empty?

farther north we stopped at Ruby Beach, reminiscent of the Oregon coast because of the tall sea stacks that were just off the beach, though this scene was wilder and more serious seeming, the climate cooler and perhaps stormier. Farther north we paused at Kalaloch Lodge above another wonderful beach and then leaving the National Forest followed the highway inland through a heavily logged area of clearcut, second, third, and fourth growth forest, passing through Forks, bigger and more prosperous than I'd expected, with signs here and there taking advantage of the *Twilight* book and film phenomenon. Past Sappho where Route 113 splits off to meet the Straight of Juan de Fuca coast and provide access to Cape Flattery and Neah Bay, the northwestern-most point in the lower 48 states, where the terrain grows very steep in a succession of ridges, huge wrinkles in the surface of the Peninsula soon leading to Lake Crescent, about twelve miles long, impressive and beautiful with the steep mountain sides rising right out of the clear blue green water. Just before the lake we turned off the highway to look at the entrance to the Sol Doc Hot Springs Lodge but decided not to go in the twelve miles. Farther long Route 101 we turned off the highway to inspect Lake Crescent Lodge, another place we might return to in the future, perhaps with friends. We passed the turn off to Elwha dam, its removal begun just days earlier and high above it a visitor would now see the blue empty water of Juan de Fuca and then we were in Port Angeles.

For Yvonne our primary destination for the day was Hurricane Ridge, a mile high point to view the Olympics to the south and Juan de Fuca to the north. The miles to empty gauge on the dash of our new Focus showed 60. The Hurricane Ridge summit was seventeen miles up hill. I thought about stopping for gas but we were at the turn before I saw a station so we drove south, stopping at the gate, where I showed my National Park lifetime pass and I noticed that miles to empty was dropping rapidly. It made sense that we'd use more gas going up hill but then we'd use much less coming down again so my concern didn't turn into alarm until the gauge dropped into the teens. Yvonne kept asking what we were going to do and I talked vaguely about coasting downhill (I'd noticed that the road had been uphill all the way), something I thought we could do safely as long as the engine was running. Within a mile and a half of the summit the gauge had dropped to two miles to empty. Uh oh! We were about to enter clouds so there wouldn't be a view but once we turned around Yvonne was hoping we'd stop at a pullout to admire the view, but anxious now, I vetoed the idea. We were coasting downhill now and I didn't want to stop for anything.

Soon the miles to empty display showed zero. The gas gauge was pinned to empty. But the engine hadn't quit. The car was in neutral, the engine idling, using only a small amount of gas. It stayed on zero through the gate, five miles above Port Angeles, and I had to shift into drive because the road was flat for a hundred yards, did the same at another point further on and then we were at a stoplight coming into town. I used the engine to make the turn, and we were on a downhill course again, in neutral. Yvonne had found the nearest gas station, on 2nd street and I made that turn in gear and then used the engine twice more to get us parked at a pump at the Arco station six blocks down the road, and still downhill. We'd made it! Yvonne commented that this had been one of the most stupid things we'd done and though I agreed I pointed out that no harm had been done and that we now had a teaching story to tell on ourselves. She thought that less of an asset that I did.

I hadn't been convinced that the tank was actually empty. Our Ford van had about a gallon and a half when it showed empty. I was curious about how much gas the car would take. Just over eleven gallons. Since the tank held 12.4 gallons we had almost a gallon and a half in reserve. That was good to know. But why had the gallons to empty read out fallen so precipitously on our uphill leg? Were we really using three, four, or five times as much gas per gallon as usual? Or was the onboard computer mistaken? Did the program have a bug?

We checked into the Olympic Lodge and were favorably impressed and then drove out the spit protecting the harbor to the Coast Guard station gate, looked north to find the San Juans and thought the small lump on the horizon was Mt Constitution on Orcas. Looking south at Port Angeles and the steep ridge behind the city we couldn't see the Olympics but the sky had cleared and the wind abated. We parked close to Fountain Square and walked to the Bella Italia restaurant and liked it immediately, Yvonne having prawns and me spaghetti.

We'd been through Port Angeles once before on a rainy day coming from Victoria on the Coho Black Ball Ferry and didn't remember much about it. Yvonne's book group had read a recent novel that made it seem small, gritty, and redneck and she didn't see that at all. I talked about Raymond Carver's association with the town. We both liked it and understood why people would live here on the narrow strip of land between the Straight and the mountains. And we talked about the fun we had with Morgan and Opal. After soaking in a big spa outside in back of the hotel next to the pool we read for a while but not long. A big day. An interesting day.

Three-hundred-forty-three: Windy Return

"Let us step into the night and pursue that flighty temptress, adventure." – J.K. Rowling

The evening sky had been cloudless but the morning showed itself wet and windy. Outside the breakfast room at the Olympic Lodge, a foursome, each with his own golf cart, played right to left one fairway away from the fence separating the Lodge from the Peninsula Golf Club, none wearing anything resembling a rain coat. Yvonne went easy on breakfast, sharing her single pancake and helping herself to one of my over easy eggs and some fried potatoes.

Backtracking, we stopped first at the Olympic National Park visitors center at the foot of the Hurricane Ridge Road. The real time "Ridge Cam" showed the Ridge socked in; we wouldn't drive to the summit this morning, trying to accomplish what we'd failed at the afternoon before. We got directions to the lower Elwah dam and bought a bird guide we could use at home and a book on Peninsula history as well as instructions from the ranger on how to find the lower Elwah dam to view the removal project that had begun only a few days earlier. Backtracking even further we drove past the dam parking lot and then pulled into a Private Road to turn around, Yvonne noticing that a sign read "Dorothea Morgan." Morgan's great grandma and his grandpa Gene lived here. What a coincidence. Parking in the dam lot, we walked a few hundred yards south on a wide path in the blowing rain, intermittent heavy equipment noise coming through the forest that separated us from the river. At the overlook we could see the parts of the lower dam through the trees but not much. Yvonne explained that we were here for historic reasons. This was the first dam on the Peninsula that was being removed, now too expensive to maintain given the power it could produce and to allow the salmon to return and the river to feed its nutritive silt to the marine life where it emptied into the Straight of Juan de Fuca.

Passing back through Port Angeles eastbound, we turned off on the Old Olympic Highway, and drove east and north to the Dungeness Spit, a National Wildlife Refuge, and the world's longest natural sand spit, a place to hike and bird. The countryside had changed from the Port Angeles area, forest that rose almost immediately into the Olympic peaks, here flat with occasional wind breaks but mostly open, houses set far apart on five acre lots and to our eyes not at all attractive or interesting. Unlike Port Angeles to the west or Port Townsend to the east, the town of Sequim had no particular sense of identity or style, consisting for the most part as far as we could see of a number of exclusive retirement subdivisions, some built around golf courses. Sequim was legendary because of its low annual rainfall but it wasn't much lower than the two real towns on either side since the big change, and quite noticeable, was the transition from a heavy rainfall to a light area that happened west of Port Angeles over a remarkably short distance.

On the way out of Sequim (pronounced, "sqium"), we looked at the John Wayne marina in Seqium Bay, the land donated by the actor's family. Given that Sequim Bay adjoins the Straight of Juan de Fuca, a place we think of as often dangerous for small boats, Yvonne and I wondered how often the boats in the marina were or could be taken out into the big water nearby.

Driving south out of the Sequim area, now again through forest, today facing strong southerly winds, we saw traffic snarled ahead. I thought first it might be an accident and then realized that a tree had come down across the highway leaving only one lane, to our left, that had to be shared by cars going in each direction. One man, dressed in Carhardt overalls, was working to clear debris from the road. I pulled over and joined him and then two more grey heads joined us but of the hundred or so cars that passed in the next ten minutes none seemed to have the time or inclination to pitch in. The tree, a maple, healthy as far as I could tell, had been shattered by its contact with the highway with few pieces too heavy for one person to lift.

Three-hundred-forty-three: Windy Return

343: Volunteers clear highway south of Sequim

Port Townsend is north and east of Sequim but can only be reached by first driving south around the foot of Discovery Bay and then north and east again. Rediscovered by hippies in the 60s, Port Townsend guards Admiralty Inlet, the entrance to Puget Sound from the Straight of Juan de Fuca, Fort Worden once part of the Coast artillery, now a park and conference center and in 1982 a location for the Winger/Gere film Yvonne and I enjoyed so much, *An Officer and a Gentleman*. Victorian Port Townsend built to be a railroad terminus that never materialized is a major tourist destination for the Peninsula and had hosted its annual film festival a few days before featuring Buck Henry. After reconnoitering Water Street we chose Water Street Crepes for lunch and I ordered their Mexican crepe, ate half and later had the balance for dinner, Yvonne doing the same with her ham, cheese, and spinach model. While Yvonne visited two clothing boutiques, I spent time in the Imprint Bookstore, well stocked with hundreds I wished I had time to read, picking out a history of philosophy that made digesting its hard topics easier through its graphic presentation and then Raymond Carver's *A New Path to the Waterfall*, written shortly before his death in 1988 and edited by his wife, Tess Gallagher.

Fort Worden and the nearby lighthouse were nearly deserted, the gale force winds blowing up Puget Sound, driving nearly everyone indoors. Yvonne, concerned that the ferry might be interrupted by the weather suggested we try for an earlier departure than the 3:45 reservation we'd made. While having lunch in the creperie, we'd seen the ferry out of place and apparently being driven by the winds toward the rocky shore. The locals, with us, stared out the big plate glass windows at what looked like an impending disaster. The booth attendant told us that ferry service had been temporarily suspended but since we had no choice but to get to Whidbey Island and then drive to Anacortes, we parked in line and both fell asleep waiting. At about 3:15, after a 45 minute wait the *Chetzemoka* began to load passengers and vehicles and we drove aboard looking forward to inspecting this new addition to the Washington fleet. We'd seen the superstructure of its twin, the *Salish*, under construction at Langley, in the spring when we'd spent the weekend on Whidbey Island. Cruising out of Port Townsend, the ferry was buffeted by wind and high waves and we could see the Coast Guard heading southeast on a parallel course perhaps to stand by for the Chetzemoka or the *Salish* that we could see had already left Keystone on Whidbey Island. The captain took the ferry south to get behind Marrowstone Island, out of the wind, and then turned north again toward Keystone. With the tide now at ebb wind and water were moving the same direction so the waves rarely reached six feet but did come over the bow occasionally, at one point drenching the big window we looked through perhaps 25 feet above the Sound. The ferry service had been suspended, we learned, because the flood tide, running against the wind, had piled up waves Washington State Ferries decided would make the trip unsafe or at least uncomfortable for the passengers. Now, finally underway, the captain, over the loudspeakers, advised the pas-

Three-hundred-forty-three: Windy Return

sengers to stay out of the elevator and be careful walking the decks while underway.

The drive to Anacortes took about an hour, few cars in line for the 6:30 sailing to Shaw and Orcas that turned into a 7:15 departure. We spent most of the time in the car reading, having eaten our crepe leftovers in the ferry line. It was after 9:00 before we got home and almost immediately got into the hot tub. We'd had a big day.

Three-hundred-forty-four: More Wood

The simple hearth of the small farm is the true center of our universe." – Masanobu Fukuoka

Overnight the sky had cleared and the wind had dropped but the mild temperatures remained. As I walked out the south gate in the early morning light I could see that the ground was blanketed in brown fir needles and small green branches — but nothing big. The floor of the storage tent was a little wet near the open entrance, open to keep the mink out since they like privacy. I'd need to do something to protect the opening from the November and December storms. On Eagle Lane I noticed that Gary had finally finished the hydrant there. The doors to well house #1 were now properly locked and I now had a key to the six well houses and the water system storage room in the community center. Gary had left it in the *Huginn* while we were traveling, wired to the steering wheel. The tank level was a bit over 13', just right, and Gary had backfilled over the new piping he'd put in to connect well house #4 with the main line on the other side of Circle Road. I could check these items off the water system to-do list. On the other hand, there was still no sign of a meter at Larry's lot and the Sunnyside hydrant hadn't yet appeared. The island was very quiet, appearing deserted but it wasn't. Jim and Nancy, Tom and Liz, and Lou were at home and as it turned out, CeAnn was up from Bainbridge Island supervising repairs to their decks.

We'd bought a package of maple-look laminate flooring at the Silverdale Costco on sale with the thought that we might replace the living room carpet and the adjacent dining room, kitchen, and hallway hickory-look laminate and by the time I returned from my walk Yvonne had already opened the package and laid panels down here and there for color comparisons. The new flooring looked nice but we concluded independently that it didn't work for the house. The color was too light next to the white-wash kitchen cabinets and too similar to all the cherry bookcases we had in the living room. We were disappointed. I suggested we bring out the bamboo flooring we'd bought several years back to see whether it might make sense, in perhaps a different shade but the new flooring excitement had faded. We wouldn't be doing anything soon about the living room (and perhaps other) floor(s).

344: Outside Yvonne's garden above Raven Cove

Yvonne reported that the 75 gallon water tank was full and she suspected the 450 gallon tank also now had significant water but complained that the water pressure from the latter was inadequate to push water out through the small holes in the soaker hose she was trying to use with the bigger tank. I had no suggestions.

Three-hundred-forty-four: More Wood

The mail we collected from the Post Office the night before returning from our Peninsula trip contained five Crane Island Association completed annual bills and payments so I processed them through QuickBooks. I'd collected about $20,000 so far, nearly a quarter of our expected revenue, and expected most of the balance to appear within the next few days, before the end of September. Three bills were awaiting payment so I processed those as well and printed the checks for mailing, not yet able to do electronic banking.

Yvonne had begun work on the Garden Club Yearbook and couldn't find last year's Pages source file she'd use for this next generation so I used Spotlight to locate it and a bit later, when Yvonne wasn't working on this project, I made a CD backup of all her files and then created seven new folders on her desktop and sorted all her files on the old iMac into one or the other of them and explained what I'd done, hoping that she'd be less frustrated with a more orderly arrangement.

The weather was beautiful but wouldn't last and besides I wanted to have the Ford F150 back on Orcas to use so it made sense to pick up more firewood on the island now. I drove first to well house #4, backing in close to the little building and cut up most of the silver fir that had fallen near the door last spring and dumped it into the bed of the truck and then parked in Circle Road near its intersection with Eagle Lane, about a quarter mile from our house and cut up two good sized silver firs that had fallen the previous fall, suspended above the ground by their own branches or other trees and thus not rotting as quickly as they would if in contact with the ground. I wasn't enthusiastic about the silver fir because I suspected it wouldn't burn well and wouldn't create much heat but it was available and dry. As I worked I saw someone through the trees walk up Eagle Lane and turn the corner on to Circle Road, CeAnn as it turned out, and she told me about the trouble she was having with their old SUV on the island, apparently the result of a bad starter that husband, Howard, would replace when he came up in a few weeks. In the meanwhile their decks were being repaired. By the time I finished with the two trees, I had filled the bed of the pickup above the level of the sides, the wood scavenging process having taken three hours. Unlike the week before when it had been very dry I was not pestered by yellow jackets. Perhaps their season was over.

Walking to the house from where I'd parked the truck I saw that the back gate was open and Yvonne wasn't in sight but as I approached the gate I saw that she was working at her pond using a handled colander to sift out fir needles floating on the top of the pond, blown there by the past day's big wind. We were both happy to be back home working outdoors, the air inextricably aromatic, a fragrance like mushrooms Yvonne observed. With no or few flowers blooming it was certainly a byproduct of some kind of organic process, the rotting of everything dead around us being recycled into new life.

Three-hundred-forty-five: To Town

"What you do makes a difference, and you have to decide what kind of difference you want to make." – Jane Goodall

First hints of dawn and the sun's rising seemed to take forever on this cool morning, 46°, Tuesday's heat having leaked away into the cosmos overnight under a cloudless sky. And though by afternoon the thermometer in the Focus told me the outside temperature was only 62°, it felt much warmer. I was late leaving Crane for Orcas and even with sunglasses could hardly see because of the glare of sun on the water directly in my path and I was happy that logs in the water were rare this time of year, much more common in the winter when higher winter tides driven by high winds lift logs off the beaches and carry them out into the Salish Sea until they find another resting place.

The previous Wednesday my bike ride from the Crane Island parking lot to Howard's in Deer Harbor had taken eighteen minutes; today by car only four but I was ten minutes late anyway. Walking along Howard's garden I especially noticed the huge, perfect cabbages that begged to be picked and made into coleslaw or perhaps stuffed and baked. Chris was on one of the couches, Howard on a chair and offered me a cup of strong black tea as I sat down, the little space heater warming the room against the morning cold. Neither David nor Brian appeared this morning and hadn't recently, Brian because he had so much trouble walking, and David, I didn't know why. I'd have to ask him. I told about how Yvonne and I had taken Morgan and Opal to Ocean Shores and what Yvonne and I had seen driving up the Peninsula Coast and how surprised I was at the beauty of Ruby Beach and La Push, which we didn't see. Howard told a tale of coming into the La Push harbor at night, dangerous even by day because it's necessary to approach it parallel to the beach thus subjecting the boat to severe rocking as it passes through the trough of the waves, never a recommended procedure because of the danger of broaching, that is turn over. He and his shipmates radioed the local Coast Guard three times to guide them into the the harbor, something they're supposed to do but Howard and shipmates had no reply and found out the next morning that the on duty officer had been asleep. Responding to my story about apparently running out of gas ascending Hurricane Ridge Chris told stories about finding his boat's tank needle pinned when returning from Speiden Island though he and Lynn made it to Deer Harbor — and how he had coasted into gas stations totally out of fuel. At least foolishness had company.

Leaving Howard's after making arrangements to meet Chris later at the Library to talk about eNotated Classics, I drove Deer Harbor Road to Crow Valley Road behind a van obeying the speed limit but let myself relax and enjoy the morning and the pleasure of driving the well-handling little Focus. At the lumber yard I looked for spitting wedges in the tool section, and not finding them, asked for help and was directed to the garden department. I needed two for the log splitting I'd be doing off and on fall, winter, and spring and now had only one, the cast aluminum one I'd badly chipped from too many sledge hammer blows, that I suspected it wasn't designed to suffer, probably intended for felling trees not splitting. I found a black steel model like the reliable wedge I had at home and picked out two yellow plastic Oregon wedges as well, that I'd use, in imitation of John's technique, the next time I needed to fell a tree. I was a little disappointed not to have more to shop for at the lumber yard, a favorite place.

I'd intended to drop off the ten gallon propane tank that had run out of gas the day before (I had two more, filled, at home) but the attendant at Crescent Service appeared at the big propane tank quickly so I just waited the few minutes it took him to fill the tank and put it into the truck. At KeyBank I spent about half an hour talking with Patti about the Crane Island accounts and safe deposit box or boxes. She explained exactly what I needed to complete the account signers forms and confirmed we had a box at the Friday Harbor branch and that the Crane Island Nature Preserve had one at the Eastsound branch. Now in my fifth year on the Crane Island Association Board, we'd talked off and on about the safe deposit boxes, no one quite sure what was in them or who had the keys. I had promised the Board at the last meeting that I'd find out and I was getting closer. I remembered to buy the *Islands' Sounder* and the *Seattle Times* at Island Market for Yvonne, the parking lot no longer filled as it had been in the summer.

345: Early sun texture

Three-hundred-forty-five: To Town

At Islanders Bank I dropped off the completed account application forms from Dan, Martha, and me and confirmed what else I needed to provide to open an Crane Association account here, primarily a list of the officers I could get from past meeting minutes and an official document with our tax ID. Once the account was created the bank would prepare signature cards to be circulated amongst the three of us. Lynn was at the desk in the Library, volunteering as she did every Wednesday morning but Chris hadn't returned from a computer problems call so after she handed me a copy of *When Everything Changed* to take to Yvonne to give to a young woman of Yvonne's choice, I visited with Phil, Library Director, who told me Tom was mending from his heart attack though the stent hadn't done the job on its own so he'd had to return to the hospital for an angioplasty. Phil invited me to the Library public budget hearing the next Tuesday morning but I declined, telling him I would wait to see whether Tom, who had asked Lois and me for advice, followed up. Then Chris appeared and we spent the next hour in the Library conference room talking through my emerging vision for the business, our appearance to come at the MLA January meeting in Seattle, getting help from Susan for the website, and finding a web server expert to provide the technical help neither one of us had. He'd talk to Randy about the two interns at OPALCO. He wasn't interested in eNotating *Moby Dick* as a sailing/whaling book but did think that doing Joyce's *Ulysses* as an Orcas community project had merit, especially from a marketing point of view. His question: could it be done with a leaderless group?

Back home, after stopping at the post office to leave off and pick up, and after a late lunch, I donned my Carhardt overalls and drove the F150 to the Crane Community Center where I'd had my eye on another silver fir that had fallen less than a year before and looked promising as a source of fire wood, something my chain saw confirmed as I made my first cut. Cutting and loading the logs into the bed of the pickup didn't take long and once back home I carted the wood to the front yard near the saw buck to add to the pile I'd created from the cutting and hauling I'd done the day before, about enough for five weeks burning in the wood stove. I fetched a tarp from the storage tent and covered this new

Three-hundred-forty-five: To Town

pile against the coming rain and re-stacked the bark pile and covered it with a tarp as well, intending to chip the bark some time in the indefinite future. By 5:30 I was done and ready to come in for dinner.

Yvonne reported that Larry had called wanting a copy of the spreadsheet she'd created for the Food Bank fund drive so he could record the donations coming in, the PO Box stuffed full this morning with $4700 so far. Yvonne explained that she and Bev would track the donations and report to him. He didn't have to take that on. She was delighted that the appeal she'd written and the process she'd created and managed showed so much success so quickly. She'd done a great job. Now she was working on the Garden Club annual year book and using last year's Pages file as a template had almost completed the new file, needing only confirmation that her membership list was complete. She's also taken a walk around the island that I couldn't join because I wanted to finish my wood cutting and hauling project. She'd also baked two beautiful loaves of one hour whole wheat bread and an apple pie and then cheese enchiladas covered with her homemade green chili sauce but she felt she hadn't done enough for the day. Trying to reach Cresi again she found that the phone number she had wasn't working. She wanted to take the high school senior, her grand niece, to look at colleges, something the young woman wanted to do but didn't have the resources for but now Yvonne couldn't reach her.

Coming soon: I no longer needed the pickup on Crane. It was time to make arrangements to move it back to Orcas.

Three-hundred-forty-six: Dirty Job

> *"To me, a lush carpet of pine needles or spongy grass is more welcome than the most luxurious Persian rug."* – Helen Keller

After breakfast and after catching up on the introduction of the Kindle Fire online, the risen sun and fine morning invited me outside for a walk around the island. I took my camera — because you never know — and I hadn't gone far, just to my usual left turn on Circle road, and I saw that the sun was visible straight through the forest here and there making those particular spots look like they were on fire. I'd seen this phenomenon before — it was especially striking at the summer solstice when we spent the sunset at the west end of the island with Ken and Kate who had come over from Deer Harbor for dinner — so I took some telephoto shots. The tank was at 13′ — good — and when I descended the other side of the little hill next to the barn and could see the meadow, the morning had set up another shot for me: ground fog had risen off the meadow to about ten feet and behind it the sun, the forest on fire, filtered through the trees. Then I saw almost nothing the rest of my walk — partly because I was thinking about eNotated Classics and partly because there were no deer, birds, people or other wildlife to bring me out of my reverie.

Later Dan called to say he'd come up from Issaquah and had scheduled the Mud Puppy (the barge that Gary and Wilma recently sold to Phillip) for Friday afternoon to take the fire truck off Crane and to the Orcas fire station for maintenance. Would I pick him up at the station early in the day when he dropped his pickup off so that he could return home to America? Of course. I told him I was looking to take my pickup off the island and we talked about whether it would fit with the fire truck. Phillip then called responding to a voice mail I'd left him two days before and said he was confident both would fit. Thirty-eight feet were available in the bed of the converted landing craft. I told him I would measure both trucks and get back to him. When I walked to the fire station I ran into Dan who had the same destination in mind and he helped me measure the length of the fire truck — 21 feet and a few inches. Back home I measured my pickup — 20 feet and a few inches. It wasn't likely both vehicles would fit unless the ramp was down. Having neglected to call Phillip back he followed up later and said they did from time to time operate with the ramp down. I'd have the truck at the concrete ramp on Friday at 3:00 with the prospect of getting it to the ramp at Cayou Quay marina. The tariff? Same as what Gary charged — $150 per hour which I'd split with Crane Island Association.

Yvonne had been disappointed with her lily flower bed against the deer fence just south of the studio deck. It just hadn't produced and she blamed the tree roots that had grown up into the bed of imported top soil. Her plan was to dig the first eight inches out, put down weed block, sift the removed soil, and more from the pile of top soil I'd brought in the truck in June that was hiding under a bright blue tarp next to the forest green tool shed. It was always hard for her to dig and digging was something I'd enjoyed doing as long as I could remember having been happy to spade the garden in the spring for my mother in our yard on Washington Street in Lombard, a Chicago suburb. I shoveled the soil onto a tarp on the deck and Yvonne sifted it into a wheel barrow. I was digging too deep and making too much work for her she said and we agreed on a depth — the height of the blade. She loved to work outdoors, she said, but she was losing her enthusiasm for heavy yard work.

While I loaded cabinet doors into the bed of the pickup in the sunshine near the two shops where they'd been stored since we pulled out the old and put in the new IKEA kitchen the previous fall, Yvonne motioned to me from where she was working next to her pond. A mink had come by, oblivious of human presence as usual, drunk at the pond and then made its way through the barely visible three inch black plastic pipe that drained a low spot on the west side of the driveway to the east side, a small grassy area just above the little pond. A wildlife sighting up close and personal.

Three-hundred-forty-six: Dirty Job

346: Rising sun burns through the forest

Nancy reported that she'd have to decline Yvonne's dinner invitation because Jim wouldn't stop working, having in mind that they'd be leaving in four weeks for the winter and his house and major remodeling were open to the elements. I took Yvonne to Orcas for choir practice about 3:00 and then spent time arranging my Crane Island Treasurer files, having an increasingly clear idea about what mattered and didn't and to help the process began to create an overview of the annual bookkeeping process including what I would need to do (or any Treasurer) and what the accountant would do. I couldn't find the recent years' Federal tax returns or 1099 transmittals and sent four emails off to Pandora asking for help. I was determined to organize the process so that it was foolproof and easy to turn over to someone else.

Three-hundred-forty-six: Dirty Job

After heating up leftover chicken and cheese enchilada leftovers and rice and beans, I opened the envelope from Angel and found signed contracts and a note. She was ready to begin annotating Kipling's *The Man Who Would Be King*. I'd already downloaded the HTML file from Gutenberg and now ran it through a filtering process that built a paragraph database and then exported it in HTML but formatted for import into Co-ment and did that. After a couple go-rounds the Co-ment file looked good. It was ready for Angel so I had Co-ment send her an email to register for the service and an email with additional explanation. The only help file I'd created so far had to do with markdown formatting. I didn't know whether Angel would catch on immediately but suggested she experiment and then we'd talk.

Chris had talked with Randy about our recruiting one or both of the young men that had or were working for OPALCO on their technology and Randy gave his blessing to our talking with them about moonlighting on our project. I'd written Jens about Susan redoing our website, he'd passed the note to her and we were scheduled to talk the next morning. Falling into place?

Three-hundred-forty-seven: Beachcombing Treasure

"A man is rich in proportion to the number of things he can afford to let alone." – Henry David Thoreau

The sunrise this morning was extraordinarily beautiful and I took a dozen pictures that couldn't capture its luminous presence. First I took a telephoto picture of the first ferry, four rows of lights against a black background with a red/purple sky above Mount Woolard and reflected in the still water below. Then I included more of the sky and water so that the complex gray fish scale cloud pattern was visible above and below. straight ahead the double horizon (the second one inverted below the first) was sandwiched by red above and below and then a mottled gray above and below. But it wasn't just the beautiful colors. I felt something as well, something enormous, pervasive, powerful, and expressive.

Not wanting to be late, I left the house by 8:15 and drove into the fire station lot in Eastsound just before 9:00. Dan's pickup was already there, with his canoe inverted and strapped down to take home to repair, but he was inside. As I entered the lobby he invited me in to say hello to Patrick who I'd met on Crane a year and a half before when he'd taught a CPR session and I participated in a mock disaster practice session with Crane folks and paramedics from Orcas — including a rescue helicopter flying in to make the practice authentic.

CeAnn had called Dan before he left Crane to say that Freddy, a friend from Bainbridge Island who was repairing their decks, had hurt his back or at least caused some painful condition to re-emerge and might need to be evacuated. Freddy's wife and a family friend met Dan and me in the Crane Island parking lot on Orcas and I took them and Dan to Crane and let them know I was available. Dan drove them in the rescue vehicle to CeAnn and Howard's house and left it for their use should that become necessary. Later in the day, Yvonne and I saw the two women leaving Crane in CeAnn's aluminum boat on their way to the pharmacy to have a prescription filled.

Just after noon Yvonne went to Orcas for the Friday afternoon knitting group convening at the Deer Harbor Community Club and I worked on an online photo album for the Labor Day weekend when Ron brought Aileen and her sons Icarus and Isa to see Crane and meet us. I was due at the barge ramp next to Dan's house at 3:00 to try to fit my Ford F150 on the *Mud Puppy* with the fire engine Dan would load to drop at the Orcas fire station for maintenance and then get in his truck parked there, get on the next ferry and go home. I'd loaded all the doors from the old kitchen cabinets into the bed of the truck and now added two trash cans, their tops secured with bungee cords, and drove to the barge ramp below the north end of the air strip. Dan had brought the fire engine from the community center and parked it. No sign of the *Mud Puppy*. We chatted and then I noticed an aluminum fishing boat hull half on the gravel beach, ripe to be swept away by the first fall storm. I asked Dan whether he knew the owner and he said he didn't and then I added the observation that whoever owned the boat would lose it. He thought that was fine — because the boat had been adrift and cast up on the beach — no one claiming or wanting it — so it might just as well go someplace else. I'll take it, I said, and he thought that was fine. I'd move it to the community dock later. The two of us put the boat in the water and then towed it to the dock next to the barge ramp and tied it up. Since the barge still wasn't in sight I drove home, picked up the four horse power two-stroke outboard I use with the Ranger sailboat, its fuel supply, a pair of oars, some life vests and drove back to the ramp. We could now see the *Mud Puppy* coming from Deer Harbor a mile and a half away. I mounted the motor on the aluminum boat and loaded the fuel tank, oars, PFDs, and line. I'd come back later to pick it up.

Jake and Matt pulled the *Mud Puppy* up to the ramp and Jake explained that there'd been a miscommunication and they had been waiting for us at the Cayou Quay Marina ramp in Deer Harbor. After Matt put down dunnage so there would be clearance on the ramp for the fire truck while Jake used the engines to hold the barge against the ramp while Dan backed on the fire truck. Then I pulled the F150 head in, putting a piece of plywood I'd brought along between the front bumpers of the fire truck and the F150 to prevent them for damaging each other. Jake raised the ramp part way from the bridge, Matt secured it with a chain and we were underway. I backed off at Cayou Quay, drove to the Crane parking lot on Deer Harbor Road and called Yvonne with my walkie talkie so she could pick me up.

347: Approaching the Cayou Quay ramp in the Mud Puppy

Yvonne walked home to call Cresi in eastern Washington and I walked up Dock Road and then Circle Road to the barge ramp, walked to the dock next door, got in the salvage aluminum boat, started the motor and was on my way to the community dock. I was delighted with how fast the boat would go with the little four horsepower motor and how high the gunnels were. This three bench boat would be comfortable in even somewhat rough water. I set up some mooring lines and fenders to hold the boat to the west side of the eastern arm of the community dock Y and was home by 5:30, Yvonne almost ready to come looking for me.

She had reached Cresi and she'd pick her up in Ephrata Friday morning and they would spend four days looking at colleges. Yvonne was determined to help this young woman help herself. After dinner we walked to the community dock and took the new (old) boat out for a spin. Yvonne wondered about justifying the moorage fee and I said we should try it for a month and see if we used it and save money on fuel since the little motor would use almost none compared with the *Huginn*'s Volvo engine. I could see myself using the new boat to go to Deer Harbor and certainly to the Crane dock on Orcas. Yvonne saw a boat that could hold six we could use to transport the family (along with the *Huginn*) to Jones Island for a picnic. We'd be able to pull the aluminum boat right up on the beach. I was pleased at what the day had brought, having thought for some time that a boat exactly like the one I'd brought home would be a perfect emergency or second use boat for us — and I'd scored it because the *Mud Puppy* was late. The boat was someone's loss but since it had been abandoned on the high seas (at least that's how I saw it) it was available to anyone who took possession. I'd done that.

Three-hundred-forty-eight: First Fire

> *"There is no exquisite beauty... without some strangeness in the proportion."* – Edgar Allan Poe

Our Ford pickup was now back on Orcas in the Crane Island Association lot on Deer Harbor Road. All the cabinet doors Yvonne had removed from our old kitchen cabinets before I took the kitchen apart were in the bed of the truck and two big cans of recycle and one full plastic bag were housed in the back of the cab. It all had to go to the transfer station, the dump as far as we're concerned. And the two cans of trash and plastic bag still in the privy also needed to go to the dump. About 7:00 I took the trash to the community dock in our cart and stashed it in the *Huginn*'s cockpit. Shortly Yvonne was up and ready to go. The transfer station wouldn't open until 10:00 but before then Yvonne wanted to stop at a moving sale someplace in Deer Harbor.

The morning was mild and partly cloudy. It would be a nice day. We'd had almost no wind for several days and the tidal current, though not slack, wasn't very noticeable in the Crane Island harbor. A large swirl of floating bull kelp had worked its way into the "V" where the two fingers of the dock join at the foot of the ramp to the fixed pier that leads ashore and some kind of scum covered the water here and there, part of the life cycle of this watery world. On the Orcas dock I pointed out the five inch wide fish head I'd found in the Pronto, removed, and set on the dock close to the bull rail at the bottom of the aluminum ramp, the eyes staring into infinity and passed on to Yvonne that Wilma had described it as a bottom feeder (its "chin-neck" was grey and flat as a pancake while the rest of the head was a mottled green/brown like seaweed — maybe a rockfish). I was surprised an otter hadn't eaten it overnight but that told me both that the head wasn't good eating and that more food was readily available. Yvonne kicked the head into the water for the crabs.

Three-hundred-forty-eight: First Fire

We each dragged a trash can up the ramp and I carried the trash bag. As we readied the truck, Howard and CeAnn drove into the lot having come from Bainbridge Island this morning and having probably taken the ferry from Kingston to Edmonds, driven to Anacortes and then made the 7:35 ferry. They'd gotten up and going very early. I asked how Freddy was doing. CeAnn didn't know and they hadn't called their Crane house yet this morning. Knowing that their boat was moored on Crane because their friends had been using it, I asked how they'd get across. The *Pronto* maybe. I was glad I'd removed the fish head from the old Boston Whaler row boat. Since they didn't ask for help getting across and since their friends could come and get them, I didn't volunteer to interrupt our moving sale/transfer station process. When we returned to the lot later on, the Pronto was still in its place.

The moving sale was next door to Howard and Sheila, though they had left for a week of rented motorhome cruising in eastern Washington with Howard's older sister who had come for a visit from England and wanted to see more of the American Northwest. The moving sale didn't have much to offer and all that Yvonne could find to buy was a white vinyl three-ring binder and a desk lamp for a total of 75 cents. But then Kate drove up in her green RAV4 and I asked when they were coming for dinner and she and Yvonne talked and decided it would be the next night, Sunday.

The F150 tank was about one-quarter full and that partly the result of my emptying what was left in a five gallon can before driving it to the barge ramp the day before. We had time to kill before the the 10:00 transfer station opening so I drove north on Crow Valley Road to the lumber yard and bought $40 of Passing Gas gasoline (a little more than eight gallons) and we drove to the entrance to the transfer station on Orcas Road (the road from the ferry landing to Eastsound) and parked outside the locked gate, first in line and half an hour early. Yvonne wanted to talk about people who resent others' good fortune or the rewards of hard work and delayed gratification, having felt it from some of her relatives and not happy with their implied or expressed criticism, comparing those experiences with ones we had on Orcas where people of means and those with less seem to get along and even appreciate one

Three-hundred-forty-eight: First Fire

another. I didn't have any wisdom to offer. While dumping our recycle into one of the big green dumpsters, Yvonne suggested that we offer the cabinet doors to the Exchange rather than dump them on the floor of the garbage building (to be plowed into the dumpster below and at the back of the concrete floor.) I suggested she let me finish with the recycle and she take a cabinet door down to the Exchange next door and see if they'd take it. I drove the truck to the space in front of the scale that also leads, to the right, to the Exchange parking area, to wait for Yvonne's signal. No one was behind me. I saw the attendant take the door and display it against the Exchange fence and Yvonne motioned me to drive over. Making a dozen trips or so, we stacked all the doors against the fence and then drove onto the scale, waited for the green light that indicated we'd been weighed "before", backed into the dumping floor building, chasing out a dozen ravens, and left the contents of the cans, bag, and odds and ends. Back on the scale for an "after" reading and then to the attendant's booth to pay the $22 fee, a bargain. At the Deer Harbor Marina, I bought the Saturday and early edition *Sunday Seattle Times* while Yvonne checked our Post Office box across the street. First dropping off Yvonne and the four empty cans in the lower lot, I put the red F150 back in its regular spot in the upper lot, unoccupied since we'd brought the truck to Crane in late June. On Crane I'd cleaned the truck outside and in and though the outside had gotten a bit dirty the inside was pleasant compared with what it had been over the winter, some kind of mold having taken hold especially on the vinyl door pulls, probably because, in part at least, the inside of the truck was too damp. I'd bought a chemical dehumidifier and now opened the plastic bag of white pellets and poured them into the canister and put it into a square bucket that would catch any overflow.

Back on Crane and after lunch Yvonne, on the couch, felt cold. How about a fire? We hadn't had one since May. It was now the first of October. That seemed reasonable. We had a good supply, much better than at any time in the past, so I brought in a basket of wood from the front porch with some cedar kindling and noticed that the fire starting gell wouldn't flow in its plastic bottle so I found some alcohol in the bathroom, poured about a cup full in and shook the gel until it mixed.

Three-hundred-forty-eight: First Fire

348: Orchard remains

The fire made the house cosy and Yvonne was soon at work on her knitting, sitting in her wicker chair facing the water, having started a scarf at the first fall session of the Deer Harbor Community Club knitters the day before. I sat in my wicker chair next to the wood stove finishing work on a photo album of our previous weekend's trip to the Peninsula with Morgan and Opal, having finished one for Labor Day and Ron, Aileen, Icaras, and Isa's visit. Almost everything was put away and ready for the fall rains and winter. With our first fire fall had truly begun.

Three-hundred-forty-nine: Evacuation

"The fog comes on little cat feet. It sits looking over harbor and city on silent haunches and then moves on." – Carl Sandburg

About 9:15 CeAnn called. Could I help them move Freddy off Crane so that Freddy, his wife, and their female friend could make the 12:10 Anacortes ferry to get back to Bainbridge Island across the Sound from Seattle? Yes, absolutely. Though the fog that had rolled in from Harney Channel over the previous hour making it impossible to see more than 100 yards, that was enough, with the *Huginn*'s GPS system to find our way to the Orcas dock. And since the fog was bright that meant it wasn't very high and likely would melt away soon. By 9:30 the fog around the house and the area around Pole Pass was gone though it lingered at the east end of West Sound and in Harney Channel continuing to envelope the ferry landing. A large power boat pointing into the fog sat at its edge, the captain having made the decision to wait for the fog to lift, probably a wise choice to be patient and one we had not made ten years before returning from Sydney in our pocket trawler, *Gumption*, when we encountered a fog bank lying on Harro Straight, the shipping channel for freighters traveling between the Straight of Juan de Fuca (and the Pacific) and Vancouver, BC, to the north. Though other boats heading toward Speiden Channel were waiting out the fog I decided that we could make our way through it with our GPS and radar — and we did — but not before a nerve wracking 30 minutes of worry that we would be run over by a freighter as we passed in front of it.

About 9:45 CeAnn called. They were ready to take the rescue vehicle Dan had left at their house to the community dock. I told her I was on my way and walked across the meadow to the dock and down the ramp to the *Huginn* to make it ready. I had my camera on my belt to take pictures of the evacuation. As I looked north toward the west side of Pole Pass I saw something peculiar moving through the water to-

Three-hundred-forty-nine: Evacuation

ward the northwest corner of the marina's cove, a point with a shore pine that had grown out over the water and a spot with rocks that dry at low tide and thus a dangerous place to take a boat. The strange shape, no bird, resolved itself into a deer with antlers, a buck swimming from Orcas to Crane, using the most sensible route it might take, the shorter crossing to the breakwater not acceptable because the buck would have a very hard time getting out of the water and then walking among the big rocks. I took four pictures. Though I knew the deer made this trip, perhaps often, I had never seen it until now. The buck emerged out of the water on the short beach left by a nearly high tide and nonchalantly climbed the bank to the west and was gone, to appear later munching salal at the head of the dock.

The white Ford Expedition with the words "Crane Island Fire and Rescue" painted on its side drove into the parking lot and I walked up the dock to help. Howard pulled the folded wheel chair Dan had retrieved from the community center/fire truck garage and set it up next to the passenger door and Freddy slid off the seat, stood briefly, and then sat down in the chair. He could barely walk but he said he was in much better shape than two days before. Down the dock at the *Huginn* I climbed into the cockpit, entered the cabin and brought out the two passenger seats that slide onto mounts on the engine cover and Freddie lowered himself carefully into the cockpit and then took the port side seat, with his wife and family friend following. Howard and CeAnn got in their aluminum skiff and our flotilla of two made our way through Pole Pass to the Orcas dock. Howard wheeled Freddy up the ramp, I took two photos, and then everyone was gone, on their way to the ferry landing and perhaps medical care for Freddy. Back on Crane I parked the fire and rescue vehicle in its designated spot closest to the dock.

The fog was gone but the air remained thick, nothing at a distance in clear focus, and the sun, which had hinted at making a full appearance was now hidden behind multiple layers of clouds but the air wasn't cold and the day felt safe, relaxed, and in the house cozy, still warm from an early fire in the wood stove. Noah called, especially to let us know they wouldn't be hosting Thanksgiving, the situation with Natasha's brother casting a shadow over possible family gatherings there. Yes, of course, we'd love to have you all come here. We went on to talk about his book, *Cedar Rain* that we now had a loose leaf copy of, how Yvonne and I would read it and make suggestions and that I would create an ebook version of it as one way we'd approach it.

349: Howard backs Freddy up the Orcas-side ramp

Wanting the Livingston out of our cove for the winter, since if left there it would certainly be carried away by a winter storm, I rowed it to the flatter beach in the cove just north of our property, pulled it up the bank toward the cross-meadow path when Yvonne joined me and helped me carry it through the salal narrows to its over-winter spot next to the path on our lot and we set it on four logs face down. Since this almost foggy day felt so good I decided to clean out the "new" aluminum skiff at the dock but quickly got frustrated with trying to remove the gravel and dirt it had picked up when Dan and I turned it over on the beach at the barge ramp two days before so I motored it to our beach, from which I taken the Livingston, pulled the aluminum boat out of the water and then went up the ramp and stairs to the path to the house, pulled most of the garden hose off its spool and lowered the hose, nozzle first into the cove. The 100 foot hose had slack to spare. The boat's transom had a plug but I saw no ready way to remove it so after hosing out the boat I bailed the stern, now carrying five gallons of water perhaps, and in doing so removed the gravel, dirt, twigs, needles and other debris that had found its way into boat. Then after remounting the motor and attaching fore and aft lines and two old fenders starboard I dragged the skiff back into the water and then pushed from the bow, jumped in, rotated the motor to vertical, started it and zipped back to the Crane Island marina.

Yvonne had baked an apple pie for Jim and Nancy as appreciation for Jim's helping me pull the Ranger out of the water and lower the mast and I called to make sure they were home, waited half an hour for the pie to cool and then carried it in a Costco bag to the dock, being very careful not to tip it (per Yvonne's instructions) and took the skiff through Pole Pass and then down the east side of Crane Island to Jim and Nancy's, tied up at their dock and carried the pie up to the house, both of them meeting me as I stepped off the dock. They were pleased. Jim had covered the roof with felt and for the first time since they had bought the house the roof didn't leak, the old, glass roof having always leaked no matter what Jim had done with the glass panels the architect/builder/owner had been so enthusiastic about years ago in a fit of bad judgement. Jim was expanding the cottage and had probably a year's work on it to do but that would be interrupted by their wintering in Mexico, though Nancy explained that would be late this year because Jim needed to make the house rain proof before they could leave.

I was at the Orcas dock in the *Huginn* by 5:20 and spent a few minutes with an adjustable wrench putting a second 3/4" nut on a bolt that held together one of the two hinges connecting the first and second newer dock floats together and as I finished, Ken, Kate, and eight-year-old Caleb, their grandson, came down the aluminum ramp, Ken carrying a basket of homegrown chard, tomatoes, and cucumbers. Yvonne served us all broiled cinnamon chicken with golden rice pilaf, raita yogurt cucumber sauce, and a tomato, cucumber, and goat gouda cheese salad, with fresh baked apple crumble for dessert. Caleb played with the marble chutes kit I'd brought down from the studio loft, building five-foot high contraptions and I talked with Ken and then Kate about the Northwest art panel we'd bought in Seattle recently and what little I understood about the principles that lay behind it from books by Bill Reid and Bill Holm. Later conversation turned to the local, national and international economy that had affected them directly and negatively as realtors and leveraged property developers. Projecting what we saw today, that we were having a hard time imagining would improve, the future looked grim for retirees, with a pattern of capital spend down and distressed real estate sales going on for years, collapsing the lives that had been conservatively planned and deflating everyone's assets. We ended, about 10:00, when Caleb said he was tired and wanted to go back to their house to go to bed, trying to convince ourselves that the smaller world many of us were now entering might have benefits we couldn't now conceive. Did we want to spend some time at Long Beach, the sand spit town just north of the mouth of the Columbia river, for free, in the house of a friend? Sure, why not?

Three-hundred-fifty: Sitting, Thinking, Learning, and Writing

"Difficulties are just things to overcome, after all." – Ernest Shackleton

Cloudy, the sky spitting, the deck wet, but a very mild morning that dried out during the day. Still no significant sign of the fall rains. Plans for our long drive trip, at least three and a half weeks, are now clear. We'll leave the 19th for Ashland, stop in Winter, California to see Heather, stay for a week in Los Osos with son Eric and family, then a long weekend in LA with James and Keith, on to Tucson to see Joyce and Larry, a stop in Santa Fe or Albuquerque, then a weekend with sisters Marcy and Julie in Colorado Springs, part of a week with old fiends Alan, Tessa, Dave, Ann, Dean and Barb in Boulder and then home by way of Harstine Island with Noah and family.

Yvonne's plans to take Cresi, Yvonne's grandniece, to visit colleges this weekend had firmed up though she wouldn't be surprised if the project fell apart. No one in Cresi's family had been to college and Yvonne wants to show that world to her and help her with the application process — if she's sufficiently interested. So the plan is for Yvonne to leave Thursday, stay with friend Julie in Ellensburg and visit, pick up Cresi Friday, come back to Ellensburg for a tour of Central Washington University, go on to Renton to stay with friend Kathy, then visit Western Washington and the University of Washington over the weekend (the order isn't clear) and stay in Jeni's apartment she's vacating to see Adrianna with Corrina in New York over the weekend. Sunday Yvonne will put Cresi on a bus back to Ephrata. Saturday or Sunday I'll take the ferry to Anacortes and Yvonne will pick me up coming south from Bellingham to spend two days in Seattle at Jeni's cat sitting Lola. Yvonne saw on Facebook that Cresi's sister Maria (and her baby) were planning to drive to Centralia Monday to see their mother Gina —

when Cresi should be in school — lending an element of uncertainty to the college visiting (and applying and attending) process.

Yvonne continued to work on rebuilding her south flower bed, having dug it all out, with some of my help, and now, having lined the bottom with weed block to keep the tree roots out, is filling it back in after sifting what she took out and adding new topsoil from her covered pile back by the tool shed. She said again that she wasn't enjoying this work. We walked the island together after lunch and as expected didn't see a soul or any wildlife except for a few birds but it was perfect weather for walking, cool enough but not cold.

I'd begun the process to add our six books to the Apple iBooks catalog. We were now a registered publisher with Apple but when uploading Slocum's *Sailing Alone*, the same ePub file I'd loaded successfully to Barnes and Noble through their PubIt site, the Apple verification program found a number of ePub errors, the messages cryptic and without a key. A web search eventually took me to Sigil, ePub editing and publishing software that could run the same verification routine and then show me exactly where it found problems and then let me change the underlying HTML code to try to dissolve the errors. All the errors were related to one problem: I needed to put paragraph tags within the blockquote tags because the later can't really have any content; they can only contain other content-allowed tag sets.

I had looked at Sigil more than a year before and found it impossible to understand and useless. Now, either it had improved significantly or I had a much clearer idea of how ePub worked. By comparing Amazon's Mobi format and ePub in Sigil (and what had come out of the Calibre conversion of Mobi to ePub) I realized that the two formats were almost identical and I would need to experiment again with generating ePub out of my software rather than using Calibre to effect a conversion and possibly determine whether ePub, the more exacting format in some ways should be the base file and Mobi the output from a Calibre conversion. In any case it was enormously encouraging to see the whole eBook landscape more clearly and to have found a very versatile tool in Sigil to see inside the ePub black box and be able to easily tune the content.

Three-hundred-fifty: Sitting, thinking, learning, and writing

350: Fence at Becker's farm

Three-hundred-fifty: Sitting, thinking, learning, and writing

The signature card process at both KeyBank and Islanders' Bank were on hold until Dan and Martha signed the forms and until Martha provided the Board documents I needed so thwarted in that direction I called KeyBank to sign up for online banking — through which I could get statements and pay Crane Island Association bills. I couldn't understand what the telephone service representative was saying and Yvonne, who I called in from her flower bed work, couldn't either except that she seemed to be saying I could sign up through their website and that someone else already had — probably Mike when he was Treasurer. OK. That worked and would save me time.

James called while riding the bus from the UCLA campus in Westwood to the apartment he shared with Keith in West Hollywood and we talked his whole trip home and then continued. He was waiting for paperwork to continue his lab work. Keith was grading his first USC undergraduate philosophy essays and was appalled at the illiteracy in some cases and the plagiarism in others. They looked forward to seeing us in a few weeks.

I had nearly finished reading my first Hardy biography and now had a much better sense of him as person and author, both impressive and fallible, and was beginning to have some sense of what I might write about him and *Tess of the d'Ubervilles* to add to what Howard was doing with the annotations.

I had spent much of the day in my wicker chair in the living room with my MacBook Pro on my lap, in the morning with a fire in the wood stove, and overall very happy with the research and thought process I was going through with eNotated Classics and Crane Island Association related technology. I'd spent a good bit of the past four months outside or house projects inside. I would now be spending much more time sitting, thinking, learning, and writing and I looked forward to it.

Three-hundred-fifty-one: Recital

"Storms make trees take deeper roots." – Dolly Parton

There were signs of overnight rain and the wind was picking up. This would be my first use of what Yvonne suggested we call the picnic boat to commute to Orcas Island, picnic because she imagined us taking some of the family to Jones Island in it for a picnic, the others coming along in the *Huginn*, a small but serious powerboat with a cabin. The gunnel of thirteen foot aluminum boat with a high prow, plenty of freeboard, three plywood bench seats and a triangular seat in the bow had been significantly but not fatally damaged well above water line through some kind of collision perhaps but cleverly patched with an upside down 1984 Washington license plate. This wet morning the picnic boat had begun to collect water and I worried that it might be leaking. I dipped my finger into the bilge water and tasted it: no sign of salt. I untied the fore and aft mooring lines from the cleats on the dock, leaving a line midships tied to the dock bull rail, got in the boat, rotated the ancient Evinrude four horse power, two stroke from horizontal to vertical, primed it by squeezing the bulb on the line from the mixed gas and oil tank, pulled out the choke, turned the throttle on the tiller to almost full, and then pulled the starter rope four times until the engine started, and then pushed in the choke — and almost fell over as the boat lurched. I'd forgotten to put the transmission in neutral and it had started forward, then stopped, constrained by the center line I'd left tied. The motor died, I put it in neutral, got started, untied the boat and then found myself pushed by the wind toward the *Huginn* on the other dock finger, the wind moving the lighter bow faster than the heavier stern, so that I was completely turned around. Two summers before the wind had pushed me backward in the Livingstone, the motor shaft hit a rock and the whole motor fell off the boat and I had to pull it out by its security line and ended up taking a kayak to Orcas to get to a Library Board meeting. Now, bound for another Library Board meeting, I was determined to avoid disaster, so I shifted the motor to reverse and backed the picnic boat away from the *Huginn* toward the open end of the dock Y toward Pole Pass, then around half a circle, shifted into forward and I was soon heading into the wind and against the tide toward the Orcas dock. The prow bounced from wave to wave and I wondered whether I'd be able to use the oars I'd put aboard should the motor fail. I had a floating seat cushion for a life preserver. But I wasn't cold. I was having fun, a little adventure. Tied up at the Orcas dock, I bailed the stern with the plastic bottle I'd cut the bottom out of, and then lifted the package of laminate flooring that we'd tested against colors in the house, didn't like, and Yvonne would soon be returning to Costco.

I hadn't attended a Library Board meeting in almost two years, since I'd finished my five year term, the last as President of the Board. Tom, the current President, had asked Lois, immediate past-President, and me for help with the budgeting process, looking for advice about the budget Phil, the director, had submitted for approval. Before we could meet to do that Tom had suffered a heart attack, been airlifted to St. Jospeh in Bellingham, gone through three stent procedures, had more treatment to come, and abruptly resigned from the Board at the insistence of his doctor. Joan, the Vice-President, had asked Lois and me to attend this public hearing meeting to offer whatever we might have said to Tom, now out of the picture. As it turned out, Joan was also absent from this day's meeting. Besides Lois and I, Pierette, also a former Board member, and Tony, the Library IT director were the only members of the public to appear. I had only scanned the proposed budget and the notes Lois had made for Tom and hadn't thought about the Library budget and process for some time but it began to flow back and I found myself with lots to say, the most important probably, that the Board should use the ten year projection spreadsheet Lois and I had put together to see the effects of the budget on the future. It wasn't enough to have a balanced budget for the next year; they needed to look out ten years and see whether, given that budget and best assumptions, the Library was financially sustainable without having to go to the voters for a "tax levy lid lift," that is permission to raise the Library taxes by more than 1% per year, in these times likely to fail, with potentially dire consequences for the health of the Library. I had a good time, met the new Board member, and contributed something.

351: Early ferry at the Orcas Landing

The ride in the picnic boat back to Crane, with the wind, wasn't a problem but after lunch when Yvonne and I left Crane in the *Huginn* for Orcas the wind was blowing much harder and now that the tide had changed direction, flowing out, east through Pole Pass, the waves were building up, crashing over the breakwater. It was no problem for the *Huginn* though at one point spray covered the windshield but I imagined myself in the picnic boat, the bow skipping from wave to wave. It would work. It wouldn't have been a problem.

Three-hundred-fifty-one: Recital

Yvonne dropped me at the Eastsound sporting goods store and went on to Rainbow Services to arrange the printing of the Garden Club yearbook and then to the Food Bank for the monthly Board Meeting. Sister Marcy's husband Paul's birthday was a week away. I bought him a headlamp, something he didn't know he needed but would eventually appreciate, and then went next door to Ray's Pharmacy where I found a 99 cent birthday card and four 99 cent Halloween cards Yvonne had asked me to buy — along with the *Seattle Times*. From Rays I walked to Islander's Bank to get Yvonne $100 in cash for her upcoming trip with Cresi and then found our Ford Focus in the Community Church lot next to the Food Bank building, put my purchases on the back seat, and then walked through the Island Market parking lot to the KeyBank Eastsound branch where I deposited the eight checks that had recently come in for the Crane Island Association, Patti working today as a teller, and remembering me and addressing me by name. Then I went on to the Library, crowded this afternoon, and finding an empty table, pulled out my MacBook Pro from my backpack as well as a file folder with this year's billing information, and began to work on reminder emails to all the Crane Island Association Members who hadn't yet paid their bills — due September 30th, now four days late. I attached PDF files of what I had sent them in paper form: an explanatory cover letter and an invoice and a car and boat registration form they were to complete and mail back with a check. The process wasn't difficult and I was happy to be able to do the reminders by email rather than paper mail but it was tedious and I finished only a few minutes before Yvonne came to pick me up.

The Rock on the Rock Choir was assembling at the Orcas Center, first for practice and then a recital at 6:00. I came inside with Yvonne to read (another Hardy biography) but with no good place to sit I opted for Enzo's, promising to return by 5:20. As I ordered hot chocolate I noticed that Lois and spouse were sipping coffee and we talked a bit about the Library Board meeting earlier in the day and then they left to drive to their house on Buck Mountain, almost at the top, 1467 feet above sea level and a 1000 feet lower than adjoining Mt. Constitution in Moran

Three-hundred-fifty-one: Recital

State Park, and experiencing a different climate than those of us living at sea level.

Back at the Orcas Center I sat in the lobby waiting for the choir to finish its rehearsal, reading about Thomas Hardy, when Margot came in to collect two photos that were part of the Orcas Camera Club show. I'd noticed the photos on the lobby walls and liked them and then Margot explained there were many more in the Madrona meeting room so I followed her in, looked at hers, and then all the rest. I was impressed. I'd been struck by Rick's, hanging in the Library meeting room, as a one-man show, some having been taken from the Orcas Center for that purpose, and they were very good as well. Then I went into the auditorium and found Yvonne. The show was almost ready to begin.

I had brought my video camera and filmed the three solos and then the three songs the choir did: "Unforgettable," "California Dreaming," and Bono's "One." The best concert yet: strong voices, in sync, on pitch, and expressive. I'd put the performances up on YouTube. Eleven of us met after at the Madrona Grill and I sat next to Dawn, Brian's daughter, having come to see her husband, Sheldon sing. With Sheldon and Yvonne across the table we talked about Brian, and especially his insistence on driving when at least some of the time, because of his illnesses and medication he's not fit to. After his accident a few months back, Dawn badgered Brian to give up driving but he'd denied needing to. Now Dawn was writing the Washington State Department of Motor Vehicles to ask them to rescind Brian's drivers license and she asked me to read and comment on the letter draft. She had described Brian's various medical problems and the prescriptions he was taking but hadn't, I thought, summarized her case adequately at the beginning nor asked the DMV explicitly to ban her father from driving at the end. She and Sheldon thought the suggestions useful.

We were home by about 9:00, the wind having diminished considerably and with some moonlight filtering through the clouds we made our way from the Crane dock on Orcas, through Pole Pass to the Crane community dock and then home, the night mild, as the day had been and after a hot tub dip Yvonne was asleep before 10:00 as I read more about the interesting man and writer who was Thomas Hardy.

Three-hundred-fifty-two: Loss

"We live only a few conscious decades, and we fret ourselves enough for several lifetimes." – Christopher Hitchens

Too cloudy for a visible sunrise, now about twenty minutes later than it was just twelve days ago on the autumnal equinox, this year September 23nd. The world felt very dark outside while I ate breakfast and read the *New York Times* online. Later in the day I'd read the Time's long obituary on Steve Jobs, Yvonne having brought me the news after she saw it on a Seattle news program and we talked about what a remarkable person he was, his fall from grace and his return as a new person, his family, his fierceness, values, insight, and ability to lead and the enormous contrast between Steve and the political class.

Though the rain didn't come it was close all day long, the air misty, sometimes turning into light rain for a time. About 9:00, I walked the quarter mile to well house #6 and at Wilma's emailed suggestion left Gary a manila envelope with the water pumping and usage details for 2007 and 2008 that he'd lent me to scan and send on to Dave for inclusion in his application to the state to increase the number of water taps potentially allowed on Crane. I'd asked Gary to replace the knob key lock on the door to well house #6, the only one without a combination padlock, and he had, so I could use the padlock access key that he'd provided me a few weeks before to get into the little building.

I made a fire again just before breakfast at 6:00 and it lasted until noon raising the house temperature from the 65° thermometer setting to 71, making the house more pleasant and cozy, the absent sun not doing that job this day.

Right after lunch, Yvonne declining to go along because she was too busy preparing for her departure for Ellensburg and a weekend trip with Cresi looking at Washington colleges, I set out for a walk around the island, confirmed that the community water system tank was at the right level (close to thirteen feet) and it was. Another very quiet day, fall color still only on the verge of showing, mostly in big leaf maples and only here and there. The change in light would affect the trees certainly but so would the temperature and the overnight lows for the most part remainded in the high 40°s or even low 50°s.

352: Dawn will break the gray

Yvonne had pointed out that a Netflix DVD was waiting for us at the Post Office in Deer Harbor on Orcas Island. I wasn't enthusiastic at the prospect of making a special trip but then decided I would fill a can with gas at the marina to have for the old outboard on the old aluminum skiff, pick up Crane Island Association annual bills and payments at the PO and also time the travel between the Crane community dock and the Deer Harbor Marina dock, something good to know —

and try the picnic boat, what Yvonne wanted to call it, on a longer trip that I'd tried so far. All that added up to enough to justify spending the time.

By the time I was ready a light rain was falling and I considered changing from my Carhartt jacket to a rain coat but the rain wasn't likely to strengthen. Putting a three gallon red plastic gas can in the dock cart along with a life jacket and vinyl covered seat cushion/floatation device and carrying the oars I'd gotten from the Livingston, too short for the picnic boat but which could be used in a pinch if the engine failed, I pushed the craft down the wood chips covered path from our house through the trees and then across the meadow to the dock.

The wind calm and the water almost still, the rain drops created short-lived concentric circles on the surface of the Salish Sea on top of a plaid the result of hundreds, thousands of other drops at the overlapping of their circles. A cormorant rose out of the water just north of the No Wake zone buoy off Cal's dock and an occasional seabird flew overhead sometimes landing on the water some ways off on a mission. I'd made this trip many times before but always inside a cabin and at higher speed and I savored the nearness of the water and the unimpeded visibility of this beautiful place. Though I kept my right hand on the outboard's tiller behind me, it almost wasn't necessary, the boat holding to its course north. The light rain wet my face, and that felt good, though somehow my paint and dirt stained Levi's stayed dry, perhaps my body heat evaporating the far spaced drops as fast as they fell.

I tied up at the County portion of the dock near the ramp, took my backpack, and walked up to the pier and then to the Post Office where I found six bill payments in the Crane box and the Netflix DVD in our box. Back at the marina dock I moved the picnic boat to the fuel dock area and filled the gas can. At home I'd pour a gallon of the gas into a smaller can and add two-stroke engine oil to make a new batch appropriate for the old Evinrude outboard.

The outbound trip, dock to dock had taken thirteen minutes, not much longer than it would have required to take the *Huginn* through Pole Pass to the Orcas dock, tie up, walk to the car and then drive it to the Post Office, but used much less gas, barely noticeable on the gauge of the two gallon red tank in the stern. The return trip also took thirteen minutes to cover the distance the San Juan County Assessor's Internet mapping system said was 6944 feet or 1.3 miles as the gull flies or about six miles per hour. Not too bad.

Yvonne made a spinach, cheese, onion quiche for dinner that I'd live on while she took her road trip with Cresi, maybe supplementing it with spaghetti or even eggs over the next few days. I'd miss her but I had lots to do, having started in earnest to go through the process to clarify what the eNotated Classics business was and how to show it clearly to college faculty in a way that meant something to them at the January Modern Language Association meeting. It was hard work that couldn't come strictly from analysis. A muse was also needed.

Three-hundred-fifty-three: Disturbance

"There is a way that nature speaks, that land speaks. Most of the time, we are simply not patient enough, quiet enough, to pay attention to the story." – Linda Hogan

As I laid the fire just before 6:00 and making breakfast, I had a sense of satisfaction having split this particular wood almost two and a half-years before. Chris had hired an arborist to fell a dead Douglas fir and then sliced it up himself but didn't know what to do with it, not having a fireplace and asked me whether I wanted it. Sure. I made two round trips — pickup to Orcas dock to boat to Crane dock to yard via dock cart — on a sunny May morning — struggling with some of the sections from low on the trunk, barely able to lift them. But I did — trying to be careful of my back — a weak spot for many people, especially the gray-haired variety. The process took hours. When lifting the second to last section out of the *Huginn*'s cockpit onto the dock, I was careless about how I lifted, not straight up and down but to the side — and something gave way in my back. I managed to finish the unloading, dragged the cart back to the house, took some ibuprofen, and got into bed. Within a few days I was fine — but now more careful.

Yvonne was ready to leave earlier than she expected. I carried her suitcase and she a Costco bag with returns I guess. I didn't know. She had packed a piece of quiche, leaving about a third of the pie to tide me over for the next few days. We were out the door by 7:20, the sun having risen (according to the almanac) but not visible through the thick clouds. As I approached the community dock in the weak light, I noticed that the water was absolutely flat, a mirror reflecting what was behind it, in all directions, even in Pole Pass. It was slack tide and low. Nothing was on the water to disturb it. Not a breath of wind disturbed the surface. I saw double: a double breakwater, double docks, a double Orcas Island. As I walked from the pier down the ramp to the dock the water in the cove trembled slightly. I was reluctant to disturb it further-but Yvonne had to get to Orcas — and no matter — though time and tide waited right now, it wouldn't wait for long — whether I had anything to do with it or not.

353: Tasty morsel on the Orcas dock

For the first time I could see the *Huginn* plow a furrow through the Salish Sea and it spread behind the boat out to the four corners of the world — or so it seemed. Yvonne jumped out at the Orcas dock — I might be meeting her in Anacortes Sunday to go to Seattle or more likely she'd be coming home Monday after taking Cresi on a college tour. On the return trip the glass surface of the Sea had been replaced by a complex pattern of ripples now being reflected back from the Orcas and

Three-hundred-fifty-three: Disturbance

Crane shores and the tides had resumed their predictable goings and comings through Pole Pass, showing up as a thin layer moving west on the waters of Deer Harbor. Walking up the ramp and then through the gap in the recently repaired split rail fence, I had an overwhelming sense of beauty, rightness, attachment, love for this extraordinary place.

After lunch I found a small carton in the storage shed to mail Paul's birthday card and head lamp present, signed the former, adding a note, and wrapping the latter in birthday tissue paper from the supply we'd been drawing on for at least five years. Stuffing the carton into my backpack with a manilla envelope Yvonne wanted mailed I carried the maroon pack, fancy orange life vest, and too-short oars to the community dock, dropped them into the aluminum picnic boat, and then after checking the gas supply, got the small motor started and cast off, heading almost due north to the Deer Harbor Marina. At the Post Office I interrupted Pat's temporary replacement who rung up postage for both mailings — less than $4 — and handed me the contents of our overfull box. Checking the Crane box I found only one new annual bill and payment. The return trip to Crane was uneventful, two cormorants, some distance apart had separately lifted themselves out of the water (where usually only their neck and head shows) flapping their wings furiously, feet walking on the water at first, and then like landing gear raised into flight position as they flew only a foot or two above the surface often in shallow curves, plopping into the water again hundreds of yards away to resume their fishing. On the way out of the Crane marina I'd noticed a cormorant on Stu and Martha's mooring buoy, two hundred yards to the west, wings outstretched to dry them as cormorants often do because unlike other marine birds their feathers don't create a dry suit to hold in body warmth. The cormorants aren't insulated against the cold northern waters so they have to pay attention to warming up. On the other hand, because they're almost neutrally buoyant, they can dive more easily than the varieties of ducks we'll begin to see soon as they return from Canada and Alaska to winter on our waters.

After dinner and spending the whole day thinking and writing about eNotated Classics and Classics Unbound, Inc., what they were, what would matter to MLA attendees at the January Seattle meeting,

Three-hundred-fifty-three: Disturbance

and how we could tell them effectively, I heated up a piece of quiche, watched tributes to and discussion about Steve Jobs and his legacy, and then as it was getting dark put my head lamp in my jacket pocket and set off on my usual circumambulation of the island. Quiet everywhere. Lights on at Ilze's cabin on the north side. Josh must be back and continuing the remodel that's gone on for more than a year. At least the cabin is now insulated. Yvonne called about 8:00 to tell me she'd arrived safely at Julie's. I wasn't lonesome yet and I had plenty to eat but my fantasy of working sixteen hours a day while Yvonne was gone hadn't panned out. After ten hours or so I couldn't stand any more.

Three-hundred-fifty-four: Slogging

"I am not afraid of storms, for I am learning how to sail my ship." – Louisa May Alcott

As the world outside becomes visible again after withdrawing to some mysterious place for the night, I see the water in our cove quiver, the light wind teasing its surface, refusing to leave it alone, light rain puckering the shallow puddles on the brown painted deck, clouds, their feet close by with heads thousands of feet above.

Yvonne reported in as she approached the turnoff for Ephrata to pick up Cresi to take her on a tour of Central Washington University in Ellensburg and then again from Renton when she couldn't reach Kathy on the only number she had in her cell phone. Cresi had to be back in Ephrata Sunday to return to school and Jeni had decided not to go to New York to see Adrianna, back from France, so Yvonne would be coming home Sunday; we wouldn't take a few days in Seattle.

Noah had sent all Borgian units a link to his newly published short story "Lifting" in an online literary magazine. It was tightly written, as usual featuring a cast two generations away from Raymond Carver's world but with the same struggles, the last sentence surprising and delighting me, unsuspected but inevitable given the set up in the first few paragraphs. Tess Gallagher's introduction to Carver's posthumous poetry collection, *A New Path to the Waterfall* mentioned his connection with Tomas Transtromer, seven years his senior. Transtromer was still among the living, Carver gone in 1988 from cancer, and Transtromer, the Swedish poet, partly paralyzed by a stroke, had won the Nobel Prize for Literature — and knowing nothing about him I read his Wikipedia entry and some of the many articles and blogs that had just been published, some quoting his poetry, direct, perfectly accessible, pointing to the mystery beyond words that isn't much farther away than the tips of our fingers and on which can lean back and rest if we let ourselves. One comment described how Transtromer had found an answer to life's

Three-hundred-fifty-four: Slogging

essential mystery by being acutely present to make it real and I could sense Emerson, Thoreau, and Whitman just out of sight.

On January 5th we'd be setting up our booth at the Modern Language Association annual meeting in the Seattle Convention Center, Perhaps 7500 would attend, some to interview prospective faculty, some seeking jobs and to make connections, many to read papers on sometimes arcane topics or participate on panels. As I looked through the program of more than 750 programs, an enormous number, I was struck by how few had to do with applying technology to teaching and how many I thought I could sit in and understand, even have a conversation about, but not have any desire to take further. One phrase appeared many times, "digital humanities," referring to the use of technology in literary research (my mother's master's thesis used word counts in Whittier's poetry). Perhaps provoked by imagining myself at the MLA talking to faculty to interest them in what we were doing, a dream later overnight had me explaining to a group how and why I hadn't completed my PhD, failing to write my dissertation, the last step. The reality was, I'd always felt, that I didn't belong in that world. It was interesting, certainly, and attractive in that way, but not something I would actually want to spend my life doing. For me it was too much talk and not enough action, too ephemeral. Further I had no confidence that I could really do a good job with the research and teaching. I would be too superficial, too much wanting to go on to the next thing before mastering the present. But I couldn't explain this to the small group I was sitting with in my dream. I didn't want to insult them about their life choices. On the other hand I was irritated at the woman who was forcing me to explain myself and why I hadn't gone on to be a philosophy professor. What business was it of hers?

At the same time, the noosphere was now packed with Steve Jobs saying over and over again

Three-hundred-fifty-four: Slogging

354: Och's meadow looking east

"Your time is limited, so don't waste it living someone else's life. Don't be trapped by dogma — which is living with the results of other people's thinking. Don't let the noise of others' opinions drown out your own inner voice. And most important, have the courage to follow your heart and intuition. They somehow already know what you truly want to become. Everything else is secondary."

Jobs had run against the current. So had I in my little way and I was still doing it and at times making people around me suffer for it.

So what was Classics Unbound, Inc. really about? And eNotated Classics? And why should all the professors, associate professors, assistant professors, teaching job applicants, and grad students care? And how do we tell them in a way they understand and respond to? And then what do we need to do to be ready for the convention three months away? Two years before I'd come up with the core idea of adding a layer of background, research to literary classics, accessible through links from the primary text, possible with ebooks in ways that were clumsy with paper. Nothing revolutionary but a way to do "new things, new ways," to give serious, though not specifically academic, readers something they didn't know they wanted but would love and appreciate just as Silver Plume, the electronic insurance library I'd designed wasn't an incremental change from something the industry already knew but something completely different that offered new benefits.

Two years before it had seemed to me that annotated ebooks had some application to teaching and over the previous few days I got clearer how to do that using technology at hand or nearly so. We'd offer an electronic classics library enhanced with book/chapter/paragraph numbering to facilitate reading collaboratively on any combination of devices — so long as they had at least part time access to the internet through decent browsers, presenting the books through codex (page oriented) or web page (scroll oriented) reading software, the former convenient for reading, the latter for more intense studying, including annotation. The base library of public domain books and base annotation software would be free to libraries, schools, and faculty but we would charge subscription fees for access to our eNotated books (sold and distributed individually by Amazon, Barnes and Noble, and Apple), to advanced annotation capabilities, custom book loads, or on-reserve excerpts and collections, and ebook building — either from students' work or for faculty who wanted to publish, unless it was to publish an eNotated Classic, in which case it would be free and we'd share revenue, putting the new ebook into retail and subscription inventory. At the MLA we'd show our two faces: retail ebooks and a free + subscription services library, pointing out its relevance for reading, studying, translating, teaching, editing, and publishing. I was putting together narrative, tables, and diagrams that described and explained this integrated service for presentation to Chris, David, and Jens. It made sense to me; I couldn't help myself, the thinking process so much work for my tiny brain that I'd have to get up from time to time to pace around for relief. In the afternoon I made a circuit of the island, scaring up two deer who fled into the nature preserve at the west end of the island and seeing the lights on at Ilze's cabin, a small fire smoking outside, and someone at work with a power tool I couldn't see and didn't recognize the sound of. I didn't walk up the driveway to disturb whoever it was. Perhaps Josh. I didn't want to talk to anyone at the moment.

Three-hundred-fifty-five: Looking and Not Seeing

> *"Nature will bear the closest inspection. She invites us to lay our eye level with her smallest leaf, and take an insect view of its plain."* – Henry David Thoreau

In the early morning light the madrona outside the living room window is dark gray, a crisp silhouette on a light gray background. Farther away, on our side of Raven Cove, the big Douglas fir that has grown right out of the rocky bank is a little grayer, its outline less distinct and across the cove, on Margaret's side, the gray of the trees and the opaque screen behind them possesses even less contrast. Fog envelopes the world.

Dew frosts the deck's glass railing panels. Nothing is moving except for a few small branches in the fir to the left of the madrona, plucked at randomly by micro breezes. The rocky cove wall looks much higher than it is because much of it is reflected in the almost still water of the Salish Sea. A slight hint of peach glows through the fog above, the deck and chairs wet, the two chairs on the point on their backs blown over by last week's wind.

By 8:30 the fog is gone, only mid-level clouds remain here and there and by afternoon even they are mostly gone as the day conducts its typical October temperature cycle from 48° to 58° and back again.

After lunch and after sitting thinking and writing all morning about eNotated Classics, Classics Unbound, and the January MLA convention, I made myself go outside, in Carhartt jacket and faded orange Grand Canyon billed cap I got there years ago at Bright Angel Lodge when Yvonne, James, and I passed through on our way to California. Now, before Yvonne and I left for California and points east, I needed to better insulate the spa plumbing between the pump house under the deck and the spa itself above it and to the side, its sides about a foot higher than the deck. In June Yvonne had noticed that something had torn insulation from the underside of the box that contained the pipes, rats likely that were trying to get into the pump house and frustrated by the metal screening I had stuffed into the open areas where the pipes enter the pump house, so I pulled out all the fiberglass insulation I'd put in to supplement what I thought had been an inadequate job by Dean when he installed the spa twenty years ago and used only black cylindrical foam around the white PVC pipes — but not everywhere — leaving some pipe lengths completely exposed. So I had put fiberglass batting above the pipes and below the pipes, stapling screening below to keep the batting from falling down to the ground. What I hadn't thought of is that rats would nest in the fiberglass and they had. So it all came out as well as the screening that held it up.

We'd soon leave the island for a long road trip and it was conceivable though not likely that temperatures could dip below freezing and the power fail simultaneously for an extended period of time that though not at all likely to affect the spa itself, insulated by the cover above and the skirt below or the pump house, fully insulated, so I needed to do something to improve upon the insulation system I'd removed in June. I crawled underneath the spa platform, about three feet off the ground. Fully enclosing the area would be complicated because of the geometry of the pipe box and its intersection with the spa skirt, the deck, and the pump house below. I walked back to my shop and looked for relevant supplies. I had some hardware cloth, screening, sheet metal, and plenty of scrap wood. And in the pipe stack in back I found two lengths of pipe insulation — which I carried back to the house. This wasn't going to be easy. I looked harder and finally paid attention to the fact that there were three pipes that passed through the pipe cover box and then took the door off the pump house to see which did what. One pipe carried heated water to the spa and another back. A third pipe carried air from the blower to the tub, something we rarely used because it squandered heat. It was the third pipe that Dean had only partially insulated. The pipe left the pump house, then turned straight up, higher than the water level in the spa, then turned parallel with the top of the spa, then straight down and then at a right angle through the skirting. Of course! The inverted U would keep water from flowing out of the spa to the air pump. Dean had only insulated the part from the spa to the top of the U, the only part that would contain water that might freeze. That made sense. A few small locations on the two water flow pipes needed more pipe insulation and I used my grandfather's knife to slice the insulation I'd brought into sections the right width. Then I put a piece of fiberglass batting on the area where all three pipes entered the skirting, where I couldn't use pipe insulation. If the rats wanted to use that area as a place to hang out, so be it. They wouldn't be getting back into the pump house because of the metal screen I'd stuffed around the pipe entry points. When I'd opened the pump house door I could see that nothing had been in there since I cleaned it out in June. Instead of a big job, it had been a small job. Instead of Dean's work needing improvement, I had only to patch it.

A year and a half before we'd gotten a new spa cover. I had four tie down straps six inches in from the corners. The previous cover had two straps in the middle. I hadn't given the spa people instructions about straps and didn't even try working with the four straps because the pipe cover box would make it impossible to install a strap at that corner, so my workaround was to use rope to tie down the cover when we'd be gone in the late fall, winter, or early spring because of the potential for high wind to lift the cover off and blow it away. I'd need to use rope again when we left for California and that seemed unacceptable given that I had straps that were unused. I looked closer and now could see that the clips at the ends of the straps were inside receptacles I could remove, screw onto the skirting, and then click the clips into to hold the lid securely. Of course. It was all there. I remembered that I had a bag of small screws in my shop that Yvonne had saved when she removed doors from the old kitchen cabinets when we remodeled. They were the perfect size. I did the three easy corners and then looked hard at the corner with the pipe box. I wouldn't be able to run the strap straight down the skirting but I could run it to the side, not ideal since it would allow slack but acceptable, especially given that the other three corners were fine. Good.

Three-hundred-fifty-five: Looking and not seeing

355: Rush hour

Finally I used siding nails I found in Yvonne's tool and supply store in her pantry in the studio to secure a piece of siding that was trying to fall off the spa pipe cover and reattach another small piece that had blown off the kitchen bay just below its roof.

And then I took a walk. The tank was at 13 feet. Good. Returning along Dock Road, Blair drove up in his old VW van with a younger man, I assumed his son, aboard coming from the community dock. We talked about how slow Waterfront Construction was about repairing the hinge between the breakwater and east floats on the Orcas dock and that the next Board meeting was a week away. He was having boat trouble. His SeaSport would turn over but not start. His kicker, the small outboard mounted on the transom and backup wouldn't start and the outboard on his backup aluminum skiff wouldn't start. Three for

Three-hundred-fifty-five: Looking and not seeing

three. He'd called IMC in Fisherman's Bay on Lopez and they were coming over. I told him I was around and could help if he needed ferrying. Three for three.

Three-hundred-fifty-six: Report

> *"If one advances confidently in the direction of his dreams, and endeavors to live the life which he has imagined, he will meet with a success unexpected in common hours."* – Henry David Thoreau

Yvonne called not long after 9:00 on her way north. She dropped Cresi at the bus station in Seattle for her trip back to Ephrata after the two of them toured Central Washington University and Western Washington University with a quick stop at the University of Washington in Seattle and a visit with Jeni. She intended to make the 10:35 sailing for Orcas and if the line wasn't long would stop for gas in Anacortes. She'd call me as she came into Anacortes and I'd reported the status of the Orcas line in the Anacortes ferry holding area by checking the ferry cameras on the Washington Department of Transportation ferries web site. She'd call back in half an hour when she got to Anacortes. I pulled up the ferry cameras page and saw that the Anacortes four island lines were virtually empty. She wouldn't have a problem this Sunday morning.

A week or two before Yvonne had given me a new household task; daily scrubbing of the tile floor in the shower to keep the grout clean. Her instructions were to use a stiff brush and do half the floor every other day and then use tile cleaner once a week. But she'd issued special instructions for this weekend when she was gone to clean the floor tile with Stain Solver, an oxy bleach I'd bought to try on the cedar siding that had darkened over the years before putting on a new coat of pigmented stain. She'd used it with some success to clean the house decks where they were turning green and I'd used it to clean mold from the *Discovery*'s vinyl dodger, but I had yet to try it on the siding. I watched a video on the Stain Solver website that demonstrated how to clean a bathroom tile floor and could see that it was a truly miraculous product and exactly what I needed for the shower floor.

Three-hundred-fifty-six: Report

As per instructions I made up a batch in a big measuring pitcher by adding the powder to hot water and then poured it onto the tile carefully and then let it sit. Not all the Stain Solver charged water stayed on the shower floor of course but ran down the drain. Maybe I'd need to build a cofferdam around the drain. I'd just have to see. After letting the Stain Solver do its thing for a while I got in the shower and began to systematically scrub the floor, left to right and then top to bottom, scrubbing all the rows and column of grout. It was hard to tell whether I was doing much good so I did it again and then let it sit.

Then I heard the phone ring. It was Yvonne. Glancing at my MacBook Pro screen I could see that the ferry line was still virtually empty. She replied that she already knew that because she was already in line. Impossible. She couldn't have covered all that distance in such a short time. She told me she'd called three times. Why hadn't I answered. I was in the shower. But I said I'd call in half an hour. I didn't say it but I was certain she couldn't get from Smokey Point to Anacortes in half an hour so I thought I had more time. She said the ferry was late and would be the *Evergreen State*, usually running the inter-island route but today replacing the *Yakima* which had been pulled from service, who knew why. I checked the ferry site for bulletins. Yes, the *Evergreen State* was late and getting later. She'd call from the Orcas Ferry Landing when the *Evergreen State* docked.

I went back to the shower and rinsed the floor and then noticed brown hair in the drain, not mine, of course. Yvonne had said she'd tried to remove the drain cover in the past but couldn't find the right screw driver. I looked and saw that the screws needed a square drive bit. I tried what I had in my tool drawer and then what I could find in Yvonne's tools in her pantry. Too big. I then walked out to my shop, found my super drive bit collection and brought it back to the shower, trying several before I found the right one. I'd also brought the garbage container from the kitchen and dropped the hair ball into it, scraped off the bottom side of the chrome cover, rinsed it and then screwed it back down.

Since the picnic boat gas tank was less than half full I took the can with gas and oil I'd mixed for my chain saw and carried it to the dock and emptied it into to picnic boat's gas supply. A younger man and his son had come down the ramp and I recognized them the day before from Blair's van but didn't know who they were. John and Liv's son. Yes, I could see the resemblance. I told the eleven year old about how I'd salvaged the picnic boat and he said several times what a wonderful boat it was. He was eager to help his father take down the mast of their sailboat, almost never used over the past several years and beat up from the storms that had knocked it against the dock. They'd take it back to Bainbridge Island where they'd get more use of it. Can I help? Don't need any. Thanks.

Not long after I ate an early lunch — poached eggs on cheese on toast — the phone rang. The *Evergreen State* was at the Orcas Ferry Landing — and looking out the living room windows I could see that yes indeed it was. It would take a while to get off the ferry, drive to Deer Harbor, stop at the Post Office, and then drive to the Crane parking lot. I had half an hour but would need to leave time to take the picnic boat to Orcas and it was a bit slower than the *Huginn*. It was close to fifteen minutes before I got myself out of the house, took the oars leaning against the entrance wall and walked to the dock. The motor started right away and then died. Three times. I left the picnic boat and walked around to main dock finger, got the *Huginn* started and ran it faster than usual to make the crossing, feeling slightly embarrassed that I was creating a wake in the No Wake Zone I was supposed to be encouraging if not enforcing. But I had a higher potential feeling of embarrassment if Yvonne arrived in the lot before I did.

At the Orcas dock Blair and Molly were unloading their aluminum skiff, having got its motor started but not that of their SeaSport, even with telephone help from IMC on Lopez Island after Ian proved unavailable at West Sound Marina because he was involved in the day's youth regatta. After briefly chatting I carried some of their belongings up to the lot and Yvonne drove in shortly. She didn't have much to carry so we were soon back on the dock visiting with Blair and Molly in two parallel conversations. Home and after putting her things away Yvonne sat on the couch. She was tired from all her driving and non-stop talking. I had successfully started the motor on the picnic boat deciding that last time I hadn't hand pumped enough gas into the line. I experimented with a knob that might be a richness setting finding the position at which the engine seemed to run smoothest and with least visible oil smoke. I checked the decal on the motor cover. Yes, it did call for a 100:1 gas/oil mix. My chain saw wanted 50:1 so what I'd added to the tank actually had too much oil so I brought down the can of regular gas I'd filled a few days before and added about a gallon. The engine started and ran well.

356: Circumnavigating Crane in the "picnic boat"

Back at the house I suggest to Yvonne we make a circumnavigation of Crane Island. It was a beautiful day, all the morning clouds having moved on or dissolved. Yes, she'd like to go and off we went through

Three-hundred-fifty-six: Report

Pole Pass, then right down the east side of the island, right again into Wasp Passage where we picked up the west wind and some wakes from passing boats. I pointed out each property, Yvonne knowing most of them, As we turned north again at the west side of the island, passing Dave and Caroline's we saw three women sitting near the water to the side and below their shared dock. It was Stacy, Chanel, and Kelly, perhaps on a mom's weekend off. We waved and then Yvonne yelled out who we were and we all waved again. The wind was cold now and Yvonne was as bundled up as she could be. Now turning right again at the northwest corner of the island, Mt. Constitution came into view, a little less than four miles away as the raven flies, crystal clear, transmitter towers bristling. A beautiful day in a beautiful place.

At dinner Yvonne told me about her trip, good visits with Julie and Kathy, and then Maria, good campus tours, and very good conversation with Cresi, her grandniece who had just turned eighteen, whose mother had abandoned her at seven as an addict though they were now reconciled; her father a disabled addict, who was determined to survive, who never asked for anything, who wasn't the least bit judgmental, was polite and curious and sweet, and focused on becoming a parole officer, perhaps to finally save her mother, which of course she couldn't do because it appeared Gina was dying of kidney failure. Cresi liked Western the best. Once she left central Washington she wouldn't go back. She'd live on the west, green side. Yvonne had gotten to know Cresi and was impressed with the young woman. Nothing false or sour. She would do OK. And maybe, especially if she went to Western, she could be included in our family circle where there was always room for one more.

Three-hundred-fifty-seven: Change in the Weather

> *"When we try to pick out anything by itself, we find it hitched to everything else in the Universe."* – John Muir

Yvonne had had to water her garden in the later summer and early fall, August and September, using community water, which we'd have to pay for at the end of the current annual billing cycle after July 31, 2012. It would cost us more than $600 compared with our entire water bill for 2011 of just over $1000. From June 1st through October 10th we'd had a total of just over 2 inches of rain compared with New York's 35, Chicago's 13, Denver's 7, and Seattle's 4. Yvonne reported that the lilacs at the Post Office where she's a volunteer groundskeeper as she is at the Deer Harbor Community Club, have suffered drought damage. On the other hand even with so little rain almost everything, even the grass, especially in shaded areas is green, the natural vegetation having selected itself as drought resistant. It's the foreign plants, the ones that make Yvonne's garden so attractive and which she studied about, shopped for, prepared the soil for, and then so carefully tended that suffer and they'd simply die without supplementary watering.

The deck around the house was wet when I could first see it after 7:00 in the morning and was wet to a lesser or greater degree all day. By early afternoon we were having real rain, though not the downpour other regions are used to but more of a drip, not even drizzle, that might amount to half an inch over 24 hours, but it was something. Usually at this time of year the summer drought gives way to the fall rains with late October, November, and December especially productive. With a chance of rain predicted almost every day for the week ahead perhaps we were at the edge of the rainy season, when the good rains replenish the aquifers we've been draining and the danger of wild fires drops to zero.

Three-hundred-fifty-seven: Change in the Weather

357: Early morning fog hides Bell Island

Yvonne had received the final Garden Club membership information and needed to finish layout of the club yearbook so she could pass a PDF file to Carol at Rainbow Services for printing. She and I had struggled with the process the previous October when she took over the job. We'd tried Microsoft Word and been intensely frustrated and I eventually found that Apple's Pages was much simpler and once I'd set up a page template Yvonne needed only flow the contents into the right pages — that requiring some planning because the club yearbook would be printed from 8 1/2 by 11 inch paper folded in half to make a 5 1/2 by 8 1/2 booklet. Last year the booklet had 32 pages printed from 8 sheets of paper. Page 1 and page 32 (front and back covers) had to be side by side, page 2 and 31 and so on would be the inside of the front/back cover and so on pages that appeared together in the book were usually not together in the file.

Three-hundred-fifty-seven: Change in the Weather

The Garden Club had grown over the last year and the membership list would no longer fit in the space Yvonne had allowed last year. The booklet would need to be slightly redesigned and I could see how the pages should be rearranged. Yvonne was worried about wrecking the layout by fiddling with it but as I prepared to make the changes the phone rang. It was Sebastian. Could I move up the time for our meeting from 4:30, the time he felt he needed to be on the interisland ferry returning to Friday Harbor where he lived? The *Yakima* was out of commission and the *Evergreen State*, normally the interisland boat, was standing in and the *Hiyu*, much smaller, with a capacity of only 35 cars was substituting for the *Evergreen State*. He had intended to take the 8:05 but was now worried there wouldn't be space and he wouldn't be able to get home. I thought I could get to Eastsound, to Enzo's by 3:00 so we agreed to meet then.

Our little ebook business was looking for technical help and Sebastian, an immigrant from France, had been highly recommended and was also willing to consider moonlighting for us gratis, looking for an eventual reward as an owner. Enzo's was noisy and that plus his French accent made it hard to understand him but I think we did well enough. He hoped that eventually his OPALCO job would be in Eastsound rather than Friday Harbor because they wanted to live on Orcas where his wife had relatives. They were both surprised he said at how close the San Juan's are to one another physically but how far socially with far less traffic between the islands than to Anacortes, the local travel time and inconvenience being almost as great as the travel to the mainland. So though they lived on San Juan Island, close by to Orcas, they didn't feel that way nor have the interaction with Orcas people they'd expected.

It was a struggle to carry the four bags of groceries I'd picked up at Island Market after meeting with Sebastian, carefully following Yvonne's list, down the ramp to the Orcas dock with my pack on my back and a small carton that contained printer ink cartridges I'd received from Costco. I didn't want the paper bags to get wet in the rain and especially not to put them down on the wet dock as I climbed into the *Huginn*'s cockpit and then opened the cabin door so I got aboard slowly and carefully and all was well.

When I'd left the house earlier in the afternoon I'd noticed that the bottoms of the two sections of the front bamboo gate had been forced apart presumably by a deer trying to get in though I saw no sign of damage to Yvonne's garden. Either Yvonne or I had neglected to bungee the lower parts of the gate together. About noon when looking out the kitchen window cleaning up lunch dishes I'd been surprised to see our local doe, her two fawns close on her heels, hot footing it past the front of the house and then down the path along the cove to Margaret's house. I expected to see something in pursuit, a dog perhaps, that belonged to someone visiting the island, but nothing seemed to be pursuing them. They'd been spooked but by what? Looking at how the gate had been tampered with I conjectured that they'd been trying to get in, maybe even had come in the front yard, heard something they didn't like and then wiggled back out and ran for their lives around the front of the house, facing the water, along the ten foot cliff, a narrow space in spots but one they frequented often and are confident about. As I walked into the house to the aroma of homemade soup simmering in the kitchen, two shopping bags in each hand, I told Yvonne about the near break in. She was not amused.

The good rain continued and was still falling as we soaked in the spa about 9:30, after a film we didn't like and before reading books we did, Yvonne with *When Everything Changed* and me another Hardy biography.

Three-hundred-fifty-eight: Birthday and Farewell

"The shortest distance between two people is a story." – Patti Digh

A wet morning, 52°, clouds drifting north to darkness, the south promising clearing — but not for long, the rain returning and leaving a very welcome quarter inch.

Continuing the process that occupied most of the previous day I continued to edit Barbara's draft of an *eNotated My Antonia*, hooking her quotes in three essays to their location in Cather's text so that reader can enter essays from passages in Cather's text or vice versa. The process got complicated for a few passages in which Barbara wanted to cite in all three essays, making markup of Cather's text complicated because one link can only go one place. I went on to clean out annotations Barbara had intended to use in an essay but hadn't (they had to be deleted) and removing leading text from her glossary-type annotations that repeated the passage text being annotated. Once the book looked pretty good as a compact website I converted it into MOBI and EPUB formats and confirmed that it looked and worked OK in the Kindle and EPUB worlds and then sent it all to Barbara to look at — and then Jens, Chris, and David. The publication of the *eNotated My Antonia* was in sight, pending proofreading, testing and corrections and the addition of images including one as cover art.

Thomas had written that he had finished his translation of Mann's *Death in Venice* and was ready to sign an agreement and get started with the annotation process. That process would begin soon. Howard's sister was leaving and he'd be getting back to annotating *Tess of the d'Urbervilles* and Angel had begun *The Man Who Would Be King*. With Cather, it was conceivable that we would have ten eNotated Classics available by the beginning of the year to show off at the MLA convention. With the three newest books using the online Co-ment service, I'd need to write a routine to take the downloads and turn them into books, not so hard but probably requiring several full days at work.

After a short walk around some of the island, at 5:30 we took the *Huginn* to Orcas, then stopped to pick up the mail and then because we were early for Howard and Sheila's dinner party, drove north on Deer Harbor Road and pulled off at the Deer Harbor Community Club, looking at the lattice panels intended to hide the propane tank and recently donated green steel fence posts to hold them up. As promised, the lawn had been recently mowed. Yvonne would host a yard cleanup Saturday but I'd miss much or all of it for a Crane Island Association Board meeting.

Chris and Lynn were already inside with Sheila and Howard and his sister from a London suburb just inside the M25 motorway who they'd traveled with through Oregon and Washington in a rented motorhome over the previous week. This evening was her birthday (she was seven years older than Howard) and the next day she'd fly from Orcas to Seattle provided a low ceiling or fog didn't interfere. One of the high points had been the descent into and emergence from the 3000 foot deep Grande Ronde canyon in the Blue Mountains of eastern Oregon in their rented motorhome on a narrow road. Even though she'd been to the United States a number of times she still couldn't get over how big the country was, especially in the West.

Don and Terri appeared shortly, when we were well underway with Yvonne's hors devours, and then we sat down to Sheila's chicken, baked potatoes and carrots, and homegrown beans and Lynn's spicy carrot soup. Don and Terri had continued to work on their sailing/adventure/recipe book, something I thought had lots of promise and we talked for a while about electronic books and publishing and I offered to meet and recount what I'd leaned in the last two years. Sheila had recently allowed herself to pursue the artistic expression she'd mostly suppressed for thirty years while she raised a family and worked and had to be practical. Two recent small art quilt projects were on display, one a sad full moon, and both beautiful and from my point of view requiring impossibly exacting technique. Lynn also did quilting and

Three-hundred-fifty-eight: Birthday and Farewell

sometimes knitting with Yvonne at the Deer Harbor gathering Friday afternoons. We talked about the TED talks on the internet and Sheila wanted to know about Brian Greene's talk on "The Hidden Reality." I described Google's nGram viewer and what it revealed about Nineteenth and early Twentieth Century authors and book titles as well as changes in word use over time. Howard recounted the time when he was four years old and tasted cashews for the first time, lifting a few from a pile in a store and his sister scolding the shopkeeper's security enforcer for picking on a little boy.

358: Bell Island twice

Walking down the ramp to the Orcas dock we didn't need our headlamps. The full moon sparkled in the mirror of the Salish Sea,

Three-hundred-fifty-eight: Birthday and Farewell

Jupiter also impressive a close companion. I didn't need the spotlight as we cruised to Pole Pass and then through it, turning left into the Crane marina. Walking home across the meadow and through the trees to the gate, we didn't need our headlamps. In the spa, the moon and Jupiter lit the deck, trees, and grounds, all but the brightest stars invisible overhead. We were happy soaking in the hot water and having had a chance to socialize with our friends. Goodnight moon. Good night stars.

Three-hundred-fifty-nine: Smaller Portions

"If you want to fly, you have to give up the things that weigh you down." — Toni Morrison

The *Huginn* needed gas and Yvonne, knowing that our MasterCard had entered a new statement month, approved the purchase, so I took the SeaSport to Deer Harbor and on the way, leaving the wheel and stepping out of the cabin into the cockpit, got a good look at the full moon setting in a patch of blue sky, a small distant cloud partially covering its face, while opposite the risen sun, though completely obscured, provided intimations of its glory by radiating rococo orange shafts through a tear in the gray clouds. Mooring the *Huginn* on the west side of the Cayou Quay Marina, I walked the 300 yards to Howard's, David slowing down as he drove past me gawking. Entering the honeymoon cottage Howard handed me a mug of hot English breakfast tea he and Chris were already sipping while David held a bottle of water. Why?, I asked him. Why no tea? We hadn't see him in several weeks. What had happened? As he unspooled his story, Brian struggled through the door with his cane, hunched over, and took the folding chair while David faced Chris and I faced Howard from the two couches against the wall of the little room, a tiny space heater on the floor opposite me blowing warm air to chase off the cold and damp.

David was determined to lose weight and keep it lost, something he hadn't managed in all his previous attempts though Maxine had succeeded. No caffeine, no alcohol, no flour, no sugar — and smaller portions that would total less than 1500 calories for the day. He had set a goal of getting back to his half-century ago wrestling trim and besides changing his diet was working on changing his habits more broadly. He had decided he was a food addict and had enrolled in a twelve-step over-eating oriented plan. Had he joined a cult? What was a cult? If it

Three-hundred-fifty-nine: Smaller Portions

was, it was a good one for many people. Chris weighed in, pulling up his calorie counter app on his iPod, his tool for limiting himself to 1000 calories per day. Brian testified that he'd lost twenty pounds since January. Neither Howard nor I had much to say being at or close to our youthful weights. We talked about addiction more broadly, each with examples of the sometimes fatal damage it can do. Brian's fifth free-rent-for-cooking-and-housekeeping bargain wasn't working out (surprise!). She wouldn't cook the way he wanted or what he wanted and made a terrible racket in the kitchen. We looked at each other but didn't repeat the advice we'd given him many times before: charge rent, pay for help — and then you'll get what you want.

I wanted to talk with Chris and Sebastian before our Friday planning meeting so he drove me back to the marina and we walked down the long dock to his sailboat and climbed into a warm interior. He didn't know much about Sebastian except that he had been well-received and was doing a great job with his technical and support assignments. I told him about the meeting I'd had at Enzo's on Monday and that I'd been disappointed that he wasn't an expert in web servers and applications. Ah, so maybe we need to find someone else, Chris observed. Maybe not. He's got the right attitude — technology serves users not the interests of the expert. I explained that I'd told Sebastian I'd get back to him, having left him with the suggestion that he study Co-ment since that's what we would want him to set up and run on our server area. We'd each learn something in the process: he'd see whether he could do it and whether he liked the process; and we'd see whether he could do it and whether we should have confidence in him. He said he was willing to take a risk to be in position to acquire stock in our little enterprise. Once he proved himself we would be willing to take a risk that he could and would help us over time. That made sense to Chris.

He showed me the page numbering problem he'd found with our books in iBooks: the page numbers in the iBook table of contents didn't match the page numbers of the pages themselves. We had no problem with the page numbers Nook generated. I spent some time later in the innards of one of our EPUB files, making changes, and testing the results. No change. After more than a week our test book, Slocum's *Sailing Alone*, still hadn't shown up in the iBook catalog. Low priority?

359: Crane marina breakwater, fog bank hides Blakely Island

Crossing to the adjacent marina, Deer Harbor, I splurged on $100 for gasoline, about 20 gallons, and then sped back to the Crane dock, the sky beginning to clear, a day with great promise. Tying up all the way in on the main dock I walked over to the picnic boat on the finger going off at an angle. Lots of rain water that took me about ten minutes to bail. Then home where Yvonne told me she had just called Howard's looking for me. I hadn't forgotten that she needed to use the *Huginn* to

Three-hundred-fifty-nine: Smaller Portions

cross to Orcas for the annual Deer Harbor Community Club Auxiliary luncheon that she'd made apple crumble for. At dinner she'd report on who was there and what they had to say, everyone having a good time. The men I knew might enjoy getting together that way but it would neither occur to them nor be organizationally possible.

The day was very nice now but I spent the afternoon working on Crane Island Association bookkeeping for Saturday's Board meeting, an email from Martha to the eight others of us that the meeting was on to which I replied by offering our house as a more comfortable venue than the community center. I paid all the current bills and processed all the member completed invoices and payments. A surprising 17 out of 49 had yet to respond to either my paper or digital mailings. I'd have to make phone calls. So far I'd deposited about 80% of what we'd budgeted for revenue so the trend line looked promising.

Right after dinner, warmed up by homemade soup, Yvonne asked whether we could get a walk in around the island before dark. Of course, let's go, and I left the little bit of cleanup for later and put my headlamp in my pocket. Along the way, Yvonne had been startled several times by birds darting in and out of the trees and bushes we could barely see. By the time we reached Dock Road and close to home and under the trees we could barely see the hard-packed gravel road under our feet. Then we walked through the break in the split rail fence glowing silver, a bright path across the water from Orcas Island, the harvest moon well above Mt Woolard, Jupiter a striking companion. Later the moon and Jupiter joined us in the hot tub, adding dazzle to the clear hot water.

Three-hundred-sixty: Can You Hear It Now?

"The sun never says to the earth, 'You owe me.'" — Hafiz

The green glowing display of the alarm clock on our dresser said 2:20. Though I couldn't remember its content once Yvonne poked me awake I was having a good time and very busy in my dream with some project with a group of people. My sense on awaking, as it often is, was that I hadn't been asleep. I knew what the poke meant. I'd been snoring — excessively. To explain myself apparently I heard myself say that I didn't hear anything which part of me knew to be absurd, another unreasonable rationalization and excuse for why I hadn't stopped snoring on my own. Since Yvonne only complains this forcefully when gentler measures don't suffice, I knew the polite thing to do was get out of bed and let her get to sleep. I closed the door to the bedroom and went into the guest bedroom where I knew I could find a duvet on the shelf in the curtain covered closet and a pillow as well. In the living room the moonlight streamed through the big skylight that runs fourteen feet along the crest of the roof above the huge fir beam that holds the lesser beams four feet apart that support the tongue and groove ceiling. I made a bed on the couch but when I couldn't fall asleep after ten minutes decided I might as well do something useful, put on a jacket over my flannel pajamas and went into my office to work.

I'd left some loose ends with the Crane Island Association accounting and I wanted to tie them up. Somehow I'd entered some bills twice or three times and they were showing up on the General Ledger I'd need to provide the Board for the meeting Saturday. I had to find a way to expunge the errors so for the first time I read the QuickBooks user documentation. It would be no problem. I wouldn't have to create journal entries. I could just delete them and I did and could now produce a fine General Ledger and an Aged Receivables list that highlighted the members who hadn't yet paid. I printed to PDF files and at 5:14 sent the two reports to Martha for distribution to the Board and then spent half-an-hour entering August and September water usage Gary had sent me in a spreadsheet generated from meter readings that Wilma and Edi had taken two weeks before into a month by month spreadsheet format I'd used for the two previous years to send to members so that they could see their usage and accumulating charges they'd pay after the end of the fiscal year next July. Our water usage, at 12,000 gallons for two months was much higher than anyone else and our running total was already over $600. Awful but the result of Yvonne wanting to save her garden from the long drought we'd experienced, finally broken now we hoped. The water report went to Martha for distribution at 5:41. Then I wrote up a report about the water committee doings and then the finance committee progress and projects. I found a "winterizing" document about preparing the water system in one's vacant house for cold weather that had been sent to members the previous fall, added more advice and sent the three reports to Martha at 9:00. I was pleased to have finished documents the Board needed for the Saturday meeting. Martha, also sitting at her computer apparently had forwarded the files to the Board not long after she received them.

More loose ends remained: I had a $25,000 Crane Island Association deposit to make at KeyBank and I wanted to see whether I could complete arrangements for authorized signatures of the Crane account and that at Islanders' Bank I wanted to set up a new account where we'd move cash to get a better interest rate. After lunch, with a brief shopping list from Yvonne I motored the picnic boat to Orcas, past a big power boat and its tender behind it floating just west of the pass, not a good idea even with the reduced traffic of mid October. Someone came out of the cabin and seemed to pull the tender closer to the cruiser. Why? The wind was out of the west and incoming tide from the east creating a little excitement for my light aluminum boat. High cross winds would be a big problem.

360: Buck swimming from Orcas approaches Crane

Lou's old Boston Whaler was at the Orcas dock as it usually is on Thursdays when he makes his Orcas visit to see friends, pickup groceries, and do his laundry. Four new Crane Island Association completed bills and payments lay in the Crane post office box. That would mean fewer collection calls. The day was sunny, almost too warm for a jacket, and since I didn't have a specific time I needed to be in Eastsound, I moseyed rather than rushed, enjoying driving our sporty new Focus, and noticing the now definitive color changes in the big leaf maples, green to light green to yellow to brown, not crisp colors or divisions, more blurred, more water color than acrylic.

At KeyBank, Patti took my deposit and then explained that the meeting minutes and officer listings I'd brought with weren't adequate. The Board meeting minutes or an addendum needed to specifically identify who was to be on the account. I have to think about how to accomplish that at the upcoming Board meeting. At Islanders' Bank, Kathy said I had everything I needed to set up the new account — except copies of drivers licenses from Dan and Martha and a check to make a first deposit. Yvonne's list called for cream cheese and two newspapers from the Market and hose end repair kits from Ace Hardware. The return trip to Crane in the picnic boat into the clean west wind was bracing. The rest of the afternoon I wrote up a status report for the following morning's meeting and sent it to Jens, David, and Chris. We'd already sold a few books on Barnes and Noble and *Sailing Alone* had finally entered the iBooks catalog with the good news from Chris that when he bought and downloaded it, the page numbering was as it should be. I didn't need to do any HTML/EPUB debugging. Our drafts moved directly to iBooks on an iPad wouldn't work correctly but those purchased would. That was just fine. As I wrote up my report to supplement the eight or so documents I'd sent them two days before relating to the MLA convention and our booth there I was impressed with all that had been accomplished in the last month. An email forwarded by Jens from a retired University of Arizona professor who had read *The eNotated Metamorphosis* and admired both the form and content of the book and who wanted to sign up to do Dante was very encouraging.

In the afternoon Yvonne had sent off the Garden Club yearbook PDF to Carol to print, relieved to have it done and happy enough to tell someone calling with change request that it was too late. She'd made headway with her garden, replanting lilies in the bed south of the studio fence that she had worked so hard to improve. She'd cleaned out her worm ranch and turned on the winter heat for them. All the hoses were disconnected from the hose bibs. Our homestead was almost ready for our departure and long road trip coming up the next week. Yvonne made us salmon and white potato and sweet potato french fries. We couldn't finish the salmon so while I cleaned up the dishes she threw it into the cove for the crabs or mink. She said it was too old to have as leftovers. A long day and I fell asleep reading about Hardy by 9:30, the moon later this evening but still silvering the Salish Sea outside our windows.

Three-hundred-sixty-one: Who Are We?

"It's never too late to be what you might have been." — George Eliot

The northwest wind helped blow me through Pole Pass against the tide in our salvaged aluminum skiff with an old four hp motor. I was early for a change and was at Chris' door on Cayou Valley Road, three doors down from where we used to live, by 8:50, with ten minutes to spare. I parked the Focus in the parking area at the garden level next to their BMW MINI Clubman station wagon, about a foot shorter, and walked upstairs to the front door and Chris let me in after I tapped the knocker on its brass plate. He'd set his iPad2 on a picture stand to serve as camera and display screen for our conference call with Jens. David, having calendared the meeting for the next week changed his schedule to attend this one. Then Jens was on the screen from his office at Wellesley College. Except from some screen freezes once in a while the iPad and Skype app worked well. not interfering with the conversation and exchange of ideas.

We reviewed current operational issues first: bank balance, near publication status of *My Antonia*, Susan's probable unavailability to remodel our web site, Sebastien's interest in being involved to do technical support and the idea of a joint experiment putting Co-ment up on a local server, Amazon and Barnes & Nobel sales statistics, problems and apparently solutions listing our book in the iBooks catalog, Jens' experience using his two Kafka books in his fall class as well as Co-ment as a platform for an annotation assignment (something we'd know more about in a few weeks) , and Co-ment as a step in the new annotation project process as a partial replacement for my eNotator software.

The main focus of the meeting, however, was to discuss our corporate identity, how that was relevant to the Modern Language Association members that would be attending their national meeting in Seattle in early January where we would have a booth on the exhibit floor. I'd prepared a number of documents, several dealing with our identity, suggesting that we had (or could have) two — one a retail enhanced electronic book business and the other a subscription annotation platform business as a new, promising bit of pedagogical technology. Jens acknowledged that both businesses could provide valuable services to faculty that were interested in using eNotated books in their classes, becoming an eNotator, or in using our tools to engage students in texts by annotating them. But Jens, Chris, and David also felt that we should have only one name, eNotated Classics, that we didn't need to offer a library of non-eNotated classics, that we didn't need to provide both codex (page turning) and scrolling (word processing or Web page-like) reading and annotation environments, and that we should look for teachers who would like to experiment with us not suggest that we already had a product and fully understood annotation as a pedagogical tool. In effect they pruned away most of what I suggested we do beyond presenting ourselves as an enhanced ebook classics publisher. With the field cleared we were left with developing a logo and then creating a matching brochure-style website and support documents. I thanked them for the important edit they'd provided to my expansive imagination.

After Jens said goodbye and David left, Chris used his relatively high speed Internet connection (ten times faster than mine) to download the latest iTunes for my Mac and then the new iPad operating system that he thought was a valuable update. Since my MacBook Pro didn't have our music on it (the iPad had been linked to the older MacBook Pro that had died six months ago) so all the music on the iPad was erased. When I got home I found a utility program on the Internet that would copy music from our iPod, which still had the music library, to my MacBook Pro and then sync iTunes with the iPad and everything was back where it should be — but now with the new operating system on the iPad.

Three-hundred-sixty-one: Who Are We?

361: Bull kelp in the Crane harbor

I'd used the picnic boat to commute to Orcas but late in the afternoon when Yvonne and I left Crane for Orcas we took the *Huginn*, since we'd be coming back in the dark. Becky and Kevan had already set up the community club for the October potluck when we arrived and the big room quickly filled with people we'd known in some cases for fourteen years, others new or visiting Deer Harbor. Ken and Kate had brought along their granddaughter, Trinity. Pat, from the Post Office, Jack and Pat, back from California and soon bound for Arizona, Cal, thinner than I'd seen him still missing Clarina, Erik and Pam, Pam and Bob, Bev and Dave, Bob and Sue, Karen and Clay, Howard and Sheila, Chris and Lynn, Jim, with MS, attended by a care giver, Gene and Judy, and more, including a man visiting from Oakland accompanied by an old friend, his wife who had to do some teaching to return to soon, who explained that he was fighting cancer and felt he'd stumbled into some other reality where the world was quiet, people cared about one another, and that wasn't directed by the commercial, political, or religious ideas and mood flow of the larger America.

Becky and Kevan had announced they planned to marry in April, he for the first time, right on schedule, he told me, having thought many years ago it would happen in his 50's, the end of them around the corner. He would move up from Bellevue and freelance in website and perhaps book design, something he knew a great deal about. Aha! Months ago I had told him about eNotated Classics. Would he like to know more? Yes. First checking with Yvonne I invited the two of them for Sunday supper.

When we walked down the Orcas dock ramp, the moon, though no longer full, made our headlamps superfluous. Another moonlit cruise to our home island. Another hot water soak in the moonlight.

Three-hundred-sixty-two: Here and There

"The most difficult thing is the decision to act, the rest is merely tenacity." — Amelia Earhart

About 6:45, I began to set up the Polycom conference phone that I'd retrieved from a cabinet in the community center/fire station for the Crane Island Association Board meeting later in the day thinking that I could use it for my call with Jens at 7:00 but I couldn't get it to work. I was eager to use it because it provided much better audio fidelity than my old Panasonic that had a speaker phone function but I couldn't get the Polycom, that I'd bought for the association eighteen months before, to work.

Jens reported that on Thursday he'd be discussing the annotation project he'd assigned his Kafka class and he wanted to be certain he had answers to the questions they might ask. They want to print out the *Hunter Gracchus* text with their annotations, for their own use perhaps and to it turn in to him for their assignment so he and I tried out the five different printing options and as I suspected none was appropriate; they contained the information but not in an attractive form. I told him I would be writing a program that would do what he wanted but not immediately but questioned whether the students really needed to put their work on paper, especially short of their final product which wouldn't come until later in the semester. But they'd need to project their work on a screen to the class and explain it, Jens said. If not printed out, could a computer file be created that they could send him to set up for display. I pointed out that a file was really no different than printing; and right now that's a problem. But why not just project the Co-ment screen — where they'd been doing their work? He agreed that would probably work. But what about his reviewing their work. Didn't he need a file or print out.? He could already do that, I pointed out, since he had access to each of their files on Co-ment. But they don't know that, he said, and in any case he hadn't looked at what they were doing with their Kafka files. Neither one of us had fully thought through all the implications of teaching via online annotation. Given the current circumstances in this alpha test, he decided he'd tell his class I'd now provided him with access to their files, true in the sense that he hadn't quite understood he already had could and that they do their work, show their work, and he'd review and comment on their work all online. Though we wouldn't know for a while whether online annotation with class and then teacher interaction was an effective approach to teaching literature (at least in part), it would have been impossible, practically speaking, without the new technology. He was satisfied with the conceptual solutions we'd come up with and I was very interested to learn about the students' reactions. And we finished our call.

For the next hour I fiddled with the Polycom conference phone. Probably a few Board members had come to Crane for the weekend and would be coming to the house for the meeting but most would probably be at home attending by phone. Before I got the phone and we began using a conference call-in service, attendees had to appear physically and often couldn't so we struggled to convene quorums and even when we did those not attending were out of the loop. I found that as I inserted, pulled out, and then reinserted the ethernet type cable between the power source and the desktop unit, sometimes indicator lights were illuminated but not as they ought to be and in any case the unit wouldn't turn on. I took the cover off but couldn't see anything problematic and more cable fiddling created the same results. I brought my Panasonic phone out from my office. It would have to do and it did.

I reported on member receivables; we collected almost $72,000 of the $82,000 budgeted with about 10 of the 50 yet to pay. I'd begin making collection calls soon. Dan suggested I sent a registered letter to Harris Bank in Chicago rather than try to talk to them. They'd foreclosed on one of our members and had taken the house in March. Then I reported on the water system — everything OK in the sense that the background leak was at its normal 4000 gallons per month level (it would take 6 minutes to fill a gallon) and I recommended not trying to find and fix the perhaps multiple leaks unless forced by the County or State because it would be expensive, more a slight nuisance than a threat to the system. Then back to the finance area and discussion of the paperwork the two banks wanted.

362: The picnic boat and its license plate patch

Martha would send a special email meeting document to the Board members asking them to vote on a resolution for KeyBank for Dan, Martha, and me to be signers. Dan and I would sign the two banks' application forms, I'd photocopy his driver's license and send the package to Martha to forward to the banks — but then Dan and I forgot to take care of it before he left. I'd have to send the package first to him and he would forward it to Martha. Had we all actually lived on Crane it

Three-hundred-sixty-two: Here and There

wouldn't have been such a problem. Blair told us that Waterfront continued to promise attention to the torn rubber hinges on the Orcas dock and that he had some non-slip paint and would re-coat the two aluminum ramps soon, depending on the weather. Pat had been thinking about the Crane roads and gravel and now thought that rather than barge over a two-truck load it might make more sense to bring over a whole barge full, store it and use it over a period of years. He'd report back at the next meeting in January. Dan said that the Orcas Fire Department, with which Crane has a close connection, would be changing one of their radio frequencies very soon and would lend us two portable radios we could use to talk with them (since the ones we had on Crane would now be useless though our pagers would still work). After the meeting and Mike's departure, Dan, President of the association this year and I talked about the water system leak and what, if anything, should be done about it, Gary's good intentions about our water system and attention in times of crisis but inability, apparently because of over commitments, to complete his projects on a timely basis. We'd just live with it. We hadn't ever talked about Tom but I had with Jason when he was President over his three year term. Dan said he thought Tom had changed over the many years he'd known him, once having been happy and content apparently and then becoming paranoid and one by one becoming estranged from most of the community, especially those on the Board.

About 11:30 I took the picnic boat to Orcas and drove the Focus to the Deer Harbor Community club, walking into the kitchen just as everyone was serving themselves turkey chili and Pat's recipe cornbread for lunch. They had quickly finished their clean up at the Deer Harbor Post Office, owned by the Community Club, and were nearly done here at the Community Club a half mile north on Deer Harbor Road. Sheldon, Bob and Sue, Howard (his mustache not yet grown back since he'd accidentally shaved it the day before) and Sheila, Becky and Kevan, Pam, Bev, Yvonne, the grounds manager and cleanup Jefa, with others having had to leave before lunch. Pam reported that son, Taylor, was enjoying his freshman classes at UW at Bothell and after Bev described how good it felt to be at Community Club functions like the potluck the evening before and at today's cleanup, I told her that Yvonne had been talking about that very thing the night before and that we both agreed Bev was largely responsible as visionary, spark plug, and taskmaster. It was true and I think she liked hearing it. I used the hose to water the earthen bank that had been scrapped clean of vegetation to create more parking space when the new septic system had been installed and Pam scattered a little grass seed before running out. Yvonne watered her plantings and then I spooled the hose. We were done at the Community Club, we both stopped at the Post Office (me to check the Crane Island Association box for member payments), and then I parked the pickup in the Crane lot above the road, turned the battery switch to disconnect, checked the cab dehydration system, grabbed Yvonne's battery powered weed-whacker and fence post drivers and with Yvonne, who'd parked the Focus in the lower lot, carried everything down the ramp to our two boats and then led with the picnic boat in our parade back to Crane.

Home again, and after emptying two wheelbarrows full of "bad" root infested soil Yvonne (and I) had removed from her south flower bed, and bringing two loads of top soil from under the tarp where I'd put it in July when I brought the pickup over, I walked around the Island, noting that the tank level was at 12 1/2 feet, down a bit because of weekend visits, found a Hersey candy bar wrapper near Dick and Nancy's cabin (in the four and a half years we'd lived on Crane I'd come upon only one other candy bar wrapper and basically zero trash), noticed that they'd put up a net on their grass tennis court — with no ball stop-fence (how does that work?), and studied a burn pile at Skip's — fortunately with a power shovel idling nearby — though no human was visible.

Though I wasn't enthusiastic about watching the documentary on Dietrich Bonhoeffer that had arrived from Netflix the day before I found it encouraging as well as horrifying, knowing that he was an important theologian and martyr but not why. We were surprised to learn of the influence Reinhold Niebuhr at Union Theological Seminary and the Abyssinian Baptist in Harlem led by Adam Clayton Powell senior had on him in coming to understand the importance of acting from an understanding of the Sermon on the Mount to lessen pain and increase justice. Bonhoeffer's conclusion that to witness his faith he had to join a plot to kill Hitler and was hung because of it, while so much of the clergy in Germany were passive at best, must have come only after an enormous internal struggle with his earlier Gandhian non-violent resistance philosophy. Bonhoeffer taught that the goal wasn't an other worldly relationship with God but a this world relationship with other people, the community, and for him the real body of Christ — an orientation toward others rather than oneself. That made so much sense to me even without a Christian metaphysics.

Three-hundred-sixty-three: Chetzemoka Visits

"The bird that would soar above the plain of tradition must have strong wings." — Mary Wollstonecraft

Just about dawn the *Chetzemoka*, named after a Port Townsend area friendly Native American chief and blessed by Native Americans when put in service, passed behind Bell Island on its way to Friday Harbor on San Juan Island, a distance of about eight and a half miles by way of Wasp Passage, south of Crane Island, and then San Juan Channel, at its north end separating San Juan and Shaw Islands. Even in little light the *Chetzemoka* was visibly different from the other ferries moving among the San Juans; its greens greener and whites brighter, lines crisper, its silhouette showing only one stack center instead of at each end.

We'd ridden the *Chetzemoka* between Port Townsend on the Peninsula and Coupeville on Whidbey Island a few weeks earlier on a very windy day, ferry service suspended for a few hours while the tide reversed direction calming the waves slightly. In March we'd seen it leave Whidbey while we parked at the ferry landing and then from Fort Casey State Park and its lighthouse just north, as the *Chetzemoka* crossed Admiralty Inlet, entry point to Puget Sound and Seattle from the Straight of Juan de Fuca and the Pacific. The day before we had peeked over the Nichols Brothers' fence in Freeland, on Whidbey Island, at the superstructure of the *Salish*, its twin then under construction and put in service in July.

Why was the *Chetzemoka* now in the San Juans? The *Yakima* had been taken out of service October 7th for repairs "after maintenance crews discovered signs of abnormal wear on the journal bearing, which supports the propulsion shaft", with the *Evergreen State* filling in, while the *Hiyu* took its place on the Interisland route. Then the *Hiyu* broke down and the *Chetzemoka*, already pulled off the Admiralty Inlet run to be moved to the Point Defiance-Tahlequah route in south Puget Sound, was diverted to the San Juans. But why had it been pulled off the Port Townsend route? Yvonne and I, and many others, had seen the *Chetzemoka* come close to crashing into the rocks near the Port Townsend ferry terminal as it struggled to its slip in the high winds and waves. It didn't look right to any of us. Was it pilot error? Apparently not. The new boat didn't have what it took to serve this difficult route after being rushed into service with a fixed pitch propeller. The *Salish*, in service, and the *Kennewick*, to be commissioned in the winter had variable pitch props. The *Kennewick* would eventually replace the *Chetzemoka* but for now the route would suffer with only one ferry.

The original *Chetzemoka*, a wooden ferry built in San Francisco came to Washington in 1938, serving first out of Port Townsend and then Mukilteo/Clinton until the state took over the ferry service from Black Ball in 1954 giving the aging ferry minor roles. While being towed back to San Francisco on Labor Day 1977, in high seas, the *Chetzemoka* developed a leak its pumps couldn't keep up with and it sunk in the Pacific, nine miles off La Push in 235 feet of water.

In the afternoon I made up some new hose sections for Yvonne who wanted to rearrange drip hose irrigation of her front and back gardens from the two catchment tanks and even though the front tank had plenty of water it didn't flow well through the tiny pore; not enough water pressure. We'd have to do something better — not just to make better use of the catchment water but of the household water used for irrigation. In August and September we'd used 12,000 gallons, less than 5000 gallons attributable to domestic use. Our total catchment capacity was under 500 gallons and we couldn't expect more than two rain fillings in that dry period in any year. In other words, catchment would make only a tiny dent in our usage — which in those two months had cost $400 more than we'd normally spend. Besides catchment we'd have to significantly increase the efficiency of our irrigation process. Rather than watering by spraying we really needed adequate drip coverage that could come from catchment (via a pump?) or from the domestic supply. A project for next spring?

Three-hundred-sixty-three: Chetzemoka Visits

363: Chetzemoka heading for Wasp Passage at dawn

When I docked the *Huginn* at Orcas at 5:30 Howard and CeAnn were emptying their skiff for their trip back to Bainbridge Island, the deck repair project that had injured friend Freddy completed. Then Becky and Kevan appeared on the ramp, boarded and we headed back to Crane, twilight fading to night. After a house and grounds tour Yvonne put the salmon in the oven to bake and we talked about our lives, families, and roots, Becky, who had worked for Microsoft, from a large small town Minnesota Norwegian family and Kevin, a graphic designer, from a smaller portable Air Force Czech-Austrian family. In April, when the two married, he'd move in with Becky on the west side of Orcas with a view of Speiden Channel and the more distant Haro Straight boundary line and shipping channel.

Three-hundred-sixty-three: Chetzemoka Visits

After dinner and while working through a homemade apple pie, I demonstrated our eNotated Classics ebooks and explained to Kevan what we were trying to do and our lack of skills in the graphics design area. He showed me a website he had recently competed as a moonlighting project, the content management system he'd used, and the much more elaborate website perpetually under construction he worked on as part of his day job. By the time he moved to Orcas he hoped to be self-sufficient as an independent contractor. He was very interested in helping us and when I dropped them back at the Orcas dock, handing them a yellow flashlight, we agreed to get together after we returned from our road trip.

Three-hundred-sixty-four: A Day in Town

"Every return home is a chance to see it anew." — Pico Iyer

Another beautiful October day in prospect, a band of dark gray clouds from the horizon to about 15° above it, with orange light seeping through a tear above Mt. Woolard, the rest of the sky hinting blue. Saturday Lou had left a voice mail worried about the numbered signs on trees on Doug's property. After calling Lou to reassure him I wrote Doug asking that he send Lou a note. Doug sent a quick reply from the UW-MSU football game in Seattle (which the Huskies won) and then to Lou this morning, explaining that the numbers he saw were for frisbee golf inviting (80-plus) Lou to come by sometime and play. My guess was that Lou was offended by the colorful signs themselves since they interrupted what was almost everywhere on Crane little evidence of habitation. By 10:30 Yvonne and I were underway in the *Huginn* through Pole Pass, a northwest breeze rippling the surface of the Salish Sea. At the Deer Harbor Post Office, I found two envelopes in the Crane Island Association box, one a bill and the other a member dues payment. Our box contained a non-delivery, "sorry to miss you note" and I handed it to Pat who was loading mail into boxes that she could only access from the front. What was it? I wasn't expecting anything. From Chase, our credit card and mortgage supplier. Was something wrong? I asked Pat what she thought the implications were of the announced USPS downsizing. She knew only that more than 250 distribution centers, including Everett, would be closed and eventually many post offices.

I opened the envelope in the car. Chase wanted to refinance our mortgage at 4.25% — at no charge. Likely story — but an effective marketing ploy to use overnight mail. In Eastsound Yvonne parked at the Island Market and I took my pack and walked to KeyBank to make a

Three-hundred-sixty-four: A Day in Town

Crane deposit, saying hello to Patti and taking one of her business cards for use later. I found Yvonne in the Market and got the cell phone I'd need to call Chase and bought a sesame bagel and had the young blonde woman waiting on me add cream cheese. At Islanders' Bank, a block away, I dropped my bagel on the floor as I walked in the door, picked it up, brushed it off and set it on the counter at an open teller's location while I made a credit line deposit Yvonne had charged me with. In the outer lobby I used my debit card to withdraw $100 for our upcoming road trip and then continued to eat my bagel, finding almost no floor grit in it. A path at the rear of the bank lot leads up hill to the Library where I returned a book Yvonne had provided me and then went outside into the sunshine, finding a south facing bench on the grass from which I could call Chase. Their letter called for almost immediate response. Why were they willing to lower our mortgage payment? Part of a retention initiative. That made sense to me. The week before I'd begun an application process with IngDirect, finally thwarted because of some software problem with our zip code the service representative promised would be fixed within five business days at which time I could reapply. The 3.25% loan had a significant defect though; it would only last five years, so I hadn't pursued it. Chase offered 4.25% compared with our 5.85% current mortgage but with a 30 year fixed term (not that we would live to make the 360th payment). By the time I completed my conversation with Chase, it seemed they were committed. I'd need to download some papers, sign, scan, and return them as email attachments and also send along a scan of our 1040 tax return.

Back in the Library I talked with Phil briefly about Tom, Board president who had recently resigned because of heart trouble and who, according to Phil's morning email, had now suffered a stroke and was hospitalized. Bad.

To complete the signature arrangements at KeyBank and open the new account at Islanders' Bank for the Crane Island Association, Dan and Martha would need to sign some forms, include driver's license photocopies for Islanders' and include the special Board meeting minutes for KeyBank. I couldn't find table space and there were few open chairs, so I sat with my MacBook Pro on my lap writing an instruction

Three-hundred-sixty-four: A Day in Town

email to Dan and Martha and preparing the forms for mailing in the envelope I'd brought with. Yvonne's cell phone rang, American Title on the other end, wanting to talk about preparing for a Chase refinance closing so I walked outside to take the call then finished the Crane email, sent it off and the walked to the Eastsound Post Office to send it off, checking first at the desk that I'd put on adequate postage.

364: Madrona berries

To complete the signature arrangements at KeyBank and open the new account at Islanders' Bank for the Crane Island Association, Dan and Martha would need to sign some forms, include driver's license photocopies for Islanders' and include the special Board meeting minutes for KeyBank. I couldn't find table space and there were few open chairs, so I sat with my MacBook Pro on my lap writing an instruction email to Dan and Martha and preparing the forms for mailing in the envelope I'd brought with. I was carrying Yvonne's cell phone and it rang, American Title on the other end, wanting to talk about preparing for a Chase refinance closing so I walked outside to take the call then finished the Crane email, sent it off and the walked to the Eastsound Post Office to send Crane mail off, checking first at the desk that I'd put on adequate postage. I had. That job done and now 2:00 in the afternoon, I wanted a snack, something to drink, and a place to work, ending up a the Home Grown Market, Eastsound's health food store and delicatessen, a funky but friendly place that Yvonne said had good fish and sold spices and grains in bulk. With a can of Blue Sky natural grapefruit soda and a sorry piece of reheated cheese pizza in hand, I walked up the stairs to the lunch room — worn out tables and chairs, uncleared lunch debris here and there but with the virtue of being deserted, having WiFi access, and windows looking over Eastsound on the sides. My Entourage inbox was stuffed with forty or fifty emails that cried for attention, if only to be discarded. One was particularly promising and challenging to answer. A Dante, Hell actually, expert had come upon Jens' Kafka ebooks and wanted to do one on the *Inferno*. My first draft offered a detailed history of our little business but fortunately after letting it rest for a while, I cut three-quarters of it, copied Jens, and sent it off to Italy where Alan was now traveling.

Returning to the Library about 4:30, Phil told me the good news that Tom was up and about, had come in to pick up some reading and that the stroke story had been exaggerated. Good. We talked briefly about the budget he'd presented to the Board, on which I had served for five years, and then at length about the CrossRoads lecture series the Library was sponsoring but was charging admission to, a fact the Washington State Auditor's Department demanded be changed immediately. The Library could offer the lectures for free and solicit donations (something that hadn't provided adequate funding even combined with help from the Friends of the Library) or could pass total responsibility to the CrossRoads planning committee, disengaging the Library, and letting the committee act independently and find its own funding. Phil felt

Three-hundred-sixty-four: A Day in Town

there was another, serious problem with CrossRoads; its programs were "elitist," of interest to a small minority of the island population, drawing small crowds, except for the most recent talk by Dmitry Orolov on "The Fall of the American Empire," one that caused a stir, letters to the editor, and consternation by members of the CrossRoads committee, one of the members complaining Orolov wasn't cheerful enough.

 A little after 5:00 I walked down the steps from the Library site on a hill overlooking Prune Alley, and through Library Park, across to A Street and then North Beach road where I saw Yvonne drive up and park our gray Focus. She was wearing a sky blue wool jacket and had just had her hair cut. I had been instructed never to comment on her hair without being asked. It looked fine to me. I let the moment pass. She wondered why I wasn't already inside with Diane and Richard. Because you said I should appear in what used to be Bilbo's at 5:45 and it was 5:40. But you were supposed to order me a margarita. I was? I had missed that part of her instructions. Inside Richard and Diane were just ordering and Yvonne's drink was included. I ordered a lemonade. Yvonne and Diane had made short work of the Garden Club Yearbook stapling project, working in one of the public rooms at the Deer Harbor Fire Station, joined part of the time by Eska. The Master Gardeners meeting and 92-year-old Emily's presentation had been sparsely attended but now that Yvonne and Sylvia had passed responsibility to new blood she wasn't going to worry about it. While with Kristin getting her hair cut, Sylvia called from Seattle to change her appointment because her daughter had lost her baby sitter and was asking Sylvia to provide day care for a couple weeks. Since Richard and Diane, from Houston, knew a great deal about Texas politics I started the discussion asking for the inside story on Rick Perry (a zero) and we went on to have an enjoyable evening and tasty food, the former Bilbo's now returned to the former owners but with a new name, Chiladas, the purchasers having abandoned the site and gone across the street to found Agave, restaurant and tequila bar. Richard and Diane would leave soon to spend the winter months in Houston to visit friends not because the weather was better and both complained about having to live in hermetically sealed houses in Huston and the bad air. Richard had talked to a group of conservative friends who had attended Orlov's Cross-Roads talk and had a different take from Phil. Orolov was a KGB agent and was patently lying about how good Russia and the rest of the world was in medical care and housing, for instance, and how bad the US was, entirely discrediting his talk. Yvonne and I were home before 8:30, water and wind calm, the waning moon not yet risen but Jupiter casting shadows. Tomorrow we'd leave for California and beyond.

Three-hundred-sixty-five: Ready, Set, Go

"Between home and now lies a border." — Ocean Vuong

Eager for some exercise before an extended period of sitting in the car, I took off for a walk around the island, carrying along the two radios and one charger Yvonne had picked up at the Eastsound Fire Station, at Dan's request, the day before. The fire truck bay was still empty — Dan would be bringing it back to the island on Friday when Howard took his truck off — and I left one radio on the bench against the east wall where the jump start battery was charging and put the other in its charger and plugged it in. Farther along Circle Road I could look back at the water tank above and saw that its level remained at about 12 feet six inches. Just fine. Many of the big leaf maples were yellow now, yellow and brown leaves covering the road. By the time we got back almost all would be on the ground. No birds today but two days before the robins especially had been abundant, flitting in and out of the madrona whose berries were now turning from light green to bright red. The madronas above the Orcas dock were especially bright with berries this year and by December would probably be picked clean.

I left for Orcas about 1:00 but found no mail in the Crane box and little in ours except for a check from James, an installment payment for money we'd advanced him to pay his prosthesis repair co-pay. Back in the Crane lot waiting for the Yvonne's friends to ferry to Crane, I saw the right turn signal flashing on a tan Ranger pickup. Odd. The driver's door was unlocked so I tried to turn turn off the signal but moving the wand had no effect.

Then Lynn arrived with Karen in her Subaru and then Nancy on her Vespa. They sat in the Huginn's cockpit in the warm afternoon sun chatting, happy to see one another and at the prospect of discussing Gail Collin's *When Everything Changed* and enjoying whatever refreshments Yvonne had in store.

One of my goals before leaving on our extended road trip was to do a septic tank inspection, using the training I'd received a year before at a class the County convened so that homeowners in the San Juans could do their own annual inspections rather than have to pay for the service. I hadn't gotten it done. It would wait for our return. Another goal, and one that I had to compete before we left, was to figure out a way to keep the rain out of the 10' x 20' storage tent without at the same time encouraging mink to use it for their privy. We'd tried to keep them out by a double layer of fencing but they'd found a way in. Then Yvonne tried removing the fencing and opening the door, turning a private space public and so far the mink had stayed away. My task, as I saw it, was to close the door enough to keep out the coming fall rain, which would sometimes fall horizontally if accompanied by heavy winds, but leave it open enough that the mink wouldn't feel comfortable being inside. I decided that any opening size that would allow an otter, raccoon, dog, or cat would probably discourage them so I zipped the two sides of the door down to the height of two five gallon buckets I'd put upside down at either side of the door, laid a plank across them, put the unzipped portion of the door across the plank, put another plank on top and then clamped the two planks together so that the wind wouldn't blow the door flap out from between the planks — an experiment I'd know the results of in four weeks.

I interrupted Yvonne's gathering and announced that I was going to turn off the water and then walked up the drive to the meter, opened the small metal cover and struggled, as usual, to turn the valve counter-clockwise, then returned the cover and walked back to the house, climbing under the south deck to turn off the one propane bottle that was supplying the stove, and then went to the south gate, closed it, put a looped cord over the top and then a bungee cord at the bottom so deer couldn't push it open. I'd already put bungee cords on the other three gates and would do the last when we left the yard to go to the dock. I'd already fastened the spa cover tie down straps and set the thermostat to 59°, set the seven house thermostats to 58° and locked the studio door and now locked the dining room and kitchen doors. Then we were all out the front door on our way to the dock.

Three-hundred-sixty-five: Ready, Set, Go

365: Morning sun, come my way

Twenty Canada geese paddled in the Crane marina cove and as we came through Pole pass an equal number floated above the bull kelp. Were they a flock heading south? Just to the east four seal heads were visible in the water, a dozen gulls on the water nearby, the seals fishing and the gulls hoping for leftovers. As we approached the Orcas dock just before 4:00, I saw Nancy J pulling out in her Boston Whaler. Had they been able to turn off the Ranger's turn signal? Yes, but the battery was dead. Parked at the Orcas dock, Yvonne, Lynn, Karen, and Nancy hopped out, and I headed the *Huginn* toward Caldwell Point and then north into West Sound, in a straight line, the marina two miles ahead. The northwest wind had almost abated, the water only slightly corrugated, a pleasure to plane over. Halfway an old green wooden sailboat with sails stowed drifted slowly east and south, three aboard sitting on the cabin top enjoying the afternoon sun and previously deserted

Sound. I passed two hundred yards to the west and I regretted a bit that my wake would soon interrupt their reverie. Parking the *Huginn* behind a C-Dory on the West Sound Marine guest dock near the fuel pump, I put my maroon pack with my MacBook Pro and assorted other electronics over my shoulder, picked up my soft-sided green suitcase I'd used on our trip to East Africa, and wheeled my black suitcase along the dock, past where the Kenmore float planes pick up and let off passengers, up the ramp, a skiff on the dock to my right and below with six inches of water in it, to the marina store where I waited for a vendor to finish pitching the virtues of the hardwood he supplied for wood repair. I reported to Betsy and Jan that I'd be back in about three weeks so they could do the routine fall maintenance on the *Huginn* at their leisure. The boat was working fine. The oil pressure gauge had suddenly failed a few months back; if it was simple to fix that was fine — otherwise I'd live with it. They had our new cell phone number and could call should they find anything peculiar.

Yvonne poked her head in the door, reminding the three of us that we had to catch the ferry, having arrived in the Focus a few minutes after I walked into the marina store. She'd already taken my two suitcases up to the car and we were off, along Deer Harbor Road and then right, south on Orcas Road toward the ferry landing. As we talked I realized that I hadn't put away the cream and sugar she and her lady friends had with their tea and biscuits. Ants would soon discover the treats and swarm on the kitchen counter and the cream would spoil. So be it.

Afterword

Orcas Island was special. Crane Island was even more special. But nothing lasts. Everything changes.

In 2014 we moved to Olympia, near son, Noah, daughter-in-law, Natasha, and grandchildren, Morgan, and Opal. Olympia is the capital of Washington, a nice small city, at the south end of Puget Sound. And shortly we had a land yacht we named *Further*, (see Ken Kesey's 1964 *Merry Pranksters*) and for the next five years, when not in Olympia, we were likely to be someplace west of the 100th meridian — from Canada to Mexico.

Further in Arizona

Afterword

Further from the inside

In many ways *Further* resembled *Gumption*, had some problems I could repair and others not but it was a great way to get around and we visited friends, relatives, historic sites, and virtually every National and state park in the West, many we had never heard of but found delightful and sometimes profound. We hiked in all of them and even a bit on the Pacific Crest Trail. The West, out of the cities, and away from the Interstates is a beautiful and amazing place — and not all of it is crowded.

Afterword

Ballard

Then by 2019 when we found we were beginning to repeat ourselves, we decided to try a fourth life, a stationary cruise in a condo building in the Ballard neighborhood of Seattle, close to our daughter Jeni and her husband Juan Carlos. The 2020 pandemic soon restricted our activities so we used our found time to walk all over the city. The University of Washington encourages seniors to audit classes gratis and we've enjoyed the courses, learned something, and are energized by being with young people. And we've gotten to know many people in this green dynamic, creative, city. We have no plans to move someplace else.

We had cruised the waters and then the highways. Now were were cruising Seattle from a condo — a stationary urban cruise — and we like it.

John Ashenhurst, Ballard, January 10, 2025

Afterword

Shilshole marina near Ballard

What's next?

Who knows?

Crane Island Journal is a four-volume memoir covering October 19, 2010 through October 18, 2011.

This is **Sumar (Summer)**, the fourth and final volume of Crane Island Journal.

Find information about **Haust (Autumn)**, **Vetur (Winter)**, and **Vor (Spring)**, on the Journal's website, www.craneislandjournal.com.

www.ingramcontent.com/pod-product-compliance
Lightning Source LLC
Chambersburg PA
CBHW070417010526
44118CB00014B/1796